THE PROVIDENCE OF GOD
REGARDING THE UNIVERSE

Mediæval Philosophical Texts in Translation
No. 43

William of Auvergne

THE PROVIDENCE OF GOD REGARDING THE UNIVERSE

PART THREE OF THE FIRST PRINCIPAL PART OF

The Universe of Creatures

TRANSLATED FROM THE LATIN

WITH AN INTRODUCTION AND NOTES

by

ROLAND J. TESKE, s.j.

MARQUETTE
UNIVERSITY

PRESS

BT
96.3
.W5513
2007

Library of Congress Cataloging-in-Publication Data

William, of Auvergne, Bishop of Paris, d. 1249.
  [De universo. Part 3. English]
  The providence of God regarding the universe : part three of the first principal part of The universe of creatures / translated from the Latin with an introduction and notes by Roland J. Teske.
      p. cm. — (Medieval philosophical texts in translation ; no. 43)
  Includes bibliographical references and indexes.
  ISBN-13: 978-0-87462-246-1 (pbk. : alk. paper)
  ISBN-10: 0-87462-246-8 (pbk. : alk. paper)
  1. Providence and government of God—Christianity—History of doctrines—Middle Ages, 600-1500. 2. Philosophy, Medieval. I. Teske, Roland J., 1934- II. Title.
  BT96.3.W5513 2007
  231'.5—dc22

                                                            2007012442

♾ The paper used in this publication meets the minimum requirements of the American National Standard for Information Sciences— Permanence of Paper for Printed Library Materials, ANSI Z39.48-1992.

Association of American University Presses

MARQUETTE UNIVERSITY PRESS
MILWAUKEE

The Association of Jesuit University Presses

IN MEMORY OF
GEORGE P. KLUBERTANZ, S.J.
TEACHER, SCHOLAR, AND FRIEND

CONTENTS

INTRODUCTION

For William of Auvergne's life and works, see the introductions to the translations of *The Trinity or the First Principle* (*De trinitate, seu de primo principio*) or to selections from *The Universe of Creatures.*[1] William's *The Universe of Creatures* (*De universo creaturarum*) is a huge work that runs from page 592 to page 1074 in volume one in the 1674 Paris-Orléans edition of his works. Although *The Universe of Creatures* is the second work in the systematic sequence of the *The Teaching on God in the Mode of Wisdom* (*Magisterium divinale et sapientiale*), it was written relatively late in William's career, probably at late as 1236 or even 1240.[2] It is divided into two principal parts, the first on the bodily or sensible universe, the second on the spiritual universe.[3] Each principal part is divided into three parts. After an introductory chapter, the first part of the first principal part (Ia-Iae) first argues against the Manichees or Cathars that the world has only one first principle (chs. 2–10), secondly argues that the bodily world is one (chs. 11–16), thirdly discusses how creatures have their origin from God (chs. 17–30), fourthly deals with the origin of various parts of the bodily world, such as the heavens and the elements, and finally concludes with discussions of the earthly paradise, purgatory, and hell (chs. 31–65).

After a short preface, the second part of the first principal part (IIa-Iae) takes up the nature of God's eternity in contrast with the sort of eternity that the Aristotelians attributed to the world. William argues against those who held that time is simply a part of the whole of eternity, distinguishes eternity, perpetuity,

---

1   *The Trinity, or the First Principle*, translated by Roland J. Teske, S.J., and Francis C. Wade, S.J. (Milwaukee: Marquette University Press, 1987) or *The Universe of Creatures: Selections Translated from the Latin with an Introduction and Notes* (Milwaukee: Marquette University Press, 2000).

2   For further details on the systematic order and chronology of the parts of the *Magisterium*, see Gugliemo Corti, "Le sette parti del Magisterium Divinale ac Sapientiale de Gugliemo di Auvergne," in *Studi e Ricerche di Scienze Religiose in onore dei Santi Apostoli Pietro et Paulo nel xix centenario del loro martirio* (Rome, 1968), 289–307.

3   In "Guillaume d'Auvergne et l'enunciabile: La solution profane d'un problème théologique," in *Autour de Guillaume d'Auvergne († 1249)*. Ed. Franco Morenzoni and Jean-Yves Tillette (Turnhout: Brepols, 2006), pp. 117–136, Laurent Cesali has well characterized the work: "Le *De universo* peut se lire comme un traité d'ontologie dans la mesure où il est une longue et minutieuse réponse à la question: Qu'est-ce qu'il y a?"

and time, explains the sense in which all things are simultaneous in eternity, and compares eternity and time (chs. 1–4).[4] William is adamant that Aristotle held that eternity was simply temporal duration without beginning or end (ch. 5); he then turns to some difficulties posed by some biblical expressions and a series of other terms that could pose problems for his understanding of eternity (chs. 6 and 7).

William confronts the errors of Aristotle and Avicenna who held that the world was eternal in the sense of always having existed and always going to exist. He presents the arguments of each of them and at times bolsters their arguments before turning to a refutation of them (ch. 8). He resolves the arguments of Avicenna (ch. 9) and then those of Aristotle (ch. 10). Next William presents a series of arguments for the beginning of the world based on religious and secular history along with a group of what he refers to as moral arguments, after which he presents a series of metaphysical arguments, which ultimately stem from the arguments for the newness of the world developed by John Philoponus, a sixth-century Christian commentator on Aristotle (ch. 11).[5] William turns to a discussion of the end of time and what will come after its end (ch. 12). Turning to the Platonic doctrine on souls, he argues against the view that they are created outside their bodies, subsequently enter bodies, and migrate from one body to another (chs. 13 to 15). He argues against the Platonic doctrine of the Great Year, namely, that every 36,000 years everything returns to its original state (chs. 16 to 18). After rejecting Origen's theory that bodies are ultimately destroyed (ch. 19), he turns to the resurrection of the body and its glorification, the characteristics of the glorified body and soul, and the state of the world at the resurrection (chs. 20 to 51).

The third part of the first principal part (IIIa-Iae), which is translated in this volume, deals with the providence of God with regard to the universe and various related questions. Its contents will be outlined below.

The first part of the second principal part (Ia-IIae) deals with the separate intelligences of Aristotle and his followers, that is, mainly Avicenna, in 46 chapters. William is mainly concerned with errors regarding their nature and functions. The second part of the second principal part (IIa-IIae) deals with the good angels in 163 chapters, while the third part of the second principal part (IIIa-IIae) deals with the bad angels or demons in 26 chapters.

4   See my "William of Auvergne on Time and Eternity," *Traditio* 55 (2000): 125–141.

5   See my "William of Auvergne on the Eternity of the World," *The Modern Schoolman* 67 (1990): 187–205, and "William of Auvergne's Arguments for the Newness of the World," *Mediaevalia: Textos e Estudios* 7-8 (1995): 287–302.

In a previous translation of selections from *The Universe of Creatures* I omitted the third part of the first principal part simply because of the length of the work, which would have made that translation a huge volume. But I said then that the third part could well be turned into a separate translation, and that is what the present volume does.

After a brief preface in which he lists many of the topics to be treated in the third part of the first principal part, William turns in Chapter 1 to the distinction between foreknowledge and providence. The principal difference lies in the fact that God foreknows both goods and evils, but exercises providence only over goods. That is, William excludes blameworthy evils or sins from the providence of the creator, because the creator does not cause them, although he maintains that the creator foresees such evils, which he permits. In a manner typical of his writing, William poses objections and answers them, often by giving examples. For instance, someone might object that God creates beings and then leaves them on their own. William replies that God gives them the powers by which they can govern themselves and that he governs them by means of those powers. He appeals to the example of a father who governs his young son by giving him a governor whom he has instructed about how to govern the son. So too, he appeals to the example of a helmsman on a ship who governs the movement of the ship by means of the helm. Hence, although God may not have immediate governance of all things, he has mediate governance of them through the powers he gave them, and to deny that he governs all things because he governs some by means of others is like saying that a helmsman does not govern a ship because he uses the helm.

Chapter 2 begins by pointing out the benefits that human beings, other animals, and even plants receive from the motion of the heavens and the changes of the seasons and finds in such things clear evidence of the providence of the creator. Frequency and universality are evidence that events do not happen merely by chance or accident. The Italian philosophers, probably the Stoics, admitted such evidence of divine providence, but maintained that providence did not extend to individual things and events.[6] William first presents the case for denying providence over individual events by a series of examples. For instance, a chariot driver certainly intends the movement of the chariot, but does not intend each turn of the wheel or each step of the horses. Much less does God intend each and every event, according to the Italian philosophers.

---

6   On the identity of the Italian philosophers, see my "The Identity of the '*Italici*' in William of Auvergne's Discussion of the Eternity of the World," *Proceedings of the PMR Conference* 15 (1990): 189–201. William refers to Cicero, Seneca, Boethius, and others by that tag. Here he refers to the Stoics against whom Cicero argued in *De natura deorum*.

Moreover, these philosophers thought that it was ridiculous to suppose that divine providence extended to the individual atoms, grains of sand, and other such minutiae. In his reply William points out the difference between the providence of a human father of a family, who cannot have care for each and every thing in the management of his household, and the providence of the creator, whose knowledge and care extends to absolutely everything. As the creator is the source of being for each and every thing he has created, so his providence extends to every grain of sand and to all the infinitely divisible parts of a continuum. The creator, moreover, not merely created and conserves each and every thing, but guides and directs them toward the ends for which he created them.

In Chapter 3 William argues for the providence and care of the creator from the activities and skills of animals. For example, he asks where spiders learned to make their webs and catch flies as their food, where ducklings learn to swim almost immediately after they are hatched, and where ants learn to store away food for the winter. If someone claims that nature teaches such activities, William points to the creator as the source of nature, claiming that, as being flows over creatures from the first source of being, so the lights of knowledge flow over creatures from the wisdom of the creator. He credits dogs, which he claims were created for the protection of human beings and their possessions, with the light of a sort of divination analogous to prophetic illumination by which they can detect the presence of thieves and other dangerous persons. Although a great diversity of lights descends from the wisdom of the creator, William warns against supposing that there is any diversity in him. He argues the case for the providence and care of the creator over the natural world by many examples, many of which, though interesting, hardly qualify as scientific, such as the claims that female cats learn to conceive from catnip without a male, that horses conceive from the wind, that eagles recover their youth, and that scorpions sting only the backs of human hands so that they do not get caught in the palms.

Chapter 4 turns to the general and diverse benefits of creatures. William asks how the creator cares for the little flies that are eaten by swallows and replies that their being eaten and providing nourishment to swallows is one of their benefits, to which the creator orders and guides them. William lists the general benefits of creatures: first, the good of each thing, such as its being; secondly, its usefulness for others. He distinguishes natural benefits of some creatures for others, such as nourishment, and the more noble benefits, such as those that come from the disciplines and the virtues and graces. He brings the chapter to a close with a discussion of the benefits of fear of God.

Chapter 5 turns to the difficult subject of the good of pain. After all, although divine providence does not extend to the culpable evil of sin, it does extend to the penal evils of pain. Hence, William endeavors to show how divine providence uses pain for various good purposes and benefits. Pain, for example, removes or reduces our desires for carnal and worldly pleasures and lessens those pleasures themselves, which can be extremely harmful to human souls. William quotes from the Hebrew and Christian scriptures and from the philosopher, Archytas of Tarentum, to support his argument that pain is—or at least can be—productive of virtue. Since souls are delivered from the evils of the vices through pains and suffering, pains and sufferings are great goods, which must therefore fall under the providence of the creator. Just as a good and wise physician gives his patient the medicine to cure him of the disease from which he is suffering, so the good and wise creator gives pains and sufferings to heal the human race from the diseases of vices and sins. Although at times we ourselves or others cause pain and suffering in us, the creator still brings good out of them, even when they are produced by the sinful actions of others, which he does not cause, but permits.

Some people might object that the creator is the cause of such sinful actions because he gave to those who inflict pains in a sinful way the power to do so. William replies by means of an example. Just as, if a king appoints an official who kills an innocent man, the king cannot be said to have caused the death of the innocent man, so the creator who gives sinners the power to inflict pain and suffering cannot be said to be the cause of such sinful acts. Scripture calls pain the water of tribulation and fire, and William uses these expressions to illustrate the benefits that come from pain and tribulation. Persons who inflict pain and tribulation are, he argues, ministers of divine providence, though they do not, of course, intend to be. Evils that do not come from the sinful wills of bad persons also fall under the providence of God, who brings many benefits out of them. If someone objects that such evils do not always benefit people, but sometimes do them great harm, William argues that the creator is not to be blamed because people misuse these benefits. Death too can be a great benefit, even for evil persons since it prevents them from adding to their sinfulness. Penalties imposed by judicial sentences produce great benefits for human society in quieting down criminals. So too, the pains and tribulations imposed by the creator produce great benefits for the human race, and if they do not benefit those who suffer them, they at least deter others. Because pains and tribulations produce great benefits, they must come from the providence of the creator.

Again William turns to examples. Just as a nurse puts something bitter on her nipples in order to wean a child, so the creator, the nurse or nurturer of the whole human race, sprinkles bitterness on the pleasures of this life in order to wean human beings from the childish or puerile pleasures of this life and to make them long for the true pleasure of the next life. So too, just as a father may punish his son to keep him from some danger, so God may punish his children to keep them from danger. As a third example, William compares carnal and worldly pleasures to a very strong wine that a good host would temper for his guests with the water of tribulations, which one should not doubt come from the providence of the creator. Finally, William points to the providence and care of the creator in natural things, especially in the production and nourishment of their bodies.

In Chapter 6 William argues that, as the word itself indicates, oppression has many spiritual benefits, since it suppresses the exaltation of pride, presses down the tendency to flighty inconstancy and mobility, and represses excessive haste by its burdens. William points to the disciplines that some Christians and even some philosophers impose upon themselves. So too, poverty contributes to chastity and sobriety and serves as a rampart to ward off the vices of luxury and dissoluteness.

William notes that people have erred about the providence of the creator because of four things: first, because of things that seem to happen by chance and that befall the just and the unjust equally, secondly, because of people, such as the insane, who seems not to be cared about by either God or man, thirdly, because of people who live bad lives according to their desire, and fourthly, because of those who seem to be totally abandoned by everyone.

With regard to the first cause of error William replies that there are no chance events and accidents for the wisdom and goodness of the creator. He argues that penal evils, which the common folk call evils, are really goods and are useful and salutary for human beings. Moreover, temporal or bodily goods, which the goodness of the creator bestows to sustain human beings and to draw them to a love for him, are comparatively small goods that the wise should scorn. The creator used such childish goods to educate the Hebrew people by their law, but now promises the lofty goods of the next life in the law and doctrine of the Christians. Death brings a benefit, even for the wicked since it brings an end to their sinning, and the fear of death is salutary against human torpor and helps one prepare for the next life.

Chapter 7 takes up response to the second source of error about divine providence and argues that the mad or insane are not beyond the care of God. Some of them are cared for by being bound or beaten so that they do not harm themselves or others, and others are sheltered and fed by their fellow human beings. Even those who seem utterly abandoned by human beings are still under the care and providence of the creator. William cites Galen on a benefit of melancholy and mentions some holy and religious men who desired melancholy because it put them in a state in which they could not sin. In bringing the chapter to a close William argues that penal evils are wrongly and falsely called evil by common and foolish people. Patiently suffering for the truth, for example, is both praiseworthy in the eyes of human beings and deserving of reward from the creator. This William mentions should suffice with regard to the fourth reason for error about divine providence.

Chapter 8 continues the topic of the previous chapter about people who live voluptuous lives and misuse the gifts of the creator. William argues that the wisdom of the creator chose to win the love and obedience of such people by his gifts and benefits rather than to wear them down by tribulations. The fact that people misuse temporal goods and turn them to the corruption of their souls is contrary to the intention of the creator. William gives examples of bodily goods that people misuse and turn to their own punishment, and he claims that such just punishments are inflicted by the care and providence of the creator. He gives scriptural and historical examples of such punishments as well as some bits of folklore that strain credulity. Even the barbarian nations display some forms of justice and thus come under the providence of the creator.

Chapter 9 argues that people who live sinful lives of pleasure amid delights and according to their own desire impose upon themselves the punishment of God, making the benefits of the creator the instruments of their own punishment, for their spiritual diseases and wounds are far worse than bodily evils, to the extent that souls are more excellent than bodies. At times, however, the beneficence of the creator can turn impious and evil persons away from their wicked lives, and William gives the example of a sinful man who despite his sinfulness was chosen for the dignity of the priesthood and was as a result so overwhelmed by the goodness of God that he committed himself to a life of the strictest religion. He argues that those who suffer scourges, tribulations, and woes of the body do not fall outside the providence of the creator for they either suffer these for the sake of justice or as punishment for their own sins and crimes. Hence, they are not abandoned by the creator. William explains how, although the creator gives a sinner the power to do evil, the creator is not the efficient cause of the malice and disorder of the sinner's will, again using concrete examples.

Chapter 10 argues that God's wisdom knows small things no less than great ones. William first returns to the examples of which fish is caught or which rabbit is snared, but soon turns to the two meanings of "to care" and "not to care." In one sense God is said to care only about something by which he is pleased or offended, that is, something that he rewards or punishes. In this sense

God does not care about which fly is eaten by which swallow or which fish is caught by which fisherman. In this sense one is said to care about something that one takes to heart or that burns one's heart, and in this sense God is said to care metaphorically in the same way he is said to be angry or placated. In a second sense "to care about" means much the same as "to pay attention to" or "to think about," and in this sense God cares about even the most minute creatures and orders them to their ends.

Chapter 11 turns to the topic of chance. Chance events, such as the encounter of two persons on a road, neither of whom had intended to meet the other, provide the key to understanding why one fish is caught rather than another or why one rabbit is snared rather than another. William points to many factors that contributed to this fish's being caught rather than that one, but insists that the wisdom of the creator sees each of them and orders them to their ends and uses, which are all known to him. Hence, there is no absolute chance under the providence of God. William points to various ways the creator conserves various species of animals, such as by the inclusion of all the kinds of animals in Noah's ark and by giving various kinds of animals different means of self-preservation.

Chapter 12 offers an explanation of why God allows evil persons to flourish in this life. William claims that many benefits come to good people from being oppressed and afflicted by those who flourish in this life and that those who are evil are given reason to admire the creator's goodness and generosity and are thus challenged to love and obey the creator. Good people are, furthermore, taught that riches and delights are minor goods that are scarcely to be considered among the gifts of the creator since he gives them even to his enemies.

In Chapter 13 William points to the benefits that come from a firm belief in the providence of God and argues that the error of those who deny God's providence causes great harm for it uproots all concern for moral goodness, destroys all the honor of the virtues, and removes all hope of future happiness.

Chapter 14 turns to some objections raised against divine providence. Some people, for example, wonder how God can care for so many and such diverse things. William replies with an example from Apuleius who argued that, just as a king or military general can set a whole army in motion with all the different tasks involved by a single trumpet blast, so the omnipotent creator moves the whole universe of creatures by one act of his most imperious will. Moreover, the spiritual and abstract substances, that is, the angels, and the first human beings were created with a natural knowledge of the divine will. William also appeals to Augustine's example of a king who, in undertaking to build a city, moves so many builders to their different tasks by his one will and command. He develops a similar example from a well-ordered kingdom and argues that in an analogous way the creator orders everything in his kingdom, the kingdom of all ages, and arranges everything by natural, human, or divine laws. Finally, he appeals to the example of a well-organized royal court in which everything is ordered and arranged by the king.

In Chapter 15 William turns to the ancient question of whether the providence and care of the creator imposes necessity on things and events. He first states the reasons that have led people to suppose that it does, namely, that it is impossible for divine providence to be deceived or to err. Hence, people wrongly conclude that everything is necessary, immutable, and unavoidable. William dismisses as useless the distinction between necessity said "about the thing: *de re*" and "about the proposition: *de dicto*," proposes a solution in terms of universality or singularity, and notes that the same thing is said with the terms "compositely: *composite*" and "separately: *divisim*." For example, if in the proposition, "Everything that God has foreseen will necessarily come about," the necessity refers to the totality or universality of the things God has foreseen, the proposition is true, but if the necessity refers to the single or individual things that God has foreseen, e.g., this or that event, the proposition is not true. Such propositions involve what William call a duplicity or a two-fold intention or meaning since the necessity can refer either to the totality of things foreseen or to particular or individual things that are foreseen. William complains that, though in his time even children were aware of such duplicities, many are now still miserably entangled in them. He also explains that necessity can pertain either to the condition or consequence or to the consequent, that is, to the whole conditional proposition or to the consequent. He points to another source of error, namely, the belief that, because a proposition, if true, is always true, it is for this reason necessarily true. Thus, even if divine providence has foreseen something from eternity, it does not follow that it is necessary.

Chapter 16 undertakes to explain how it is true that the creator has foreseen something and that it is still possible that he did not foresee it. William explains that nothing is added to God's knowledge and nothing is taken away from his knowledge. Thus by one and the same knowledge he knows or sees one of two contradictories when it is true and will know the other when it is true. Our knowledge, which is derived from the things known, is changed when we gain some knowledge or lose some knowledge. Hence, it is true that the creator knew something from all eternity and that it is still possible that he never knew it. Although the creator's providence is infallible and immutable so that it is impossible that he foresees something otherwise than it comes about, it is still possible with regard to anything he has foreseen that he did not foresee it. William again appeals to what he calls duplicities or twofold states to exclude any change, such as learning or forgetting in God's knowledge. On the other hand, although there is no newness in God's knowledge, he can truly be said to create something anew, because such creation involves no change in God, but in the new creature.

Chapter 17 warns the reader to be circumspect with regard to words used about God that signify a newness or twofold state, such as "to begin," "to cease," or "first to exist at some point." Similarly, one should avoid terms that signify an addition, lessening, or increase. For nothing can be added to the things that the creator has foreseen or subtracted from them. The creator's knowledge is essential to him and in no way adventitious; hence, there is no change in his knowledge, but our knowledge, which is derived from things, changes when we come to know something or forget something. The creator cannot, William claims, have some knowledge that he never had, but his knowledge can fall upon something that it previously had not fallen upon. He explains that the falling of his knowledge upon something is a relation whose acquisition or loss entails nothing new in him. Similarly, one thing can become equal to another thing without any change in the first thing. William appeals to the example of a king who acquires a new subject in his kingdom, but does not thereby acquire new royal power.

In Chapter 18 William turns to another error concerning words and propositions about God. Some people argue that the creator can know only what is true and only as long as it is true; hence, he begins to know something when it begins to be true and ceases to know it when it ceases to be true. Thus it seems to follow that he learns something that he previously did not know or loses knowledge of something that he once knew. Another error claims that stateables (*enunciabilia*), that is, all truths and falsities, existed from eternity apart from creatures and all the works of the creator. William is adamant that nothing apart from the creator exists from eternity. He claims that by affirmations and negations one affirms or denies what is signified by predicates of things signified by subjects. Besides natural compositions of subjects and predicates, there are rational compositions and divisions produced by the intellect, that is, affirmations and negations, and these can be true or false, possible or impossible, necessary or contingent. And by such rational compositions and divisions we can join or separate mentally what is not and cannot be joined or separated in reality. Against the error that maintains that stateables exist eternally independent of the creator, William points to the eternal knowledge of the creator that sees everything past, present, and future. He reminds his reader that the duplicity of states he has mentioned has no place in the creator's knowledge and that the providence of the creator does not impose necessity upon things. He argues that, if the necessity of future events followed from the providence of the creator, the creator would be the cause of good things and evil ones, such as "future adulteries, murders, and other such blameworthy evils." Furthermore, the fact that the creator knows that something will come about does not make it necessary that it come about. Although God's knowledge falls upon many things from eternity, it is still possible that it never fell upon any of them.

Chapter 19 takes up a new topic, namely, four reasons that led people to deny freedom and hold that everything takes place of necessity, namely, mistaken ideas about divine providence, the motion and configurations of the stars, *heimarmene* or the interconnected series of causes, and fate. Since William has already argued against the first reason, Chapter 20 turns to the second of these reasons, namely, that the motions of the heavens and dispositions of the stars introduce necessity into everything that is done in this world. William first points out the destructive consequences for human life and morality that stem from the belief that the positions of the stars determine everything that happens in the world. He secondly argues against the "lazy argument," reported by Cicero in *On Fate*, that, given such determinism, everything that we do is either useless or superfluous. Thirdly William argues that our freedom is such that we cannot be forced to will anything or prevented from willing anything, although he admits that some of our bodily actions are able to be coerced or prevented. Neither the act of willing or of refusing nor actions dependent upon our willing or refusing are, therefore, subject to determination by the motions of the heavens or of the stars. Moreover, in a *reductio ad absurdum* argument, William points out that, if the motions of the heavens and of the stars were the causes of our voluntary acts, all human sinfulness would have to be imputed to them, while human beings would be completely innocent.

Chapter 21 argues against the third reason for holding that everything that happens in this world is necessary, namely, *heimarmene*, that is, destiny or fate. William attributes the doctrine to Hermes Trismegistos, although the doctrine of an interconnected or intertwined series of causes sounds like the position that Augustine argued against in the *City of God*, when he attacked Cicero's account of fate.[7] However, from his refutation of *heimarmene*, it seems that William understood the position as a theological determinism rather than as a determinism of present events by past events, which is more what Augustine and Cicero seem to have understood by fate. For William immediately asks whether they traced the series of causes back to the first cause, which is the creator, and he insists that the first cause either acts freely or in the manner

---

7   See Augustine, *City of God* 5.8; PL 41: 148.

of nature and of a servant. Here he is alluding to Avicenna who claimed that nature acts in the manner of a servant,[8] which is, of course, a manner utterly inappropriate to the creator. William has an interesting discussion of the common expression, "being coerced or compelled by love," and argues that such compulsion does not diminish the freedom of the lover, just as the freedom of the holy angels and blessed in heaven is not diminished by their love of God.

In Chapter 22 William examines whether an effect follows necessarily, given the aggregate of the efficient cause and all the things that help it. Interestingly William remarks that the argument that the cause and all its helps make the effect necessary had led him as a youth to think that every event is necessary. Here he argues that, given the efficient cause and all the things that help it, it is necessary that the beginning of the effect exist, but that in things that come about through a temporal succession, it is not necessary that their completion come about. For the completion of the work or event requires the aggregate of many possible things, any one of which may be lacking.

Chapter 23 points out that many actions depend upon those who are acted upon and that such actions are often not contrary to the will of the one acted upon. William then claims that "a cause is said to be in our power when we can bring it about that it is or that it operates or prevent that it is or that it operates." Thus the sun is not in our power because we cannot bring its existence or its operation about or prevent its existence or operation. An objector, however, might argue that, if an effect is in our power, its cause is also in our power as well as the cause of its cause. Hence, if any cause is in our power, the first cause or God will be in our power. But since the first cause is not in our power, nothing will be in our power. Hence, if nothing is in our power, all things will exist or will come about of necessity in relation to us. In response William explains that to say that the first cause is in our power seems to imply its subjection to us and claims that we should avoid language that has even the appearance or suspicion of error. Yet, just as we can prevent the sunlight from entering our house, so we can prevent the works of the creator in us by blocking his generosity or by turning away from his goodness. Such actions on our part, however, are not absolutely in our power, presumably because God could overwhelm us by his grace. Hence, in the proper sense something is said to be in the power of the creator alone.

---

8   See Avicenna, *Metaphysics* 9.2; ed. Van Reit, p. 448. Also see Michael Miller, "William of Auvergne and Avicenna's Principle 'Natures Operates in the Manner of a Servant.'" In *Medieval Philosophy and the Classical Tradition: In Islam, Judaism and Christianity*. Ed. John Inglis (Richmond, Surrey: Curzon, 2002), pp. 263–276.

Chapter 24 turns to an investigation of fate. William explains that in one intention fate is good fortune or ill fortune, prosperity or adversity that has been preordained, predestined, or prepared for someone at birth or before. In accord with this intention astrologers supposedly can tell the fate of someone from the position of the stars at his birth. In another intention fate is taken to be what the gods or goddesses have decreed. Stories about people who heard the gods or goddesses conversing about the great future successes of someone being born have fostered belief in fate in this sense. Such persons were said to have been fated from birth.

William sets out to discover the truth about fate. He cites Cicero's definitions of fate from *On Divination*, but points out that Cicero did not explain why fate was so named. Referring back to his work on *The Trinity*, William links the name "fate" to the Word of God by which and in which the Father eternally spoke all that has been, is, or will be. Although the creator foresees culpable evils, he does not, however, cause them to exist, but merely permits them to exist.

In Chapter 25, however, William warns that, if one understands the Word of God as fate, one must be very careful in using the expression, since only goods, whether of nature or of grace, can be said to come from the Word of God. Moreover, the Christian people avoid the use of the term "fate," for it is necessary to avoid not only the errors of any impiety, but even the semblance and suspicion of such. Then William warns his readers not to be disturbed by the subtleties of sophists who say that, because the creator eternally spoke all future events, because his word is absolutely immutable, and because he cannot possibly lie, it is necessary that everything he said come about or be true. He urges them to recall the duplicities about which he has warned them and reminds them that, although it is impossible that things be otherwise than God has said, it is perfectly true that he has spoken many things from eternity, concerning each of which it is possible that he did not say it.

William returns to the error of those who held that stateables (*enuntiabilia*) existed from eternity. The error arose, he explains, from that belief that, if such stateables were true, they were true by the truth that existed in them. But if the truth existed in them, the stateables themselves had to exist since nothing can exist in non-existing things. Wanting to avoid the supposition that such truths were true by a truth that did not exist or that existed in what did not exist, such misguided thinkers claimed that true stateables were true by the first truth. William argues that they must have meant that they were true by the first truth either formally or effectively. If they are true by the first truth formally, then the first truth, which is none other than the creator, is predicated of them when they are said to be true, which clearly will not do for a number of reasons that William points out. If they are true by the first truth effectively, then some effect of the first truth is predicated of them, which is an illumination by the light of the first truth. But that outpouring of light from the first truth is either natural or voluntary. If it is natural, it will be servile and incompatible with the nobility of the creator. But if it is voluntary, then all truths will be true by the creator's will, and then such truths as that this man steals and that man kills will be caused by the creator. As William argues the point, "whatever causes it to be true that this man steals causes him to steal."

William begins Chapter 26 with six senses of truth. In the first sense truth is simply the thing signified. In the second sense truth is opposed to falsity, which is the appearance of something that is not there. Thus a false man is one who externally pretends to be what he is not interiorly. In the third sense truth is purity from adulteration. Thus silver is true if it is not mixed with something else. In the fourth sense the truth is what is left when all the accidents are stripped away from a thing; hence, the truth in this sense is what is expressed in a definition, namely, an account of the substance of a thing. In the fifth sense truth is the being of the creator in comparison with which everything else is false, since everything else has its being from elsewhere. In the sixth sense truth is the adequation of speech and reality, a definition that William attributes to Avicenna. He notes that speech in that definition can be either vocal or intellectual. As an adequation or agreement, truth in this sense is a relation between a stateable (*enuntiabile*) and its utterance.

William explains that, unlike a disposition such as whiteness, a relation does not add anything to or subtract anything from the things of which it is said. Similarly, what is said or signified does not, by reason of the fact that it is said or signified, have anything in it. In the same way what is said or signified need not exist, just as what is loved or desired does not need to exist. William then applies this to the relation of truth. For example, stateables about the future are true with such an agreement, harmony, adequation, or equality, but such agreements put nothing in things. He claims that stateables about the future, where neither the subjects nor the predicates exist, are true with such "agreement, harmony, adequation, or equality." The agreement between a statement and what it signifies is a privation or is said according to privation. Hence, he maintains that nothing prevents something from being true with a truth that does not exist, just as something is naked with a nakedness that does not exist, since nakedness is a privation. Furthermore, when stateables are said to be true, that is, agreeing with their affirmations or negations, this is not understood in terms of act, but in terms of potency. Hence, one is not forced to say that countless truths or stateables have existed in act from eternity. As something is true that does not exist, such as that a chimera does not exist, so something is true with a truth that does not exist.[9]

In Chapter 27 William takes up three topics: first, the source of the term "fate," second, the claim that being fated by the goddesses or demons should be scorned, and third, an inquiry about the soul of the world according to Plato. William notes that the laws of the Hebrews and of the Christians contain reports of revelations at or before the births of great human beings of important events in their lives. Both laws, however, avoid the use of the term "fate." The idea of people being fated from or before their births is, according to William, a leftover from the idolatry, which survives mainly because of the superstition and greed of some old women. William argues that the predictions of fate, which are supposed to be non-retractable decrees of the gods, impose no necessity on the life of human beings, since even the word of the creator does not impose such necessity. Furthermore, many such predictions prove to be false or so ambiguous that they could seem to be true whatever occurs.

Some philosophers and others have introduced many other ruling or governing powers in the sublunar world, such as the soul of the world, and since William is dealing with the governance of the world, he begins a consideration of the soul of the world. For, just as the soul of any living being governs its body, so the soul of the world, it would seem, ought to govern the world, especially since Plato held that it is a living being that understands the sanction of divine wisdom.

Chapter 28 returns to Plato's view of the world soul. Against those who claim that there is only one soul for the nine heavens, William points out that the same proof that shows one heaven is animated shows that all are animated, namely, their motions, but that the diversity of their motions indicates a diversity of movers. He argues at length against the position that there is only one soul for all the heavens, which he takes to be what Plato held. Much of the lengthy chapter proceeds in a hypothetical manner in which William answers arguments that a defender of a world soul might present. He asks, for example, why, if that soul moves the planets, it moves them in epicycles and retrogressions and so that it produces eclipses of the sun and moon and whether it does so knowingly or unknowingly. If the soul moves them in that way in ignorance, William wonders why it has not learned what it is doing, since even human astronomers have over time learned these motions.

In Chapter 29 William first undertakes to state what Plato held regarding the soul of the world. He says that in his opinion Plato did not hold that the

9   On William's theory of truth and his account of immutable truths, see Steven P. Marrone, *William of Auvergne and Robert Grosseteste: New Ideas of Truth in the Early Thirteenth Century* (Princeton: Princeton University Press, 1983), pp. 74–97.

whole world was one living being, but held that only the heaven, that is, from the sphere of the moon up, was animated. On this he thinks that Plato and Avicenna were in agreement. After deploring the claim, which he attributes to Abumasar, that God is the spirit of the heaven, he suggests that this great philosopher could not really have made such a terrible mistake, but more probably meant that the spirit of the heaven was God by participation. Then turning to the question of whether there is one or many souls of the heavens, he argues against the idea that there is one soul by which the various heavens are animated. He points out that the position of those who hold that there is one soul for the many heavens will lead them to believe that there is one soul in a plurality of human beings and that the soul is multiplied only by different accidents. William argues against the view that a variety of accidents produce numerical difference, although he admits that in this life different accidents may allow us to recognize a numerical difference. Avicenna's position on the individuation of human souls may be in the background on what William is opposing here for, as William interpreted him, the great Islamic thinker held that souls were individuated by diverse accidents, including their relation to the body.[10] Boethius, who had said that only a variety of accidents produces numerical difference, receives a benevolent interpretation.

Returning to Plato's position that there is only one soul in the nine mobile heavens, William argues that nothing prevents one soul from animating all the heavens and appeals to the example of a magnet whose power of attraction operates by mere contact and seems to be able to attract an endless series of pins. Similarly, William suggests that it is possible that the first heaven, the seat of the soul, may well pour life, motion, and other operations into the bodies of subsequent heavens.

Chapter 30 undertakes the destruction of the error of Plato who held that the soul of the world is composed of numbers and musical harmonies. William admits that our souls find great delight in musical harmonies and explains that Plato argued that, because nothing is delighted save by its like, the soul must be like such harmonies and even be composed of them. Hence, the soul of the world must also be composed of such harmonies and resound with music. Arguing against this view, William appeals to Aristotle who argued that there cannot be any sound or music in the heavens, since sound requires air, which cannot be found above the sphere of fire in the sublunar world. He further argues that, according to the teachings of Ptolemy, the motions of the spheres of the planets are not related in harmonious proportions. William also puzzles

---

10   See my "William of Auvergne on the Individuation of Human Souls," *Traditio* 49 (1994): 77–93.

over many things that Plato said in the *Timaeus* about how the soul is stretched out in the shape of the human body.

In Chapter 31 William states that, although Aristotle and his followers as well as many Italian philosophers held determinate views about the soul or souls of the heavens, the Jewish people had been content with its law until they turned to incredible myths—where William is perhaps alluding to the Talmud and/or Kabbalah. He states that the Christian people were not interested in such souls because they were concerned about their own souls. He points to a great Christian teacher, probably Augustine, who confessed his ignorance and doubt about such questions. In any case he insists that such souls of the heavens play no rule in governing human affairs. In Chapter 32 William briefly rejects any ruling power in the world besides the creator and his assistants, that is, the angels, about whom he will deal in the second part of the second principal part of the work. In the final chapter of the first principal part William denounces those Christian teachers who have held that the Holy Spirit was the soul of the world and argues that a soul is a perfection and a part of what it animates and is bound to its body. Thus William brings the first principal part of *The Universe* to an end.

William's style is often rambling and can leave the reader confused about the point he is trying to make. At times he writes more in the style of a preacher or pastor exhorting and encouraging his flock; at other times he presents clearly articulated philosophical arguments, and at still other times he reports bits of scientific data, of folklore, or even of just plain gossip. William has little patience with stupidity and errors. Some errors, he says, should not even be argued against, but should rather be wiped out by fire and the sword. He is not reluctant to refer to people in error as feeble-minded and to describe an erroneous view as one "that an unimaginable feebleness of intellect has dreamed up."

The Latin text of the *De universo* is in need of a modern critical edition. I conjectured fairly often, as I indicated in the notes, readings that I thought the sense demanded or that were at least better than what was found in the Paris-Orléans edition. I included the chapter titles in the text and in the introduction, although they are not William's work, and the chapter divisions often do not follow the logic of the thought in the way one might expect. Often the Latin is able to dispense with extra words that English demands; hence, I have added in angular brackets words that I believed were either necessary or at least helpful for clarifying the text.

Finally, I want to thank Father Martin D. O'Keefe, S.J., who carefully checked my translation, corrected my mistakes, and offered many helpful suggestions.

THE BEGINNING OF THE THIRD PART OF THE FIRST PRINCIPAL PART OF

The Universe of Creatures

by

William of Auvergne,

Where He Deals with the Providence of God regarding the Universe

The Preface

After this I shall begin to speak about the governance of the bodily universe, and especially with regard to human affairs and human beings themselves. And this is because there has been a greater and more dangerous error regarding human beings and human affairs, and many are still in error. To those with little understanding, even the prophets of the Hebrews can seem to have doubted about the care and providence of the creator, and you can read this in the books of the Hebrews.[1] Some of the more noble of the poets also wrote in their poetic books that they had doubts.[2]

I shall, therefore, set forth for you first of all questions about these matters, and I shall try to settle them, because from knowledge, that is, from sapiential knowledge there comes knowledge of the governance of God most high, as you have heard from the words of Avicenna.[3] The first of these questions is whether the blessed and lofty creator has care for all things and for individual

---

1 See, for example, the Books of Job and Ecclesiastes.

2 Virgil's *Aeneid*, for example, is full of references to the Fates; the Fates are mentioned more than a dozen times in the first two books.

3 See Avicenna, *Metaphysics* (*Liber de philosophia prima sive scientia divina*) 3 vols., ed. Simone Van Reit (Louvaine-La-Neuve: E. Peeters, 1977, 1983, 1983), 1.3,

ones and concerning all things and individual ones. The second is how he has care for the evils that happen to just and holy human beings in this life and concerning other things that are related to this question, namely, how and with what benefit or utility he allows evil persons to flourish here, I mean, in riches and delights, and similarly with what benefit or fruit he allows good persons to be afflicted here and also to be oppressed among the evil and allows the evil to dominate the good and to move against them with many sorts of tyranny and violence.

After this I shall inquire about evil itself whether it /754b/ comes about through the providence of the creator. I shall also speak here about fate and the Fates, by whom human beings are said to be fated or to have been fated, and this language is extremely common and very characteristic of old women. I shall also speak about those that are called Parcae among the poets and are named by them Clotho, Lachesis, and Atropos.[4] And I shall make you know how necessity does not come to contingent things from the foreknowledge and providence of the creator and how our free will is in no way impeded, prevented, limited, or restricted by them, in terms of willing and not willing, doing and not doing, save insofar and in what ways I shall show you.

CHAPTER 1
On the Difference between Foreknowledge and Providence,
And That All and Individual Goods and Evils Are Cared for and Ruled
By the Creator Immediately or Mediately

First of all, know that the intention[5] of foreknowledge differs from the intention of providence, because the intention of foreknowledge is broader and extends over future goods and future evils. For the blessed creator equally foreknows goods and evils, and the converse. But the intention of providence is more restricted and applies only to future goods. For we commonly say that only good things are provided for. For no one is said to

---

p. 21, where he says that "the ultimate intention in this science is the knowledge of the governance of God most high. ..."

4   The Parcae were the Italian goddesses of birth and death, while Clotho, Lachesis, and Atropos were the Greek names for the goddesses who respectively spun out the thread of life, allotted it to each person, and inevitably cut it off.

5   Following Avicenna, whom he followed on many points, William uses "intention" as a synonym for conceptual content or meaning as well as in the sense of purpose and goal. Since his debt to the great Islamic philosophy is great, I have preserved the Avicennian term in the translation.

provide something evil for himself or for another. After all, someone provides who deliberately intends to do something or that something be done. But evils are not intended deliberately or circumspectly, but rather by error.

Moreover, someone who provides something procures by an intention that it be done or come about in some way. But it is not the intention of the divine goodness that evils come about or are done, I mean blameworthy evils. But it also does not pertain to the same goodness to procure that such evils are done or come about. Hence, it is evident that evils are not provided for by the creator, just as they are not deliberately procured, although you ought not to doubt that all things, both good and evil, are foreknown by him and antecedently cognized and foreseen, and my intention here is with regard to blameworthy evils.

I shall, therefore, pursue the first question. I say, therefore, that the creator cares for all things and for individual things and for all goods and for individual goods as well as for evils, of which there are two kinds, namely, blameworthy ones and penal ones, although he does this in a different way. But it is necessary to see this by parts. For it cannot be doubted that he has care for all the things that come from him by creation, since he knowingly gives them being and conserves them. For this caring is not diminished.

But if someone says that, after he has given them being, he leaves them to themselves, not governing them thereafter or caring for them further, note this error in which many have become involved. Either the creator gave to such things forces and powers by which they are sufficient to rule or govern themselves without further care of the creator, or he did not. If he did and did so knowingly, of course, and providently, they are, therefore, ruled through his providence, since there was produced in them through his care and providence that by which they rule themselves. For they have it from his care and providence that they rule and govern themselves.

But a most evident example of this matter is found in someone who, wishing to rule his son by himself, chose for him and gave him a governor, instructing him how to rule the son and setting limits for him in the governance of the son by certain commands and rules. In this example it is evident that the father did not leave the son to himself, but rather entrusted him to be ruled by a governor instructed by him. Nor can anyone doubt that the father has care for his son, and no one will dare to say that he neglects him or has neglected him. Those things that are neglected are, of course, said not to be cared for.

Moreover, such forces or powers /755a/ are like helms by which the things rule themselves according to this. No helmsman, however, of ships is said not to govern the ship, of which he holds the helm, but is said to govern it by the helm. If, therefore, the creator holds such powers, which are helms of such things, how will he be said not to govern such things?

Moreover, he who rules the ruler or governs the governor, insofar as he is ruler or governor, undoubtedly rules and governs that which is ruled or governed by him. For the helms of ships are governed by their rulers, and this is done by their hands as by rudders of a sort, but the hands are governed by the muscles, nerves, and ligaments, and these in turn by the moving powers, and so on until one comes to the governor's wisdom, which is the helm through itself and not in need of another governor, if it is true and perfect wisdom. And it is necessary that it be this way with the wisdom of the creator, which through itself governs and directs those things that are immediately before him and through them those that immediately follow, and so on until one comes to the last things governed by the creator.

If someone, then, wants to say that all things created are not immediately ruled by the creator, that is, through himself alone, I do not oppose this, since he rules countless things through both bodily and spiritual rulers. For many human beings are rulers of others, and many angels preside over other angels and human beings, and in animals it is also found in many kinds that parents rule and train their offspring, as eagles train their offspring to fly, and hawks do so similarly. In flight many birds, such as cranes, chose a leader for themselves.

Moreover, such forces either naturally need a ruler and governor, or they do not. If they need one, the creator either provided or did not provide one. If he did not provide one although they needed one, he left them to chance and happenstance. He, therefore, knowingly willed that they be in danger. Hence, he created them for chance or ruin, and danger. But if he provided rulers or a ruler for them, which undoubtedly befits his wisdom and goodness, then either he is through himself their immediate ruler, or there are other rulers, and he of necessity rules them through those others. It is evident, then, that in those things that come from the creator by creation his care and providence has a place.

Moreover, those are most noble in rational creatures, and similarly bodily ones, which come from the creator by a most noble creation. But I understand this concerning bodily ones that are merely bodily. If he does not, therefore, have care for those that are most noble, for all the more reason he will not have care for the less noble, and thus he will care for nothing at all in the universe. For, if he does not care for the more noble ones, much less will he care for the least noble, and if <he does not care for> the highest, much less will he not care for the intermediate and the lowest.

Moreover, every creature needs the care and governance of the creator in terms of its conservation in being. But someone might say that animals that conserve their being through nourishment do not need further care from the creator, but its nature is sufficient, because, when a pig is born, it knows how to run to the dugs of its mother and to suck milk. Similarly, for grazing on grass and taking other nutriments, they do not need a leader or teacher, and on this account they are self-sufficient for the conservation of their life. Although I have already removed this objection in the foregoing, I shall also add other things to remove this objection more fully and clearly. I say, therefore, that nature, which teaches animals to seek food in that way and to preserve life, is their governor. But the most wise creator gave this to them, and he gave this, of course, so that they would be governed by it and through it. This statement, therefore, comes to this, namely, that one who says this admits that the creator governs such animals, but does so by that intermediate ruler, that is, by such a nature. However, one who /755b/ admits that the creator cares for and governs something, but does so by another intermediate ruler and governor, does not destroy the care or governance of the creator, but rather explains it.

CHAPTER 2
That the Providence of God Extends Not Only to Higher Things,
But Also to These Lower Particular Things, However Small

But with regard to the motions of the heavens, stars, and lights, with regard to the changes of the seasons, and with regard to the generations and corruptions that follow upon the changes of seasons on account of the care and providence of the creator, the benefits that come from them for human beings and other animals, which could only come about by the care and providence of the creator, are clear proofs for those who are intelligent. For the creator would have uselessly created such things, namely, human beings, other animals, and plants, if he had not provided for them food and other things without which they could not last. An example of the sort is found in an architect who not only uselessly, but also foolishly would have built a house that was going to fall down by itself and immediately, if he had not added supports to it by which it would be stabilized.

Similarly, frequency or perpetuity, and universality are most certain proofs of care and providence, and they remove chance and happenstance, as I told you in the preceding chapters, for death happens to human beings universally and always, as long as they are here. These two, then, are most certain proofs that death occurs in human beings through the care and providence of the creator. But rarity and particularity, on the contrary, are most certain proofs of chance and happenstance in relation to us, but nothing is chance and happenstance in relation to the creator, and you need to pay careful attention to this in every kind of living beings. For the generation of feet, wings, and even feathers in all the living beings that naturally have such members or helps, such as feathers and scales, are of necessity produced by the care and providence of the creator, because it is perennial, so to speak, that is, lasting as long as the creator has provided that there be living beings here. And it is also universal for each kind of such living beings. Thus it is with the generation of hair in those parts of animals in which it is usually generated.

But I call intelligence care, whether it is mediated or immediate. For how much better reason, then, will the motion of the heavens, which is so frequent and so immutable, come through the care and providence of the creator?

Moreover, it cannot be doubted that the creator foresaw or foreknew what a good the motion of the heavens would be or would have and that on this account he gave the powers for such motion. He has, therefore, provided the motion of the heaven since he procured it on account of the good, either the good that it is or the good that it has from it or that comes from it. But this comes about through care and providence, as I have already told you. This sort of motion, therefore, comes from providence. Hence, everything that by itself naturally follows from it <comes from providence>. Hence, day and night, generations and corruptions, the changes of the four seasons of spring, fall, winter, and summer < come from providence>. But these benefits are known to us; for much better reason <they are known> to the creator. Because, therefore, the intention of someone wise is to intend every good and every benefit in his work that should or can come from his work, for much better reason, this will be the intention of the most wise creator. Hence, /756a/ every good that is or ought to be from any of his works comes through his intention. Every good, however, is either his work or comes from his work. Every good, therefore, comes through his intention and is his effect, either mediated or immediate. But whatever is created by him is created through his wisdom, and on this account every good is provided by him through his care and providence.

But know that the Italian philosophers used the previously mentioned proofs to explain his care and providence with regard to the bodily universe and with regard to bodily things that are generated and corrupted under the sphere of the moon.[6] But they were not able in these ways to extend the care

---

6   See Cicero, *On the Nature of the Gods* (*De natura deorum*) 3.86, where such a doctrine is attributed to the Stoics who hold: "For the gods do not care about little things, nor do they take care of the little plots or vines of individuals. Nor did it have to be called to Jove's attention if drought or hail harmed anyone. Nor

and governance of the creator to individuals of particular things. For that this grain of wheat is generated or corrupted through the care and governance of the creator does not seem to be explained in any way by these paths. The reason is that you were not shown by them that the care and governance of the creator is immediately concerned with such things. But the intention of intermediate things is not <directed at> this. For example, the intention of the father of Socrates was not that Socrates might be generated, but rather that some offspring in general be generated, or perhaps, as someone might say, a vague individual.[7] It is, therefore, good and suited to this chapter, which I began to deal with, to investigate this.

You ought to know, therefore, that it is generally not necessary that the means, by which governance is carried out, pay attention to it, either by a universal intention or by a particular intention, as is evident to you in the equipment of a ship, that is, in the instruments of its governance, because they pay no attention at all, either universally or particularly. Moreover, when human beings are the means of governance, it is also not necessary that they pay attention to all the particulars, as the servants of the chief pilots[8] do not pay attention to the individual waves or surges that can overturn the ship or the individual drops that can flow into the bilge, because they do not think of them with a particular thought. Nor do the guides or those who are walking <think> about individual steps.

And from these examples it might perhaps seem to someone that for even better reason it is not necessary that the omnipotent creator pay attention to the individual elements of those things that are done or governed by his care and governance. For, if a chariot driver need not individually intend or think of the individual steps of the horses pulling his chariot or the individual revolutions of the wheels of the chariot he is ruling, how much less does God, the omnipotent creator and ruler of the universe, not need to pay attention individually to all the things that are ruled by his care and providence, especially since it is incomparably easier for him to rule the universe than for any charioteer to rule the lightest chariot!

Moreover, providence with regard to atoms and grains of sand can seem laughable and ridiculous, especially since no wise person cares about such small

do kings care for all the little things in their kingdoms." William might also have got this doctrine from Augustine, *The Literal Meaning of Genesis* (*De Genesi ad litteram* 5.21.41; PL 34: 336).

7 On "vague individual," see *On the Soul*, ch. 7, pt. 7; Paris-Orléans ed., II, 213a–213b, as well as below in this work, ch. 3, 761a.

8 The Latin has "*argonautarum sive archinautarum*: of the argonauts or chief pilots." I have taken "*sive archinautarum*" as a correction of "*argonautarum*."

things or even knows or wants to know the number of them. For how much better reason, then, should they not be cared about by the creator! Hence it is that some of the wise men and teachers of the Christians were considered flatterers of God, when they said that he cared for such things.[9] Notice, therefore, in these examples that were set forth for you here, that there are statements in them whose intentions you need to look at carefully, namely, that a charioteer is said to rule a chariot or the horses pulling it and that a guide of a journey <is said to rule> those traveling. For these things are not said unqualifiedly or in terms of the whole. For the horses rule their steps by their senses and estimative power,[10] and most of all by those, and in a very small amount by the charioteer. So it is with those journeying and their guide.

But concerning the father of a family and any wise person, who does not /756b/ care for the very minor things of his house, like the atoms or grains of sand, this is, of course, true. But the reason is that the attention of such a wise man is limited to those things that are useful to him or expedient for his house or for those that he has to take care of or to provide for because of his office. Hence it is that he does not care about the number of atoms and of other minutiae of this sort and <does not care> about some things, but only about those in which there is the hope or certitude of the benefits he intends.

Moreover, it is not possible for a human being to care about them individually or one by one, because he cannot even think of them. But in the creator care and providence are as remotely otherwise and as dissimilar as his goodness and wisdom are remote from human wisdom and goodness, however great they might be. For, as the largeness or fewness of things does not help the wisdom of the creator or his vision, so neither does the smallness nor the multitude of them impede it in any way. For this was explained in the first part of this knowledge,[11] and the reason for this is that the creator is not wise because of something else or from outside, but is wise essentially, that is, by that which he is, and for this reason he likewise knows the future, present, and past equally. Similarly, he knows small as well as great things, many as well as few things,

9   See Jerome, *Commentary on Habakkuk the Prophet* (*Commentarium in Abucuc prophetam*) 1.1; PL 25: 1286–1297.

10   The estimative power was in psychology of Avicenna and William a sense power by which an animal or a human being recognizes sensible things that are naturally good for or harmful to the animal or human being. For an extensive treatment of the internal senses, see George P. Klubertanz, *The Discursive Power. Sources and Doctrine of the Vis Cogitativa according to St. Thomas Aquinas* (St Louis: Modern Schoolman, 1952).

11   See *The Trinity* (*De trinitate*), ch. 9; ed. Switalski (Toronto: Pontifical Institute of Mediaeval Studies, 1976), pp. 60–62.

bodily as well as spiritual things, and conversely. Similarly, he knows particular things as well as universal ones. Hence, he sees both the individual things he created and the individual benefits of them in the ultimate degree of clarity and strength. From this it is evident that he provides all the instances of the goodness of creatures individually and bestows them individually. But this is to exist through his providence and care, that is, to be good or beneficial or to have been made deliberately and knowingly.

Moreover, in any continuum there are undoubtedly infinite parts, and as the creator provided and cared for the whole, so he provided and cared that there would be a half, and the same way is concerning a half of the half, and so on to infinity. For one who provides and cares for a house's coming to be, provides and cares that there is a wall and also for a stone's being in the wall. But it is not necessary for him to take care that the parts of the stone are in the stone. For he finds this already made apart from his care and providence. But the blessed creator found none of the things that he makes or made and found nothing made otherwise or by another. By "made otherwise" I mean "not made through his care and providence." It is evident, therefore, that the whole continuum with the universality and infinity of parts was made through the care and providence of the creator. But this is seen clearly from the fact that, since the generation of everything natural, that is, of any continuum that is generated, comes only through the generating power given by the creator for this benefit, namely, of generating, it follows that each and every part of any generated continuum comes about through the care and providence of the creator, and for even better reasons <each and every part> of any created continuum, which I say on account of the last heaven, namely, the empyrean heaven, and on account of the earth, which seems perhaps to have been created and not generated in the proper sense. But concerning the nine mobile heavens that were made in between the waters, it is perhaps more likely that they were generated or made from the waters, that is, from the middle part of the waters in the place of which they were put and set in order.

I shall, therefore, return to that point at which I was, and I shall say that, just as the parts in a whole continuum, despite their numerousness or even infinity, exist, I say, through the providence of the creator, so for much better reason <the parts> in a non-continuous whole, that is, in every mountain of sand and on the shore of any sea and on the bank of any river, <exist through his providence>. For neither their infinity nor their numerousness blocks the wisdom of the creator so that it sees it less than <it sees> finiteness, so to speak, or sees infinite things less than one thing.

Moreover, everyone who provides for his house knows how to gather stalks and straws for building a house or constructing a roof from them, although he does not see /757a/ the benefit of each straw or stalk by itself with a singular and determine vision. In the universal, of course, he sees the bundle of straw is necessary for one of the two previously mentioned purposes. For much better reason does the creator, who sees all things and each individual thing and sees the benefits of all the individuals certainly and clearly, know how to gather the tiniest particles or smallest bodies into a continuous whole or an aggregate whole. For he knows no less the benefit of each grain of sand, however small, and the benefit of the whole heap formed from countless grains of sand. It is necessary, therefore, that small and minute bodies, in whatever degree of smallness they are, exist through the providence and care of the creator. Hence, he knows the usefulness of each grain of sand, which it has in itself and by itself, and incomparably more clearly than we know those that it has in the whole. But on account of the dullness and obscurity of our intellect and its shortsightedness we do not reach such small things, just as by our bodily vision we cannot see such small things in their smallness until they have been gathered into an atrium or some other mass or continuity bound together in the totality of something. It is, therefore, evident to you from this that the creator knows the individuals of his creatures and knows the individual parts of them.

Moreover, if he cared about individual things coming to be and about their goodness and well-being, providing for each a suitable and salutary place for it, and also gave to each the power of acquiring that place, how are all the things he created through his providence and care not under his care and providence? How is it likely that he neglects to rule and govern those that he willed to exist and created?

Moreover, since he created each of the things that exist on account of certain benefits, it is necessary that he direct them and guide them to those benefits, insofar as it is up to him, and to the end on account of which he willed that they exist. I say this on account of bad human beings and bad angels, who, although they were created by him for the most noble happiness, that is, perpetual happiness, do not, nonetheless, attain that. But the reason for this is the voluntary malice by which they turn away from his rule and direction in this respect. For they are not outside his kingdom, but he often quiets them down and weakens them so that bad angels do not do as much harm as they want and bad human beings cannot carry out their lusts or desires as they wish and do not attack others. And I shall speak about this with more careful examination and at great length in the following.[12] You will, however, then hear how he weakens and quiets them down and with what benefits. But it is evident to you that a horse, which is at times released by its rider for a run and at times

---

12   See perhaps *The Universe* IIIa–IIae, ch. 13; Paris-Orléans ed., I, 1040a–1044.

reined in by him from it to a walk and is at times tied so that it cannot move at all, is not outside the control and care of the rider.

But some things have already been said to you about children, the benefits they have, their uses or births, or life. You must, however, wait for the other things until the chapter I stated. But the most kind creator undoubtedly directs and guides other human beings and angels, whom he loves, to the good on account of which and for which he created them, and he also helps them with many and almost countless helps. Animals also, which were created for the use of human beings, are turned to the use of human beings through the skills and arts that he gave to human beings for this purpose. Hence, they are guided to their end, the creator, for whom they exist, although through human beings as intermediaries. For I have already told you that whatever is the cause of an essential cause in the same kind of causality is also the cause of the effect, and I mean the cause of an essential cause.[13] Since, therefore, /757b/ the diligence and will of human beings to use such animals were caused by the creator efficiently or effectively and since he causes such a use of them in the same manner of causing, such a use is necessarily the work, gift, and benefit of the creator. But whatever is caused or given by him in that way is caused or given by him through his care and providence. Hence, such a use of animals will be through the care and providence of the creator.

Moreover, it is certain that death and life lie totally in the will and good pleasure of the creator, nor does anyone live except by his gift and benefit, and no one dies except because he causes or permits it. But whatever he does or gives, he does or gives knowingly, and whatever he permits, he likewise permits knowingly. But whatever he either gives or does knowingly, he undoubtedly takes care both to do and to give, and he also cares for the end and fruit that ought to come from this, unless it is perhaps the last gift, which is the end and fruit of all those preceding it in its order and ordering. In the same way, therefore, he makes and similarly gives all the things he makes with care or providently. Otherwise, he would produce something or allow it to be made as a pointless game or joke, which neither his goodness nor his wisdom allows in any way. It is, therefore, evident to you from all these points that the creator has care and provides for all goods from the greatest to the least and that every good other than him exists through his care and providence. For it is completely unfitting for his goodness and wisdom that he does not care for either what they do or what is done with those things that he took care to make. Otherwise, he would have made them jokingly or pointlessly, just as, if an artisan made some artifact and afterward did not care about either what it

---

13 William alludes to a scholastic adage that the cause of the cause is the cause of the effect.

did or what was done to it or where it went, he would clearly be seen to have produced it as a most foolish and most pointless joke.

But if someone says that it is not necessary that the creator care for small and minute things and that such care or caring would be ridiculous and laughable, I have already replied to you on this that, because the creator judged it good to make them, it is necessarily not ridiculous that he judges it good to care for and rule them. Otherwise, as I said, he would have made them jokingly and ridiculously.

CHAPTER 3
He Proves Providence through the Industry and Ingeniousness of Brute Animals

But in order to raise you up and direct you to the more lofty consideration of the care and providence of the creator in very small matters, consider and investigate where spiders learn or learned to spin, make threads, or weave their webs or nets, likewise where they learned that flies would fall into their webs, and that flies should naturally be their prey or food before they saw their mothers making threads, before they knew of either threads, webs, or nets, and before a fly was seen by them.

Make a similar consideration about ducks, which, as soon as they see water, immediately jump into it and begin to swim although they had seen no living being swim. Where did they learn to swim and that water is their abode, that is, one most suitable for their nature?

There is a similar question and consideration about ants. Where did they learn to store grain away, and what is more amazing, where did they learn that grains of wheat would germinate if left whole, and for this reason they divide them in pieces?

But concerning partridges it involves no small amazement that they recognize their mother whom they never saw and abandon the partridge that steals the eggs /758a/ of their mother and incubates them. But once the chicks are hatched, they leave it and unwaveringly follow the mother that laid the eggs in which they came to be.

But far more wondrous than all these is the generation of beetles. For, even when beetles have not seen other beetles generate, they generate other beetles by an amazing artifice. For they form round balls from horse manure, and carrying them to their receptacles and nesting over them, they generate other beetles.

And there are countless other artifices of animals, such as the artifice of a magpie by which it puts together its nest, which no carpenter or architect can copy.

But this amazing thing is reported, something that I admit I have not tested, but have even resisted many times, namely, that swallows and certain other birds seem to use the art of masonry for that structure.

And to raise you up further, who taught roses to weave and gird their blossoms, and lilies similarly, and with regard to every kind of seed, in accord with what Aristotle says, the power in seeds is similar to skills,[14] and for this reason they are kinds of natural skills. Hence, it is evident that all seeds are the artisans of nature or natural artisans.

Then, who taught chickens and other egg-laying animals to generate other living beings of their species by nesting on their eggs? Who taught ostriches to warm their eggs in sand in the sun and in that way to generate their chicks? Who taught bees to build their combs in hexagons? Who taught them, or what instructor did they have that honey was in flowers, and who showed them that skill of gathering it from them? Where did the phoenix learn to construct a pyre for itself from spices and to cremate itself in them so that another phoenix might rise from its ashes?

I pass over the hidden and most salutary medicines of animals, such as a toad, which first revealed in a root and sage the antidote for poison, and countless others of the sort which are read about in the books of physicians and natural philosophers. On this sort of thing I have, therefore, many times jokingly asked some people, and there is one response from them all, namely, that nature teaches animals such arts and skills. But afterward I ask them whether this nature is a book or a teacher, and again <I ask> what kind of a book and written in what kind of writing and what is its size and its volume, and I ask them about its writer, and they do not know what to answer me.

But if they tell me that it is a teacher, I ask again where that teacher learned so many and such great skills, if he learned them, because, if he did not learn them, that is, if he does not have such knowledge from someone else, they necessarily have to admit that this teacher is the creator, since only the creator does not have knowledge from someone else, and whichever ones have it have it from him. But it is very surprising that a similar artisan and teacher or a similar book has not yet been found among us. But if it is the creator himself

---

14   Aristotle does not seem to have said this, despite William's repeated claim that he did. He comes close to this idea in *Physics* 2.8.199a5–199b33, where he argues for the likeness of nature and art and mentions seeds. William, however, often means Avicenna when he says Aristotle; hence, the reference may be to the great Islamic philosopher.

who teaches such artisans, which have no need of skills in a proper comparison with our needs and necessities, how much more would the generosity of such divine goodness be due to us so that these arts would naturally exist in human beings, or at least the necessary arts so that human beings would not be forced to learn and acquire the skills necessary for them by so much watching and labor. But it is surprising if it is a book in which these artisans read the knowledge of their skills. How can they read them there? And it seems that those letters are not natural, if there are letters there, because no letters are naturally read by human beings, and natural letters cannot be anything other than natural signs. But where are these signs impressed, and who has impressed them?

Moreover, if the nature that teaches such artisans is not a subject, but in a subject, as Aristotle teaches, how does it teach since /758b/ it is seen to be unable to know anything? For who would think that an accident either knows or teaches something, except in the way that someone might say that a color teaches through sight or heat through touch and each of the other sensible qualities teaches someone who senses them through a sense or a sensation of them? But this manner is far different from the sorts of knowledge that are seen to exist naturally in the previously mentioned animals and in many others.

It seems, therefore, that one should say that, just as being flows from the first and universal fountain of being—and in accord with his good pleasure—over the being caused by him, and just as goodness and beauty and other things called good are good by his goodness over all things created and generated, so also from the light of the wisdom of the creator there naturally descend or flow down in accord with his good pleasure the lights of the previously mentioned sorts of knowledge, as their necessity and usefulness requires. In that way a certain light of providence flows over an ant because the necessity of its life requires this. For, if it does not gather in the summer, from what would it be fed in the winter? It would undoubtedly perish in the winter since outside its nests it could not seek food or its nests on account of the bitterness of the cold and tenderness and susceptibility of its own body. In the same way a certain cleverness in hunting descends like another light upon a spider. For it is evident that a spider sustains its life by the hunting of flies, and because this light would be useless in it by itself, there was added to it by the providence of the creator another light, namely, of spinning or making thread and weaving its webs, and similarly a very strong receptacle of the two where it lays, incubates, and warms its eggs.

In male and female wolves, however, their considerable cleverness in hunting is a certain natural light, and what seems to be more surprising, in dogs not only is the sense of smell more noble than in many other animals, but is also like a certain light of prophecy or divination naturally given to certain dogs by the creator so that they search out, recognize, and apprehend by this light both thieves and men in hiding. The reason for this is that the dog was created for the protection of human beings and their possessions. They are seen to show this to human beings by their solicitude and a certain friendliness, and they clearly indicate this by their barking and bites, by which they try to ward off the things that they see will harm their human masters or their possessions. Because thieves or men in hiding are among those that do much harm to human beings and their possessions, the light of such divination, as it were, was given to dogs—to very few nonetheless, either on account of the nobility of the light or the rarity of the disposition that makes them receptive of this light. In the same way someone said about the splendor of prophecy that there is very rarely found in human beings such a goodness of disposition, which is receptive of that splendor. For this reason it is very rarely found in them.

But you can be certain that this splendor does not follow upon the goodness of one's make up, but is rather given apart from a disposition. For it is given to many on account of the merit of their holiness; it is given to many for the sake of instructing others and defending them against evils threatening them; it is given to many on account of other causes that you will hear in their place. And at times you will find that this good both has been given and is being given to someone of a very bad disposition.

Just as, therefore, from the first fountain of being or from the first being, as being, there descends other being, so from the first light of wisdom, as sapiential light, there descend all these lights in accord with the good pleasure of the creator and through his providence for the benefits I mentioned and countless others, /759a/ which it is difficult for me to name and list, and many are hidden from me, and it would perhaps be tiresome for you.

You ought to know on this that the folly of augurs and such an old opinion about the truth of auguries—an opinion because of which many are still known to be in error about the truth—can be seen to have had this occasion for its existence and for being believed. It is as if from that previously mentioned light certain lights of prognostications descended upon ravens and crows and other birds, with regard to which auguries are observed, and such birds indicated to human beings by their chatter, flights, and other motions of their bodies what they forebode by these lights concerning human events. But how and in what ways this error is explained to be not only impossible, but also ridiculous will be shown to you by me in its place, if God wills. You will also hear there the causes of this deception, and they will be made evident to you.

It is also seen in this way that all things that have virtue and strength and pertain to these likewise always descend from the first virtue or strength and power—as virtue and strength and power—through his providence and as the necessities and benefits of the recipients require. Hence, in some there are weapons of defense, as in the case of oxen and cows we see in their horns, because they defend themselves by them from wolves. But there are certain weapons of protection, such as the hardness of the hide in wild boars and crocodiles, although there are other benefits of these. In other animals, however, there are teeth and claws for attacking and likewise for defending, as in bears and lions and other animals that get food from their prey and plunder.

So too, it seems that it should be said about beauties that they all descend from the first beauty, as beauty, and kinds of goodness from the first goodness, as goodness, and similarly kinds of knowledge or wisdom from the first knowledge, as knowledge, and sorts of loftiness from the first loftiness, as loftiness, and kinds of genuine sweetness from the first sweetness, as sweetness. But the reason for this is that all these are reflections of the first, insofar as they are such, and of the first, I mean, as such, as I have determined for you.[15] In the same way, all virtue is a reflection of him, insofar as he is virtue, and all goodness is a reflection of him, insofar as he is goodness, and it goes the same way with the others. Because, therefore, everything that is a reflection of him is a reflection of him only by that which falls upon it from the rays of the first, it is evident that everything that is powerful and everything that is good is such only by that which falls upon it from the rays of the first. Through the previously stated comparisons, every virtue seems to be a reason and explanation of such words.

But be careful that you do not understand by this that the first is in itself diversified in any way. Just as a source is in itself not diversified or multiplied by however great a multitude or diversity of streams <come from it>, so the first is not <diversified or multiplied> on account of the multitude or diversity of the outpourings that come from it. But be careful to understand, wherever you hear the creator called the source and creatures streams or rivers. For a stream is properly only water that flows from a source or is part of the source, that is, water of the source, and on this account the water of the source would of necessity be diminished by its flow or departure unless other water were given it. But divisibility into parts has already been removed from the creator by me, and on this no doubt is left for you.[16]

From one and the same heat there come melting in wax and hardening in clay. You also see that from the same seed that is so small, there come fruits, flowers, branches, bark, and also similar seed, although the seed is one and perhaps a simple unit, that is, of one nature. For in human seed, which is of only one nature, it seems that there appears a greater multitude /759b/ and

---

15 See *The Trinity*, ch. 7; ed. Switalski, pp. 45–46.

16 See ibid., ch. 4; ed. Switalski, pp. 26–33.

a greater diversity in its effects, that is, in those who are generated from it. For they have so great a multitude and variety, for example, hair, nails, flesh, bones, nerves, cartilages, marrow, the four basic humors, and the substance of the brain. For how much better reason will there come from the creator by way of efficiency through his most imperious word a multitude and diversity so distant and separate from him that it shares nothing <with him> either in species, or genus, or category!

But in these likenesses notice the most remotely distant unlikeness. For, although seed has very strong operative power, it is a material cause, and on this account it is corrupted in the generation of those things that come from it. But this is never characteristic of an efficient cause through itself, namely, that it is corrupted by its operation, which is proper and essential. And let not the example of the phoenix, which I proposed, upset you, because that fire that it kindles is the efficient cause of its corruption. But the phoenix is not the efficient cause of that fire essentially and properly.

Recall, therefore, the sublimity and supereminence of the blessed creator and the imperiousness of his word, about which you have heard much in the first part of this treatise,[17] and you will see how distant his most omnipotent power, excellence, and the magnificence of his operations are from other powers and the ways of their operations. Recall also that the philosophers rightly seem to have extended the name and intention of efficient cause to its exact and purified meaning. For it perhaps in that way fits only the first efficient cause, which is the blessed creator.

But because all the other animals are seen to have illuminations like those I set forth above, some with much smaller and less noble ones, and also some with larger ones, such as vultures, if what many have told about them is true, namely, that they foresee future slaughters from battles and on this account gather in places where such slaughters will take place, as if they foresee that there will be food from the bodies of human beings and horses. From all these you see that the luminosity of the wisdom of the creator penetrates and reaches not only to the last of the animals, but to the last of the seeds. For the lights that fall upon seeds are like skills, as Aristotle said.[18] Notice also that such lights are not only like arts or skills in operating, but are like commands of the creator, which the seeds necessarily have to carry out. For they do not operate from free choice, but from necessity, that is, by way of servitude, which Aristotle also said elsewhere, and otherwise generally concerning nature, namely, that

17 See *The Universe* Ia-Iae, ch. 26; Paris-Orléans ed., I, 621b–622a.

18 See above note 13. In the light of the following note one might suspect that the source is Avicenna.

it operates in the manner of a servant.[19] But no one doubts that seeds cannot produce other things or otherwise than is in them, but they can be impeded and helped to operate better and more quickly, as is seen from the works of natural magic, which are the sudden generation of fleas, frogs, vermin, and many others. But seeds are impeded in fields many times by the resistant nature of the fields so that only mustard or rye is generated from wheat that is sown.

It has, therefore, now been explained to you that not only the luminosity of the wisdom of the creator, but also his command comes to all these things. Hence, all these things that come to be in that way are generated and come to be because the creator knows and commands that they come to be. Hence, they evidently come to be from him and through him.

About this question also that was asked, namely, what sorts of cognition or knowledge are these lights, you ought to recall those things that you have heard elsewhere from me, namely, that some sorts of knowledge or cognition descend from above from the luminosity of the creator, and these are called /760a/ given or infused knowledge.[20] And those that are naturally present are both created with those to whom they are given and rightly called natural or innate knowledge. But other sorts of knowledge, which come by a gift of the creator after nature is complete, are commonly called infused. But a third sort comes from[21] things, like images reflected in mirrors from the faces of people looking into them, and these are ones that follow upon the numerousness, variety, and diversity of things, as caused by them. Nor should it seem surprising to anyone if the images of things follow upon the multitude and variety of them, and this is verified by argumentation from the cause and from proportion. For, since all things stand in relation or in proportion to such images of themselves, it follows correspondingly that, as the things stand in relation to one another, so their images also stand in relation to one another, and on this account, as there is a diversity in things in relation to one another, so there is in their images. On this account, therefore, if such things are universal or particular, the knowledge of them will in the same way be either universal or particular. But the other sorts of knowledge, namely, both innate and infused knowledge, follow upon an imitation of their cause, and for this reason one of them is <knowledge> of many genera and species, but another is <knowl-

---

19 William derived the claim that nature acts in the manner of a servant from Avicenna; see above note 8. William frequently attributed to Aristotle doctrines that he found in Avicenna, presumably because he took the Islamic philosopher as representing what Aristotle said.

20 See *On the Soul* (*De anima*), ch. 5, pt. 11; Paris-Orléans ed., II, 127b–128a.

21 I have conjectured the addition of "a."

edge> one in number and in every way indivisible of all genera, species, and individuals.

Hence it is that the lights that I have listed and named for you follow in this way the unity of it, and they do not have the lines or writing of books or aggregations of parts, just as the first wisdom does not. And I say the same thing about prophetic splendor since it is one, not divisible, and not gathered together from particular splendors, and in it and through it the prophets saw such a great multitude and diversity of things and events. In this way I also speak of these lights, although they should not be called lights in comparison with prophetic splendor. Yet in one respect they are likened to it, namely, in this unity and indivisibility. If, nonetheless, there were found similar lights in human beings, that is, of searching out, recognizing, and apprehending thieves or of spinning, making thread, and weaving webs, and of hunting, if, I say, they were found in human beings apart from instruction and teaching, no one would fear to call them prophetic splendors.

But we usually do not say that animals or seeds operate by that knowledge or through knowledge on account of the paucity of our experience in them and on account of the novelty, which common and uneducated people always wonder about and often abhor. On this account Aristotle did not want to say that there are skills in seeds, but powers similar to skills. On this account, and more suitably and by accommodated and adapted language, we do not say that those lights are knowledge or arts or skills, but rather likenesses of knowledge, art, and skills.

But if someone asks whether a spider knows how to spin or to make threads and to stretch webs and do the other things it does, he will propose a question not easily able to be determined by the untrained. For it does what it does either knowingly or by chance and apart from any intention. But if someone responds that it does what it does unknowingly, how, then, does it avoid all error in its works?

Moreover, if as Aristotle says that it is a mark of a knower to be able to speak,[22] why will it not rather be a sign of a knower to be able to do?

Moreover, what sign is there in a woman making thread that she knows how to make thread, that does not appear both better and more in a spider?

But if someone says that a woman does this by art or knowledge or skill, such a man seems to have forgotten the words that /760b/ Aristotle spoke, namely, that what is naturally such is more such.[23] Hence, natural art is more an art, and a natural knowledge is more a knowledge, and a natural skill is more a skill, and one who knows naturally is more a knower. Hence, a spider is also

22 See perhaps Aristotle, *Politics* 1.2.1253a8–1253a18.

23 See perhaps Aristotle, *Metaphysics* 2.1.993b22–25.

more a knower of such a work and makes threads and webs more knowingly than a woman who knows or has learned this by instruction from another or by her own discovery.

But if he responds that a spider does this by natural instinct, he involves himself in more difficult questions, namely, concerning instinct and nature, that is, what each of these is. For the same question remains concerning nature, namely, whether it knowingly or unknowingly prompts the spider to do these things. But if it does so knowingly, such a nature will not be in a subject.[24] For it in no way belongs to those things that are in a subject to know or to do something knowingly. But if such a nature is a subject, other questions follow concerning such a subject, namely, whether it does this by itself or by a prompting from another. But if it does it by itself, the question remains, with what benefit and for whose benefit it does so. For if it does this for its own benefit, such a subject will be nothing other than the spider. For the hunting of flies is seen to be beneficial only to the spider that carries it out, unless perhaps someone says that it also benefits human beings for the admiration of the wisdom of the creator and for philosophizing about his providence. But if such a nature does this by a prompting from another, this same line of questioning will arrive at the creator, and divine providence will become more evident in such things by this, when it has been discovered that spiders make threads, weave their threads and webs, and hunt through his prompting. But if this does not arrive at the creator, it is necessary that it come to another more noble substance than the spider is, either one or many. But if it is only one, it will be seen to be regulative of all spiders, teaching them such skills for living or prompting them to carry them out, and either this will be entrusted to it by the creator, or it will be innate in it. But by each of these paths it is clearly seen that all such skills both exist and are exercised by the providence of the creator.

In the same way, if many such substances were regulative of spiders, it cannot be doubtful that such a ruling power is either innate in them or entrusted to them by the creator. Notice, therefore, in these and similar things that one should not quarrel about words or names with those who correctly philosophize, but rather one should use them without quarrel and contention, as the community of human beings uses them. But the strangeness that common use repudiates should be fled from in every way by those who philosophize. And similarly, their novelty <should be fled from>, unless perhaps a lack or necessity forces one to coin new words, or one should at least use circumlocutions. On this account, therefore, Aristotle did not want to say that the powers that are in seeds are arts or skills, but are like skills, although he said without an intoler-

---

24   That is, it will not be an accident.

able abuse that they are certain arts or certain skills of nature. Nor should you contend about what I said, namely, that spiders know how to do what they do or whether knowledge does in that case what they do, since the common usage of human beings accepts that they know how to do and knowingly do such works and that they received so small a light from the luminosity of the creator's wisdom for acquiring sustenance of life for themselves, as I said.

But whether they acquired it through one means or several means or immediately, I do not define here, because being and life seem to proceed immediately from the creator and to be created by him, and on this account it might perhaps seem to someone that small lights, like great ones, descend upon such creatures from him, just as /761a/ the most noble lights, which are called gifts of the graces, the lofty forms of knowledge, and the virtues, are said to descend upon human beings and the blessed angels immediately from him. To this extent, therefore, it has been determined for you by this that all such things that have been named exist and come about through the providence of the creator.

But because it has been given to all bodies by the creator that they can acquire for themselves their natural places, that is, ones suited to their natures, and because the powers for this, by which they acquire these places through motion and by which they also come to rest, were also given to them by him, you should not doubt that their motion and rest exist through the providence of the creator, especially since the natural motion of each body is not so much a seeking of its natural place as a flight from what is unnatural and contrary. You see clearly, therefore, that natural bodies naturally provide for themselves for the conservation of their being, both by a flight from places harmful to them and by natural motions and inclinations with regard to salutary places. And this is the reason, as it seems to me, which led Aristotle to say that such a nature in natural bodies is a certain life, as it were,[25] because such providence is most evident in living things, that is, by which they avoid harmful things and seeks those salutary and beneficial to themselves.

And in certain animals there is seen a certain natural expertise and innate medicinal art. For who taught the toad wounded by another's bite and poison to go to a root and to rub the place of the wound on it and to be cured from the danger of the poison by such rubbing? Many believe that this same thing is done with sage.

Similarly, who taught a cat that it could conceive by its rubbing against a herb that is called catnip and could in that way make up for the lack of a male? In the same way who taught horses to expose themselves to the blast of the west wind and to conceive from its blowing and pulling? Who taught certain

25 See Aristotle, *Physics* 8.1.250b13-14.

fish to pour out their seed over their eggs after the eggs were laid in water, and that otherwise they could not generate? Finally, who taught eagles and ravens to become young again and to recover their youth in the ways you have heard elsewhere?[26] Who taught scorpions to sting only the backs of the hands of human beings, but to spare the palms, or what I believe is more correct, to fear perhaps that, enclosed in them, they might be held captive after being caught in them, which they do not fear from the backs of the hands? There are countless other things that historians of such nature have written, in all of which it is evident to you and is commonly said that they are called, and not undeservedly, certain arts and skills and abilities of nature.

But we have never heard that anyone has extended these words to the natures of inanimate bodies, and this is on account of the smallness and, so to speak, thinness of their light. For we have not heard that any of those who philosophize have said that heavy bodies are inclined or moved to the middle of the world by art or skill. Similarly, we have not heard that fire burns wood by an art or a skill of nature, although it is commonly accepted that it does this by the power of its nature, but this is, as I said, on account of its great distance and unlikeness to the arts and skills. But you ought not have any doubt now either in the case of parts, or in that of wholes, that as I said, all these things that I have mentioned to you are done by the providence of the creator, just as they also are done by his primary power. But perhaps he does not intend individual things in these, unless someone says that he intends vague singulars. For the spider does not seem to intend this thread or this web in particular.

But you have already heard elsewhere my intention concerning how a vague individual stands in a sense and in the imagination.[27] And an example of such is found in a man who is seen coming from afar, but on account of the distance /761b/ he is not yet known to be a man, but is known to be this animal that is coming. Then when he draws near, he is known to be this man who is coming and not yet Socrates. But <the individual> will be more vague if it is so far distant that it was not apprehended to be an animal, but this moving thing, and even more vague if it is not seen to be moving. For then it would only be known to be this bodily something. From this, therefore, you see that the stripping away of particular conditions and of their clothing makes an individual either vague or more vague or explicit and fully determinate, in accord with the ways of such examples.

---

26 See Ps 102:5 for the renewal of the youth of an eagle.

27 See *On the Soul*, ch. 7, pt. 7; Paris-Orléans ed., II, 213a–213b. Also see Thomas Aquinas, *Summa* 1.30.4, where he distinguishes a vague individual from a person. "Some man" exemplifies the former, while Julius Caesar exemplifies the latter.

But because the statements of the philosophers concerning the souls of non-rational animals report that they cannot apprehend universals and because they said that this is proper to rational souls and intelligent substances, it does not seem, according to them, that in the souls of animals there are imaginations or other impressions of universals similar to the artisans of operations, nor that abstraction from individuating clothing is possible for them at all. Hence, it will be difficult for them to determine whether a spider imagines a fly, if it cannot apprehend it universally, according to them. But if it imagines it individually or singularly, it seems difficult to be able to see the condition or clothing by which it individuates it, since these conditions are necessarily apprehended first individually. But what I am saying will become more evident through examples.

For if a spider imagines that a fly will fall into its web by flight, these conditions are all common and able to be shared by many. They do not, therefore, individuate the fly, and to be brief, it is not possible by these conditions to come down to this one fly. How then will a spider come down to any one? But if it does not come down to this one, its imagination or other apprehension will stay at something common or general. Therefore, the apprehension of commons or universals will not be proper to intelligent substances.

Moreover, concerning the skills that exist among us, no one says that he builds this house in particular, but rather a house. Similarly, a weaver did not say that he weaves this cloth, but some cloth. Nor does a smith say that he fashions this sword, but a sword. Much less, then, in animals lacking reason, will it be possible that there be this individuation or determination.

Moreover, since rational souls are much more noble and stronger in apprehending than souls of this sort, how will their apprehensive powers extend themselves to the apprehension of individuals, while the apprehensive powers of rational souls will be so short-sighted and curtailed that in their skills they do not attain particulars and, similarly, vague individuals?

But if someone says that spiders operate, like a blind artisan or one with his eyes closed, he also does not in this way free himself from the knot of this question, because if he operates in that way, even if he has his eyes closed or entirely darkened, he still has his imagination and the common interior sense open and unveiled. But it is <not> difficult to find in ourselves an example of the unlikeness of such imagination and intention of animals in their works, and the reason is that they intend and also imagine from within, but we do so from outside and from above in the skills that exist among us.

I have already told you in many chapters and treatises of this science that the lights that descend from above extend further and wider than those that come to our souls and the souls of irrational animals from below and from things.

On account of this they are both measured and counted /762a/ in terms of things. For of one thing there is one seeing, and of one sound there is one hearing, and of two there are two, and it is that way with the rest. And the reason is that all these come by way of modifications from things acting upon our apprehensive soul and by way of reflections from the forms of sensible things in mirrors. But souls are apprehensive and receptive of such modifications and reflections, like things that are passive and receptive of such modifications and like mirrors of such reflections.

Natural vision and hearing and the other such habits are, however, more ample and broader, although they are naturally incomplete in act and need the modifications and reflections that we said. It is that way with the lights that I named for you, and the more that you ascend in thought and consideration, the more amply will you find it spread out until you come to the purest light, namely, the light of lights, which is the most wise creator. His light is luminosity in the ultimate degree of breadth and similarly of length, as the holy and authoritative words have it, namely, that wisdom *stretches from end to end mightily and disposes all things sweetly* (Wis 8:1).

Hence it is that prophetic splendors, insofar as is possible, imitating that light, namely, the light of the lights, not only descend most amply in breadth, but also in length. On this account the prophets see not only the first things in these splendors, but also the last. It is, therefore, apparent to you from this that these natural lights are not incorrectly more extensive than our apprehensions, which come from outside, and on this account it is necessary that things precede such apprehensions as their causes. But as prophetic splendors and these lights do not come from things, so they do not on this account require that the existence of things precede them, and for this reason they extend to non-existing things before they exist. For this reason prophetic splendors also reveal past things, which do not now exist, and future things, which do not yet exist. In that way these lights also show to eagles and ravens[28] their renewals before they exist and the causes of them and the manner of operation by which they may produce or procure them. Similarly they reveal to spiders webs that do not exist and flies that perhaps do not yet exist and their falling into webs before they exist.

But if someone says that neither spiders nor other animals know or see what they do or the benefits of their works, then it rather turns out that he concedes that those things are done not by their own providence, but by that of another, and ultimately this statement comes to the point of granting that all such works are done by the providence of the creator, as I have already told you. It also follows that he says that spiders eat the flies they catch at another's

---

28   I have corrected *"cervis"* to *"corvis"* on the basis of the earlier passage.

prompting. And he will necessarily have to grant in pigs and in every kind of animal that they do not eat by a prompting or hunger of their own nature, but by the prompting of another. Why, then, do they rather do such operations by the prompting of another and not those that are the end and benefit of these, namely, eating and drinking?

Moreover, whatever can attain the end, can also attain the path <to it>, and whatever can attain the extreme can also naturally attain the means <to it>. Because, therefore, these operations, namely, to make thread, to weave nets, to lay in wait for flies, and to catch them, are the means and natural path to eating them and to acquiring nourishment from them, if the extremes are natural, the means to those extremes are similarly natural, and this by natural order. Therefore, if spiders can naturally attain the end or the extremes, they can for much better reason attain the path and the means.

Moreover, this <contrary view> amounts to saying that someone can naturally eat, which is naturally possible only by chewing, and that he cannot chew naturally. Similarly, it amounts to saying that something can naturally be nourished by food and cannot break down or digest food. On these points, therefore, you see from me some /762b/ ways of exercising your mind. But if God grants that you see something better on these points, I would rejoice and wish that it would happen to me.

CHAPTER 4
On the General and Diverse Benefits of Creatures,
Where He Discusses at Length the Use of Scourges and Tribulations

But concerning natural motions that are from the middle and to the middle—and some add a third, namely, circular motion, which is around the middle, although this rightly seems to Aristotle and his followers very improbable,[29] and similarly concerning the inclinations from which such motions come, I have already said to you that the motions do not come about through knowledge of the things that are moved, just as they do not come through their providence.[30] Nor did Aristotle want to call the principles of these motions arts, skills, souls, lives, but quasi lives, and the reason for this

---

29 William is perhaps referring to the downward and upward motions of natural bodies to their natural place, that is, toward or away from the middle of the universe. See Aristotle, *Physics* 4.8.214b14–16. Although he held circular motion of the heavens, he did not hold such a motion in natural or earthly bodies.

30 See the previous chapter.

was, as I already told you, their distance and remoteness from these things to which such names are suited by a correct and true naming.

You have, therefore, already seen from the things that have preceded that divine providence stretches from the first creatures to the least, and I understand this concerning substances—and both concerning parts and concerning whole bodily substances. And <you have seen> that it is not unsuitable or unworthy of the wisdom and goodness of the creator to care for those things after they exist, which he cared for when they did not exist, and <you have seen> that he cared for them to the point that he made them to exist, and <you have seen> that it is fitting in all ways that his wisdom and goodness guide them to such ends and benefits for which he adapted and ordered them, whether they are known or unknown to us. But this is, as I already told you, undoubtedly to rule, to conserve, and to guide them to the end or use for which the thing exists.

But someone might ask how he has care for the little flies that swallows hunt so eagerly since he does not seem to conserve them, but rather to expose them to being devoured by swallows, how he is seen to guide them to the end for which they exist, and whether their end is other than the nourishment or sustenance of swallows. I respond to this that this is really one end and one benefit of such little flies, and the creator guides them to this end and benefit by the nature of swallows, which he created as able to be nourished and sustained by eating them. And he gave to them a natural light from among the previously mentioned lights, by which they know these things in that way and also know how to catch the flies, just as they know how to eat them. The creator, therefore, conserves them for such a use, although there are other benefits and other uses, which you will hear in the following.

Nor is it unsuitable that the creator created certain animals for the food and sustenance of others or even for multiple other uses, as is seen with regard to horses, donkeys, and mules, which are not commonly eaten by human beings. But there are many other benefits of cows, sheep, and goats by which they help human beings besides their nourishment, and in order that the providence of God may be clearer to you in all things, I will tell you and list the general benefits of creatures.

The first general benefit is, therefore, the good that each thing has, whether that is being, or something else or some other things, or being with something else or with some other things. The gratuitous goodness of the creator does not intend to benefit himself in creating things, in giving them being or other goods, but to benefit the things themselves, and this is always the intention of the creator or of gratuitous goodness, namely, of goodness of such rectitude that the giver does not turn it back upon himself, that is, intending it for himself, that is, for his own good, honor, advantage, /763a/ glory, pleasure, or something of the sort, and not turning it away from such rectitude, either to the harm of his enemies or to the profit of his friends, that is, because they are his. For this consideration, namely, that they are his, is a falling off from the rectitude of gratuity and has something of the previously mentioned turning back.

The second cause of creation in certain ones is their usefulness for others, and this happens in many kinds of things. For some are able to exist by themselves and also to be useful to others, as you have heard above many times concerning plants and irrational animals, because both of them are seen to be able also to exist for the benefit and use of human beings. But others are not able to exist by themselves, such as parts and members of animals, as an eye is not able to exist by itself, and so too with a foot and a hand, but only in a whole and for the whole. Similarly, the mouth, nerves, and flesh in animals are not able to exist by themselves, but can only exist in animals and for the benefit of the whole of them. Hence, the end and benefit of their creation is seen to be the benefit for the totality of the animals of which they are parts and in which alone they are able to exist. And here I mean only natural benefits. For there are other more lofty and more noble benefits, and these are ones by which the virtues and the arranging of morals are helped, and also those goods of the graces, by which everlasting and future happiness is obtained, and this is the ultimate and most perfect benefit of all our benefits.

From this it is evident to you that the virtues and the gifts of grace are beneficial for all the others, because the usefulness of them, that is, for which they exist and which the creator principally intended, is their benefit for human beings, beyond which nothing is to be sought.

But after these, in terms of the degree of usefulness, there come in this order those things by which these are acquired, nourished, helped, conserved, and increased, and among these are good natural dispositions for them, or the goodness of temperament, natural kindness, and natural gentleness. For those who are endowed with these can readily receive the gratuitous and noble virtue of patience and of holy love, as well as of peace and serenity of heart, the contrary of which is turbulence and restlessness. And concerning all these you ought to be satisfied by the things you heard about the three kinds of virtues, namely, natural, gratuitous, and moral,[31] and those things that are related to them.

---

31   See *On the Virtues* (*De virtutibus*), Paris-Orléans ed., I, chs. 10 and 11, 130aE–
     130bH, where William distinguishes these three kinds of virtues. Moral virtues
     include the four cardinal virtues, while gratuitous virtues are the theological virtues
     of faith, hope, and charity. Natural virtues, on the other hand, are the natural
     powers of the soul. William follows Avicenna in speaking, for example, of the

In this ranking, doctrine, studiousness, and discipline hold third place, and on this account the people of the Christians, who are most pleasing to the creator, work at studies pleasing to the creator, are highly vigilant in sacred doctrines, and are seen singularly to insist upon preaching, although other peoples clearly neglect these. Nor do you have any doubt about how much sacred doctrines and preaching incite to the worship and honor of the creator, about how much they illumine the minds of human beings for the knowledge of him and of those things that human beings should love, seek, hold, and preserve, and similarly to the knowledge of those that they should flee, leave alone, or even persecute. And you are not at all ignorant of the great power of doctrine and preaching in changing the hearts of human beings and in turning them away from all error and depravity and from all the adversities and diseases of the vices, especially when the grace of the creator is present both to those speaking and to those listening.

And you have already learned of the reverence and purity of intention by which sacred doctrines and exhortations should both be delivered and heard and of how they are often heard and taught without fruit because of the contrary irreverence and impurity. But there are studies of readings and meditations—of readings, of course, in the sacred books, but meditations for each one in himself and by himself—and deliberations or examinations of those things which are done or sustained. For some leap unprepared, improvident, and only slightly circumspect into works that need to be done with much deliberation, and they incautiously rush into dangers of adversities and are cast down and lethally wounded from the fight before they deliberate and before they strap on or don weapons.

But concerning discipline a somewhat lengthier discussion needs to be had for the reason that human beings do not know the benefits of those things that belong to discipline, on account of which they flee from it as harmful and endure it with pain and bother, resisting it very much according to their strength. Matters of discipline, therefore, are those that introduce fear, pain, or oppression and that withdraw incentives to vices or block or remove access to them entirely.

You have already heard elsewhere about the benefits of fear in the chapter on its works and marvels, and it is evident of itself that fear is spiritual flight and a leap back from what is feared. Fear, therefore, is good and holy, by which one flees from everything that provokes the anger of the creator, that is, from every defilement of deadly sin. For the sake, then, of striking fear into mortals,

---

intellective virtue or power or of apprehensive virtues or powers, which leaves him with natural virtues, which really do not fit well with moral or theological virtues.

the creator created comets, fiery swords, and flaming dragons in the skies and made them appear on high. Similarly, he made portents on the earth and sea, made mules beget, and monsters to be born among human beings, such as infants with many heads. On this account they are called monsters, not only because human beings show them to one another out of the wonder at their novelty, but because they show that the anger of God hangs over human beings,[32] that is, so that the creator is seen by human beings to be disturbed from the disturbed order of things.

There are countless other examples besides these that the law of the Christians expressly contains, namely, those things that will be in the sun, moon, and stars and in other things, among which earthquakes are listed,[33] so that at that time the earth may strike fright into human beings and convince them to dread the imminent punishment of the creator.

Hence, it is evident that an earthquake is produced by the providence of the creator on account of the obvious utility, which ought to come from it for human beings, and this holds, whether it is produced by nature as you learned in the book, *On Meteors*,[34] or otherwise by the will of the creator. On this account the law of the Hebrews was given to them amid such terrors of fire, darkness, lightning flashes, and terrifying noise, but terrible events preceded it in Egypt so that they would fear the evil of disobedience and the most evil practices of the Egyptians, by whom they were reared.[35] On this account the doctrine of the Christians elegantly interprets that the Hebrews fled from Egypt with the Egyptians following and putting them to flight, so that they understand from this that they must not only flee from the Egyptian people, but also the Egyptian customs, that is, from the abomination of idolatry and the vices by which they had made themselves abominable and despicable to the creator.

Moreover, when you make a more diligent consideration about fear, you will find that above all other gifts it pushes down the human heart and subjects it to the one feared, I mean an unbending, hard, and servile heart. On this account, knowing the rebellious heart of the people of the Hebrews, the creator revealed himself to them by such great causes of fright in giving the law, as a God to be feared and dreaded, in order not so much to bend as also to break them to obedience of his law. For that people, as the creator himself says in

---

32 William links the word "monsters: *monstra*" with "show: *monstrant*."

33 See the prediction of the end times in the synoptic Gospels, for example, Mt 24: 7 and 29.

34 See perhaps Aristotle, *On Meteors* 1.1. 338a19-339a9–2.339a33.

35 See Ex 20:18 for the theophany at Sinai and Ex 7–12 for the plagues inflicted on the Egyptians.

their law, was a stiff-necked people,[36] and on this account, since they did not accept a voluntary inclination, they had to be terrified from the beginning by horrendous terrors.

CHAPTER 5
On the Good of Pain

B
ut, as you know, those things that involve pain mortify and extinguish the lusts for pleasures and carnal and worldly desires and mortify and remove the pleasures themselves from men. But you already know from others how harmful such pleasures and desires are to human beings, that is, because they captivate, inebriate, debilitate, destroy, blind, and drive human souls or human beings into every sort of insanity. You see, therefore, how salutary pain is that extinguishes these and removes them from human souls, and that it is really a medicine like absinthe that kills such worms, and it is like lye that dissolves such abominable defilements. On account of these two, namely, mortification and washing away of the vices, it seems that it was called *the water of tribulation* (2 Chr 18:26 LXX) in the prophets.

You should also know that it wipes out avarice and pride by their roots along with their seeds, and just as fire hardens and strengthens bricks and all clay vessels and arms them in a sense by their hardening, not only against water, but also against itself—for baked bricks fear neither fire nor water—so the pain of present tribulations arms and fortifies human souls and produces and gives them patience as a sort of armor. And this is explicitly found in each law, that is, of the Hebrews and of the Christians; indeed, in the law of the Hebrews the lawgiver himself said to that people, *I baked you in the furnace of poverty* (Is 48:11). But in the law of the Christians we read, *Tribulation produces patience* (Rom 5:3). For it helps human souls in marvelous ways and illumines them for wisdom. But the wisest of the Hebrews and a king of that people said in a certain one of his books that *folly is bound in the heart of a boy, but the rod of discipline will put it to flight* (Prv 22:15), and in the same book, *The rod and correction bestow wisdom* (Prv 29:15). Another of the ancient wise men says that wisdom *is not found in the land of those living softly* (Job 28:13). And from among the philosophers Archytas Tarentinus[37] explicitly said that, "where lust rules, there is no place for temperance, and in the kingdom of pleasure virtue

---

36   See Ex 33:5.

37   Although the Paris-Orléans edition has Archytarentinus, William is referring to Archytas Tarentinus (ca. 428–325 B.C.). William's source is most probably Cicero who quoted Archytas in his *On Old Age* (*De senectute*) 12, 41. For more

cannot exist." Hence, neither can wisdom since genuine wisdom is more a virtue than an art, as Aristotle said concerning metaphysics itself.[38]

Pay attention to these benefits of pains, and notice that the creator knew them and that it is a mark of the goodness of the creator that he loves our souls, and for this reason it is necessary[39] that he provide for them such salutary gifts by which they are freed and purified from such great evils.

Moreover, all the evils listed, from which souls are delivered through pains, are diseases, wounds, kinds of foulness, deformities, and abominable defilements of souls that are harmful and injurious to our souls in many other ways, and no one intelligent doubts that the creator loves and wants the health, cleanliness, beauty, strength, and the other perfections of our souls. Hence, how will one be able to suppose that he does not provide these goods for our souls by which they are so efficaciously helped to attain the previously mentioned virtues, which it is impossible that the creator not love in them?

Moreover, if you see a sick person laboring under the difficulties of multiple illnesses and if you see a salutary medicine is offered him against all of them, although he does not think about his health or does not procure or seek for some medication for himself, will you doubt /764b/ that such medicine is given to him by the goodness and wisdom of someone else?

But concerning those who inflict pains and do not intend to heal the patients, it is evident that their medicine is not given by such men as medicine, because their intention is not to heal or benefit others, but rather to injure and harm them, unless they are perhaps educators or teachers. But if you want to imagine that the universe of human beings is laboring under such illnesses that were just named for you, and if you are aware that the creator constantly sees diseases and illnesses of this sort in the human race, and if you consider the riches of his piety, let the idea not in any way enter into your heart that he neglects so great a plague in the human race and leaves it unremedied or without medicine. Because, therefore, it is a mark of the best and wisest physician always to give to those who need to be healed the remedies that he sees are most salutary and most efficacious to cure their illnesses, and because the blessed creator sees the previously mentioned pains are so powerful for attaining the previously mentioned disadvantages and are so salutary for such a sick

---

on Archytas, see Carl A. Huffman, *Archytas of Tarentum: Pythagorean, Philosopher, and Mathematician King* (Cambridge: Cambridge University Press, 2005).

38 See the Prologue of William's *The Trinity* (*De trinitate*), where he also attributes this line to Aristotle. Bruno Switalski says that, although no such text is found in Aristotle, the idea can be derived from *Nicomachean Ethics* 2.6.1106b15, 6/6/1140b24–25, and *Metaphysics* 1.2.983a1–11.

39 I have conjectured "*necesse*" instead of "*nec esse*."

person, it is necessary that he apply them to him. It is, therefore, evident from this that the pains of tribulations that are present in human beings are present in them through the care and providence of the creator.

But someone might say that these <pains and tribulations> come to human beings from themselves or come about in them through themselves or from other evils in others. For example, illness sometimes comes from overeating, sometimes from drunkenness, at times from food or drink that is not healthy, at times from excessive heat or cold and in many other ways. But they come from some people to others, for instance, beatings or blows, prisons, chains, losses through fraud, deceit, thefts, and in the same way insults and those things belonging to insults. The cause, therefore, of the being and coming about of all such evils does not seem to be the divine goodness, but rather human iniquities, malice, and ignorance. For their agents are the causes of their occurrences, and all suffering is an effect or outcome of action. On this account, therefore, those greater from among the wise men of the Christians said that the goodness of the creator does not really directly cause such actions, that is, any evil and perverse ones, but tolerates or permits them on account of the goodness and benefits of the sufferings, and on this account they said that he causes the sufferings because he foresees, loves, and approves them inasmuch as they are beneficial in many ways.[40] And on this account he tolerates or permits disordered actions. And because the goodness and benefits of the sufferings are greater and more numerous, the providence of the creator chooses a few small evils and perversities in order that from them he may elicit many more goods and much greater goods than if he did not allow them to exist at all.

In this way and in accord with this, the creator is said by some people to be the cause of evil and disordered actions because he created their agents and gave them the powers, through the misuse of which they did the actions, although he did not give the powers to them for this purpose. But you clearly see that they misuse the word "cause" and also misuse this preposition "from," when they say that evil actions come *from* the creator, for such a preposition is a mark or sign of direct origin and direct causation. A very suitable example of this is found in a most just king and his wicked prefect or praetor who knowingly and wickedly kills an innocent man. In this example, therefore, no one says that the killing of the innocent man comes from the king or through the most just king, although the praetorial power through which he was unjustly killed comes from the king. But the reason is that, although the praetorial power comes directly and through itself from the king, the killing of the innocent man does not come from it directly and through itself, but rather /765a/ through a

---

40   See, for example, Augustine, *A Literal Interpretation of Genesis: An Unfinished Work* (*De Genesi ad litteram liber imperfectus*) 1.3; PL 34: 221.

perversion, misuse, and diversion of it. For the punishment comes down directly from the power only through rectitude of the judgment and then only upon the guilty or upon those who are deservedly considered or regarded as guilty. I say this on account of proofs that are sometimes false, as witnesses are false or instruments are false. Yet the falsity of neither was apparent to the judge. Many times there is lacking proof of what is right, and from his judicial office the judge necessarily has to condemn an innocent person. An example of this is a debtor who really repaid a loan, but lacks proof of the repayment. He admits, however, that he received the loan; the judge, therefore, rightly stands by his admission that he made against himself, since he did not produce proof of the repayment. From this, therefore, it is evident to you that evil actions cannot be said to come through themselves and properly from the creator, just as the punishment of innocent people or the false or unjust judgments of a praetor cannot be said to come from a most just king or to exist through him, except by an abuse; indeed no one would say so except by an intolerable abuse.

But if you want to discover and list the benefits of pains and how pain is called both the water of tribulation and fire in the holy and authentic writings,[41] consider the acts and operations of natural fire, and you will find the spiritual operations and the benefits of pain and tribulation in human souls in a likeness and proportion to them, and you have elsewhere heard many things from me about these. From these it is also evident to you how beneficial those people are in the human race who inflict pains or the things from which pains come, because they are ministers and vessels or instruments of so many benefits, although they cause them without intending and knowing it. And at times they intend the opposite, that is, harm or harming; hence it is that, when the benefits of their ministries have ceased, they will be thrown into a place of condemnation, unless they meanwhile come to their senses and have been corrected through penance.

But an example of this is seen in the rod, which the father throws into the fire once his son has been fully trained. On this account a holy and wise man and most illustrious teacher in the people of the Christians said, Why does the wicked man boast because my father makes a scourge for me out of him?[42] If, therefore, you still know the immense piety of the creator and make a consideration on human affairs with diligent scrutiny, you will find that he trains in that way the whole human race with paternal solicitude and sweetness through evil men, as the one father trained his only son.

---

41 See 2 Chr 18:26 LXX for the water of tribulation and Ps 16:3 or Prv 17:3 for fire.

42 See Augustine, *Homilies on the Psalms* (*Enarrationes in Psalmos*) 36.2.4; PL 36: 366.

By other evils also that do not come about through evil people, such as death, plagues, famines, and barrenness, the goodness of the creator gives countless benefits to mortals, and because many things have been said elsewhere about these and will be said elsewhere, namely, in sermons and exhortations, I shall return to the matter at hand, and I shall say that, since the goodness and wisdom of the creator does nothing or permits nothing to be done without a reason and uselessly—and not even one wing of a fly is made except by his care and providence—for how much better reason will those things from which so many and such great benefits come about for us, exist only if he allows or reasonably permits them to be done and even arranges them!

But if someone says that such evils fail to benefit many people; in fact, they harm them, I have already replied to you on this in what has gone before by the table of a sumptuous banqueter who adorns and prepares his table, not only to the measure of the satiety of those dining, but in accord with the magnificence of his generosity. And I add other things here, and I say that it is the sin and failure of those who either were unwilling or did not know how to use such beneficial helps, although it should also not be readily conceded, namely, that such scourges do not always benefit, since it is very likely that a son rebelling under the rod of his father would be much more rebellious, /765b/ if left to himself.

It is also evident to the intelligent that death itself is very beneficial, even for those who persist in their sinfulness, since it is clearly good for such men to lose the power and freedom to do evil, just as it is with mad and crazy men with the loss or taking away of swords. For all the power of one who abuses it for his own destruction or that of others is like a sword in the hands of a madman.

Moreover, since the human race needs so many and such great benefits, if their malice did not suffice for making them, the goodness of the creator would undoubtedly procure them. For he would in no way tolerate so pernicious a lack in the human race. Why, then, is it surprising, if he providently, in fact most wisely, tolerates and permits such causes of goods to exist among human beings?

Moreover, judicial sentences are carried out on account of such benefits, namely, pecuniary fines, the mutilation of members, the hanging of thieves, and all the praetorial tortures, so that the evil persons may be subdued who inflict upon human beings any of the evils I mentioned, not by judgment, but out of malice, lest they disturb human affairs by their insolence to the point that it is impossible not merely not to live well, but just to live among them. It is, therefore, evident to you that the previously mentioned pains and evils are procured for human beings through divine providence, since it is evident that all rulers and judges are given by him to human beings on account of these benefits. There ought to be no doubt, then, that the other evils, namely, of pains and tribulations, are permitted and arranged by divine providence on account of the same causes.

Moreover, although many of such evils do not benefit those who suffer them, they do benefit others. For the punishment of one evildoer deters many from similar acts.

Moreover, who does not see that, if this world had only peace and delights, it would hold back human beings in itself with an inseparable clinging and would turn them away from the future goods and virtues to the point that very few would care about those goods or virtues? Human life, therefore, had to be sprinkled with both great and multiple sorts of bitterness and pains in order that so great an evil and such great harm might be turned aside from human beings. For what can be thought to be more pernicious and more harmful to the human race than that which takes away from it the good on account of which alone it was created, that is, the good of future happiness, and imposes on it the evil than which there is none greater, namely, the punishment of eternal damnation? It was not unreasonable, therefore, that the creator willed that the sweetness of this life become bitter for human beings lest it turn them away from the good for which he created them and draw them to the contrary evil. How, then, should one suppose that such beneficial and such salutary pains do not exist among human beings because divine providence procures, permits, or arranges them?

I shall, however, set forth for you many examples of this, although passing over many more to avoid the tedium of prolixity. The first of these will be a nurse, who at the time of the weaning of the child she is feeding, sees that the little one is so attracted by the sweetness of milk that it does not allow itself to be separated from her and refuses to be turned either to solid or more suitable food for it. And so, she sprinkles the tips of her nipples with something bitter, which the little one sensing on the nipples spontaneously spits out, and even takes refuge at, longs for its father's table, and afterward eats from it.

Why is it, therefore, surprising if the creator, the nurse or nurturer of the whole human race, wanting to separate human beings, I do not say from the milk of infancy, but from that of human puerility, which is most shameful and pernicious, and wanting them to long for and aspire to the table of future spiritual banquets, which are prepared for its glory in heaven, sprinkles carnal and worldly pleasures with multiple sorts of bitterness. /766a/ For their falsity and deceptiveness are so harmful and so pernicious for human beings that they completely turn them away from that table heaped with unimaginable delights, and they inebriate and drive them mad with themselves, and also defile, confuse, and disturb human affairs with wars, conflicts, and every disorder and restlessness?

Another such example is the father of a family, who seeing his son in a dangerous place and beating him often with a scourge he has snatched up, frightens him and puts him to flight from that place. You cannot doubt about this father that, if he had a great multitude of sons scattered in many dangerous places, he would multiply the scourges and scourging to do the same thing for the multitude of sons that he did for his only son. Since, therefore, the universe of human beings is like a multitude of sons by some kind of sonship, why is it surprising if the most kind creator, to whom are most evident all the dangers and all the harms of this dwelling and the delay that is harmful to human beings through their love <of it>—why, I say, is it surprising if he frightens them off and puts them to flight by a multiplication of scourges and pains lest they cling to this habitation or world?

But if someone says that God neither holds nor considers human beings as sons by any kind of sonship, although in this respect he clearly contradicts the oracles of the creator, that is, the prophetic words,[43] he nonetheless cannot deny that he at least holds them as either cattle or sheep or in some condition or relation of his ownership.[44] But what father of a family, as I said, would not act in this way with regard to his sheep or cattle, if he saw them in some dangerous place? It is clear, then, from this that divine providence is the cause of present pains in human beings.

A third example is with regard to a very strong and very intoxicating wine, to which the carnal or worldly pleasures of this present life are quite similar. For they inebriate one to the point of brutish folly and the most insane madness. But the contrary tribulations and pains are like water with regard to the power of checking the evil of such wine and of preventing it from inebriating. But no one intelligent fails to know that all human beings are certain banquet guests or at least guests of the creator; in fact, it is quite evident that they are children to whom he gives food and drink. But what father of a family would not temper a wine so dangerous to his banquet guests? Who would not provide for his children, on whom he expends the care of feeding and the costs of the foods, against a deadly destruction if he knew that it was in the food? Who would not watch out for deadly poison for his guests, except a most evil traitor and one seeking the death of his guests? But no poison is more pernicious than the pleasures just mentioned; in fact, they are more dangerous than every pestilential poison, to the extent that the blessed future life that they take from

---

43 See, for example, Ps 28:1, Hos 1:10, Jn 1:12, and Jn 11:52.

44 See, for example, Ps 78:13 and Ps 99:3.

human beings is more excellent than the life of the body, which alone[45] poisons extinguish.

Because, therefore, such great evils and dangers are alleviated most salutarily through the previously mentioned waters of tribulation and pains, you are left with no doubt that such waters of tribulation and pains are mixed into the present delights by the providence and goodness of the creator. But in order to make an end of this argumentation, I say that he who is a human being, not in name alone, but really, not nominally, is not permitted to doubt concerning any least good[46] that it comes from the creator, just as, if there were no source of light and could not be one apart from the sun, someone who knew this could not doubt concerning any light or a light, however great, that it came from the sun. Because, therefore, it was explained to you in the first part of this teaching, that there neither is nor can be a source of goodness apart from the creator,[47] it has been made evident to you that something /766b/ good or some goodness can only come from him.

It has also been explained to you in the preceding paragraphs that such tribulations and pains are not only good, but even very good. Who, however, except a man without an intellect would think that the creator neglects such great goods? I mean that he neglects them in that sense that he does not care that they exist or how or with what benefit. There are countless other examples of countless such benefits and fruits from pains and tribulations, which should be stated and explained elsewhere, and especially in sacred exhortations.

But if someone says that by these things the community of human beings is really cared for and provided for with countless benefits and fruits and that the creator undoubtedly exercises care for the universe, but not for individuals, one must respond to that man that the care of the creator and his providence for individuals is clearly seen in natural things, namely, in the composition, formation, number, connection, and perfection of the members. For there is no nature, no other power that is capable of the fabrication of the human body, and there is no doubt about the bodily nature. But about the spiritual nature one can see the same thing with a little consideration because it does not operate by instruments, since it does not have them, but by imagining or understanding alone and by willing or commanding. But the rational intellect does not admit that its being is subject to the will or to the command of anyone other than the creator; similarly, it does not admit that bodily forms and especially those of the bodies of animals are subject except to the com-

---

45 I have conjectured "*solam*" instead of "*sola*."

46 A marginal reading adds: "of the soul."

47 See William, *The Trinity*, chs. 1 and 5; ed. Switalski 17 and 35.

mand of the creator. For, far less can one command[48] to be in such a way or to be such a thing what one cannot naturally command to be.

It is evident, therefore, from this that only the power of the creator can fashion and form human bodies and those of the other animals; from this it is also evident as a consequence that their nourishment, life, and conservation, and whole remaining governance pertains to the providence of the creator. For the feeding and growth of animal and plant bodies is no less marvelous, nor is it discovered or rather assessed with less difficulty than the generation and fabrication of them. For who would be sufficient to admire so studiously and so diligently the digestion of food, its purification by frequent straining out, and its distribution with such great fidelity to the individual members and parts, as it is necessary and suited for each and as is just? By what art of arithmetic can the particles of foods and those fed be counted? By what art of geometry can they be divided, measured, and rendered apt to the members and other parts for their necessities and needs? None of them can complain that it receives less than is just or more than is just with regard to the nutritive power and the power distributive of food, except when more or less of the food due to it has been entrusted to that power or it is disobedient to the same power.

But in these three cases it is the fault of only the higher dispenser of the food. Just as when someone either burdens his stomach with more or less food than suffices for nature or puts into it food that the stomach's power is unable to cook and digest, the fault does not belong to the stomach, whatever damage or corruption occurs from these factors to the food or to the body to be nourished. But, as I said, the fault belongs to the one who poorly dispenses it to the stomach; the providence and goodness of the creator does not, nonetheless, cease in these cases, for he makes the illnesses and pains coming from this beneficial in so many ways, as you have heard.

You clearly see, therefore, from this that in the bodies of animals and the parts of them, whatever takes place naturally also takes place and is arranged by divine providence and goodness, so that multiple benefits come from them, /767a/ just as there is not a thread in your coat that does not hold a proper place in it, although the senses cannot perceive this on account of its smallness and the smallness of its benefit. So the whole is also that way in all wholes of every particular being of any kind. For it has already been explained to you in the treatises on the continuum and the vacuum that every aggregate from continua, that is, from parts, of which each is a continuum, but the whole is discontinuous, is necessarily composed of finite parts.[49] Hence, every piece of

---

48   I have conjectured "*imperare*" instead of "*imperari*."

49   See perhaps Aristotle's *Physics* 6.1.231b15–18. See William, *The Universe* Ia–Iae, ch. 1; Paris-Orléans ed., I, 684a, where a similar argument is developed.

cloth of whatever size is composed of a finite number of threads, and every pile of sand is composed of a finite number of granules, and if one thread is taken away from the cloth, something is removed from the whole of it, and a part of a certain and determinate relation to the whole cloth, although the senses perceive neither such a relation nor such a removal. But the luminosity of the wisdom of the creator measures and counts them all, and the holy and wise man did not say without reason in speaking to him, *You have arranged everything in number, weight, and measure* (Wis 11:21).

CHAPTER 6
On the Benefits of Oppression and Poverty,
And How God Gives Prosperity and Adversity in Different Ways,
And on the Benefit of Death

After this, however, I shall come to those things that pertain to oppression and to the removal of the matter of evils and to those that prevent access to these, that is, those which prevent human beings from withdrawing from evil, and just the opposite. I say, therefore, that by its intention and name oppression has many spiritual benefits. The first of them is against the most wicked exaltation of pride, which it heals when it is upon one and against which it guards when it threatens. The second benefit of it is against the inconstancy and flighty mobility by which certain people are troubled to the point that they cannot remain bodily in one place or spiritually in one state. An example of the first benefit is the compression of inflated hides and similarly a smith's bellows and all other things that deflate from compression. But there is an evident example in toads which are generated in narrow crevices of rocks and cannot swell until they emerge from there. An example of the second benefit is in light roofs of houses that are weighted down by stones lest they be carried away by winds. Similarly there are all those things on which heavy things are placed so that they are not carried off by a blast of wind or stream of water. There is a third benefit of which an example is seen in horses, whose excessive speed and rapid motion is repressed by burdens and whose pace is reduced to gentleness and moderation. And in these ways it is up to you to see and think up many others.

But ones that make human beings withdraw from sin or make sins withdraw from them are prisons, chains, disciplinary custody, and enclosures that holy men have made and still do make for themselves, intending to block every opening for sins, and wanting to keep themselves and their disciples from the approach[50] of them. And these are found only among the people of the Christians. Some of the philosophers, nonetheless, are said to have made something close to such custody for themselves, choosing for themselves dwellings apart and far from human beings, knowing how perilous is the society of the unlearned and undisciplined men for those who want to philosophize.

But poverty is as salutary for chastity and sobriety, as the removal of wood is for fires. For, the richness of food and drink and of other temporal things that serve the body, that is, for luxury and dissoluteness, and excessive /767b/ desires for food and drink are what wood is for a flame or a fire. The second benefit of poverty is a defensive rampart. For what a rampart or fortification is for a citadel that it surrounds, that poverty is for a poor man, whether he understands this or not. And just as a rampart wards off enemies and keeps them from entering, in fact even from approaching, so poverty does not allow the vices of luxury and of dissolute feasts and drunkenness to approach human beings. The fruits and advantages of poverty will be readily apparent to you from the disadvantages of riches, and you have already elsewhere learned many things about both of them from me.

But human beings have erred very greatly and still err concerning the providence and care of the creator in those things that seem to happen only by chance, and these are the things that happen in common and equally to the wise and the foolish, to the just and the unjust, such as are the perils of shipwrecks, which drown the just and the unjust equally, and deaths, and other fortuitous disadvantages. Secondly, they err about the people who seem not to be cared about at all both by the creator and by others, such as the mad, who seem to be carried along only by their madness. Thirdly, they err on the people who seem to live by whim, that is, as they want, and they only want to live badly, and are led so to speak by their stupid will or rather are driven by no one who rules or cares for them from outside, as it seems. Fourthly, they err on those who seem utterly abandoned, like a dead body exposed to the dogs and birds, for whose deliverance from those who tear them apart and devour them nothing is done, just as some paupers are torn and afflicted here in many ways with no one rescuing or defending them or even speaking against this or at least being compassionate, especially when they are very holy and just. How then does the blessed creator care for them? And if he does not care for these, then how would he care for the others?

Know first of all, then, that chance and accident are as far from the wisdom and goodness of the creator as folly and ignorance are, and on this account in relation to the creator nothing is chance. Among us, however, chance has a place, but in relation to us, and this is on account of our ignorance and lack

---

50   I have conjectured "*accessu*" instead of "*abcessu*."

of foresight. For the creator sees all things, not with a vision that is a sleeping habit, but rather with a gaze that is in the ultimate degree of alertness and actuality. Nor is anything concealed or hidden in any way from his sight. But he also does not see anything as far from himself or as near to himself, and I understand by my words that nearness and distance neither adds nor detracts from his knowledge. Hence, he sees everything uncovered and as near. It is, therefore, evident that nothing comes about so that it exists in reality that he does not know and has not also foreknown. And that his intention is that they should be good, happen, and last as long as he sees that it befits his glory and that the benefits that he wills to be from them come from them.

But with regard to evils, which the common folk call evil—and these are penal evils, that common foolish folks try to flee and to avoid or at least to minimize and to ease with all their desires and energy, such things are really goods, as you learned elsewhere, and they are works of justice and mercy useful and salutary for human beings in many ways—with regard to these, I say, there is the same intention for them as for other temporal or bodily goods, with the one exception that these are more suited for the goods of correction and the withdrawing of human beings from the evils of vices and sins, and they can be called by a most suitable name goods of discipline and of training by the creator. But other goods, namely temporal and bodily ones, are to be called goods of attraction and allurement to the divine goodness. For the goodness of the creator bestows them /768a/ on human beings either for the needs of sustenance, and this is given in common to all, or for the blandishment of attraction and allurement, and this is given specifically to human beings with a childish mind. For they are such small goods that the wise scorn them and know that they are entirely unworthy of their dignity. But childish human beings embrace them as great with total eagerness.

The goodness of the creator, therefore, coddles these people by these goods to attract them to a love and worship of him and entices them, as they gradually make progress, to lofty goods for the sake of which he created them, like a mother and a nurse and even a good father enticing children by the little gifts of pears and apples to a love for themselves and then summoning them either to the study of letters or also to other greater things. The creator in his goodness clearly used this strategy toward the people of the Hebrews. To that people as childish and as still young and unable to either know or love the lofty goods, he promised only small temporal goods, like childish gifts, in return for the observation of his law, and he threatened them only with their opposites, namely, poverty and bodily death, as if to deter children. For the wisdom of the creator did not judge that he should deal with that people at that time, as with wise people, since he knew their childishness and ignorance. For promises of such little gifts would be illusions and mockeries to wise people if they were made to them. After all, what wise person would not know that he was being mocked if a woman exposed and offered her breasts for him to suck or if she offered him three or four filberts in exchange for great and precious gifts?

For this reason, therefore, after the human race had been gradually educated both by the teaching of the law of the Hebrews and of the prophets and by natural doctrines and by other teachings and miracles of the creator, lofty goods were promised in the law of the truth and perfection, namely, goods of the next life. They are alone worthy of the excellence of the human race and its perfection, and in them the nobility of the philosophers was satisfied and similarly of the other wise people, who knew that such childish little gifts were to be scorned. And through the wisdom of God that taught them through the law and doctrine of the Christians, they welcomed with eagerness the promises of desirable goods, that is, of future ones. Similarly, deterred by the threats of great evils, they fled to the lofty virtues, understanding and most clearly recognizing in such a law the perfections that they sought. Understand, therefore, from this that the law and teaching of Christians was not given to the whole people as childish, which is evident from the promises and threats of it, because the knowledge of them does not occur in childish minds and is not grasped by them.

You see, therefore, from the things that I told you, the intention of the goodness of the creator with regard to those previously mentioned goods, because through one kind he intended the common sustenance of all human beings, but specifically the blandishment of the childish and the attraction of them to greater, namely, future goods, and their consolation to some extent over the present misery. But through the other kind he intended the goods of discipline, that is, to withdraw and preserve them from the evils of vices and sins. And I have already told you in the preceding paragraphs that there is no one for whom bodily death is not beneficial.[51] For it is deliverance from all the present evils and perils for the holy and just, the getting out of prison and chains, and the departure to the kingdom of future happiness. You have also heard from me of many other goods of bodily death. But for the evil and for those for whom the punishment of hell looms immediately after death, death is beneficial insofar as they would accumulate the punishments of a greater damnation by persisting in their evil merits from which they do not propose to come to their senses. /768b/ But I say that they do not propose to come to their senses, because whoever proposes to do this, is holy and just. For the proposal not to sin from now on and to live correctly from now on into the future wipes out and erases every stain of sin from human souls, as does the

51 See ch. 5, fol. 765b.

will by which one wills this—and I do not mean: would will this.[52] For those, therefore, who will in this way, there at times remains some satisfaction, which is also a purgation after death. But satisfaction and purgation do not extinguish and lessen justice and holiness, but rather help it in many ways and glorify it, as you have learned elsewhere.

And there is another benefit of this death that comes about in common for just and unjust human beings. For it is no slight warning for mortals to prepare for their end and departure from this life and a great exercise against human torpor and laziness, because of which some in this life are like sleeping people, who do not at all know what is done to them or with regard to them and do not want to know what awaits them. The death of others is also a strong help toward a contempt for the present life, concerning which the creator clearly showed how little he valued it and how little it ought to be for us, which he made so easy to extinguish and subjected to so many kinds of death.

Evils of this sort undoubtedly come about for the good and for the evil in common, but they do not benefit them equally. I also say that they are many times given to the unjust and to sinners in order that they might be turned away from their vices and sins by horror over the calamity and fear of imminent death. For fear has the greatest strength to drive out sins and to break human beings away from their evil ways and perversity of habit. It is evident, therefore, that it benefits and is most salutary for many sinners to perish by shipwreck. For how much better reason is it for the holy and just? But this will become more evident for you from the testimony of those who frequently sail and journey on the seas. For they clearly report and testify that their vices and sins were never so displeasing to them, that they never so grieved over and repented of them, and that they never so loved justice and holiness as when they saw that the peril of shipwreck threatened them. Since, therefore, it is incredible or unknown to no one that the creator foreknows that these goods come about for the good and for the evil in common from the perils of shipwreck, why is it surprising if the creator wills that such perils be common to them? For where the effect and benefit is common, it is not inappropriate that the cause be common.

---

52 That is, a mere velleity is not sufficient. See below ch. 20, fol. 786b.

CHAPTER 7
That Madmen Are Not Outside the Care of God,
And That Penal Evils Ought Not To Be Called Truly Evil

But I respond concerning madmen that they are not outside the care and providence of the creator since we see some of them bound or beaten so that they do not harm themselves or others and since we also see that they are fed and clothed and given other things necessary for them. For, whether done out of the natural love or the piety of those offering them or even to protect the property or persons whom they could harm if they were released, all these things are done through the care and providence of the creator, whose gifts are the love, piety, and solicitude just mentioned.

But if someone says that in such persons the care and providence is seen well enough, but that in madmen who are left to themselves, none is seen, since they are ruled neither by themselves nor by others, I respond that in certain ones this abandonment by which they seem to be abandoned is not only through the care and providence of the creator, but also through the care and providence /769a/ of human beings, and this is so because some are released from chains and dismissed as free, because this dismissal and freedom, running about and wandering, are salutary against their madness. And it has as yet not come to my attention that a madman was left to himself for another reason. But he is not dismissed if his dismissal and freedom are seen to be dangerous to others. But even if someone escapes from chains, as sometimes happens, it is evident that great goods come to him and to others from this, and there, of course, comes to him the good of more careful custody. But for those who see that he is free to his own peril and that of others, there comes a challenge to piety and beneficence toward him. And no rational person doubts that these are three great goods and ones accepted by the creator. Even if he harms someone before he is captured, this brings forth the benefits, of which you have learned, and perhaps many others.

But if he hurls himself into water or fire, this too is beneficial, as you have heard, and from it there comes through his death the good of peace and security for those whom he could have injured. Concerning the evil itself of madness, I say that it is often, in fact always very beneficial to the mad. For, if they are good and just, when they fall into madness, their holiness or goodness is secured through their madness, since they cannot sin at the time of the madness, and so holiness and justice cannot be lost by them or diminished at that time, since justice and holiness can be either diminished or completely taken away only by sins. But if they are evil and unjust, they are cared for through the madness so that their malice is not increased at that time, and on this account the punishments of future damnation do not increase for them.

But if Galen is believed, what he says in the book, *On Melancholy*, helps this argument, namely, that because of an excessive desire to see God and because of an excessive worry about this, certain people fall into melancholy.[53] That would not be possible with the goodness of the creator, that is, that from so great a good and one so acceptable to him as is the desire of seeing him and being deeply worried about this, he would permit them to fall into so great an evil, that is, the disease of melancholy, unless he foreknew that it would be beneficial for them and salutary in many ways.

But you ought to know that in my own time there were many very holy and religious men who had a great desire for the disease of melancholy on account of the previously mentioned security. Hence, since there was a certain melancholy person among them and since they tried to make his state their own to no small degree, they openly said that God bestowed an inestimable grace on that melancholy man, that is, because he placed his spiritual goods in so safe a place that he could not lose them, since such goods, as I already said, can only be lost through sins.

But someone might say that it is not impossible for the will of the creator that someone is permitted to receive evils on account of goods, and that it is not rare, but even rather frequent. For who doubts that many are killed for justice, because they acted justly or refused to abandon it? How many thousands of human beings were killed by idolaters, because they refused to refrain from the worship of the creator, which cannot be doubted to be most just, and because they scorned the worship of idols and the offering of sacrifice to them? Then how many thousands of matrons and virgins were killed because they refused to defile themselves by the lusts of corrupt men? To this, therefore, I respond that many such penal things are wrongly and falsely and even unjustly called and believed <to be evils> by the common and foolish people. For those things that are just cannot be evil, and those imposed by the judgment of the creator, for whom it is impossible to make a mistake or to be deceived, are good and most /769b/ worthy of his reward. Nor has it been doubted up to now by anyone intelligent that to suffer for the truth and justice is good, just, glorious, most praiseworthy in the eyes of human beings, and even most deserving of reward by the justice of the creator. Evils are, therefore, wrongly and damnably inflicted in return for goods, but are endured most praiseworthily. They do not, therefore, know the virtue of patience nor its rectitude and beauty, and they are completely ignorant of its glory, who do not yet know how beautiful it is to

---

53 Although Galen wrote two works entitled, *On Melancholy*, neither of them contains what William ascribes to him. I have not found any other source.

suffer for justice and that patience is the protector of all the other virtues and like a shield that receives on itself and fends off all the blows and attacks by which the other virtues are attacked and all the darts that are hurled at them, and it protects and guards them all unharmed. And these words on patience that I am saying here is the determination of the fourth question I posed just above.[54]

CHAPTER 8
That Those Living Voluptuous Lives and the Barbarian Nations Do Not Fall outside the Providence of God

But concerning those who are seen to live voluptuous lives here and according to their desire, as prostituted and exposed to the vices in every respect, you will understand how they live under the care and providence of God from this. For those who use the gifts of the creator only for pleasures and who are so given over to pleasures could in no way bear the pains of the divine scourges; in fact, they occasionally become worse through them. You can clearly see the great sorrow and the great anger with which they would waste away and be kindled, if those delights that they love most greatly were taken away from them, since they become insane from the removal of those delights.

Moreover, if they are not called to the love of the creator by those gifts that they love most greatly and over which they rejoice most greatly, but rather, ungrateful for them, they misuse them to so great a destruction of their souls, what do you think that they will do amid the contrary scourges? They would undoubtedly become insane to the point of blasphemies against the creator, and they would be perverted to the point of denying him, and they would even fall into unspeakable idolatry, as you have heard concerning many.

The wisdom and goodness of the creator, therefore, deliberately chose, insofar as it is up to him, to call and draw such men to himself by the gifts and benefits they love most of all <rather> than to wear them down by scourges and to drive them from him by the pains of the tribulations they hate most of all. For if a child is not enticed by the sweetness of milk so that it loves the nipples and clings to them, how much less would it be attracted by the bitterness of absinthe or of something else? On this account the most provident creator put sweetness in the milk of breasts in order to make it desirable and lovable for the little ones, who during their whole young age need to be nourished by its substance. The sweetness of temporal goods was, therefore, created especially

---

54   That is, in ch. 6, fol. 767b.

for this purpose, namely, in order that wisdom might still nourish the little ones in the love of and obedience to the creator, not merely in order to nourish them and fatten them in a bodily way. Nor is it right to think concerning the wisdom and goodness of the creator that he cares only for human bodies and neglects souls and that he gives with such a great effusion of generosity bodily goods, which become so harmful for the ungrateful and foolish through their ingratitude and abuse, but that, out of avarice and cruelty,[55] he does not take care to bestow those goods that are so necessary and so salutary for human beings and without which he sees that the bodily goods are pernicious. To think either of these things concerning the creator is wickedness that is to be utterly wiped out by sword and fire.

But someone might say that for many men such bodily or temporal goods do not entice or nourish love and obedience toward the creator, but rather lead to the perversion and corruption of their souls, namely, to pride, dissoluteness, and the other plagues of the vices /770a/ and for that reason ought not to be given to human beings by divine providence and care, since the intention of the wisdom and goodness of the creator is that his gifts profit the recipients, but not that they harm them in any way. I respond that the last statement is most true, namely, concerning the intention of the wisdom and goodness of the creator, and it is really apart from his intention that such human beings turn the good gifts of God to their own destruction, which they undoubtedly do through the abusive distorting of the free power given them by the creator.

But there are many examples of such a thing. God certainly gave wine to human beings for their good health, but many of them have turned it to drunkenness. He also gave fire as a manifold help to health and conservation; still, when madmen hurl themselves into it, they make it an instrument of their destruction. He also gave them water for so many and such necessary benefits;[56] still many, who plunge themselves into it, are killed. At times a father of a family gives his son a sword for his defense, and yet through madness or excessive anger, he kills himself with it. So too, solar light that shines so far and wide for the illumination of eyes is turned into a darkening of them through an excessive or superabundant gazing at it or its light.

But because it is evident that all these abuses or distortions are blameworthy and sins and depravities, insofar as they are against rectitude, it is right and just and most suitable to the justice of the creator that punishment follow up on these sins and that the gifts of God that they turned into the misuse of sin is for them the cause of just punishment. It is, therefore, most just that drunkenness or some other punishment, according to the good pleasure of the

---

55 I have conjectured "*crudelitate*" instead of "*credulitate*."

56 I have conjectured "*utilitates*" instead of "*utilitatem*."

creator, follow upon the misuse of wine, as at times dropsy follows, at times a fever, at times a deep sleep, which gives thieves the opportunity to rob or even to strangle drunks. There are also countless other misfortunes and evils that come from drunkenness. Justice is clearly seen in all these punishments, that is, of those who misuse the benefits of the creator, but his abundant kindness is seen in those who use them well. But both undoubtedly pertain to his care and providence—both those punishments that are just and those that are, so to speak, kind.

Nor is it doubted that by its natural power, which it has from the creator, wine inebriates someone—not that the creator gave such power to it for this purpose, but on the occasion of the misuse by one using it wrongly it becomes the creator's instrument of most just punishment. Hence, it is most true that those who turn the benefits of the creator into their own destruction make them the weapons of the creator and instruments of justice regarding themselves. But among the intelligent there is no doubt that such justice is pleasing to the creator. Both sorts of human beings, therefore, that is, those who use the benefits of God in a good way and those who use them in a bad way, either govern themselves rightly and orderly under his generous beneficence or suffer his most just punishments under his justice. But who does not see that under the rule and governance of the same king there are good people, to whom he gives peace and other good things, and evildoers, whom he torments and punishes by just judgment and justice.

But if someone says that the creator does not intend such punishments, it is easy for you to see that the statement of such a man is incorrect. For, since it is evident that all such punishments are just and for this reason good and pleasing to the creator, it is necessary that they fall under the intention of the creator. But the reason for this is that, since there is no source of justice apart from the creator, it is not possible to find a drop of justice that is not his gift. The fact that such punishments are just comes, therefore, from the gift of the creator. /770b/ But whatever the creator gives, he gives knowingly, prudently, vigilantly, and willingly, not in ignorance or sleep. Hence, since the creator knows, wills, and does this by his gift, they are just, and their infliction upon human beings is just, and they are, therefore, inflicted by the care and providence of the creator.

Moreover, it is certain that in a kingdom totally and immediately subject to its most just king there is neither justice nor judgment save through his providence and care, because no one has the power of judging in that kingdom save from him and through him, and this is so for much better reason, if no one has either the will or the knowledge to carry out judgment or justice save through that king. Because, then, the universal series of the ages is the kingdom of the creator and no one in it has the power, the will, or the knowledge to carry out judgment and justice save from the creator and through him, there is no judgment or justice in the whole series of the ages save from him and through him. The justice, therefore, by which those who misuse his benefits are brought to justice by such just punishments, comes from him and through him, and it, of course, comes through his knowledge and will, as I already said. Whatever justice, therefore, exists in the whole of the universe, whether in the examples proposed or elsewhere, comes through the care and providence of the creator.

Moreover, it is evident, even to those who understand little, how salutary judgments are and how necessary justice is and how many and how great are the benefits that come to human beings from them. And my intention in this discussion is concerning the judgments and justice that are carried out by judges and justices. But it cannot be doubted that they, that is, judgment and justice, are such great goods, in human affairs, wherever they exist, since he has never ceased and still does not cease to provide incomparably less useful goods to human beings. It is, therefore, necessary that, where judgment and justice do not exist or are not carried out by human beings, the divine wisdom and goodness provide these great goods either through itself or through other creatures, and this is known not only by the testimonies of prophets and authoritative histories, but also by continuous experience. It is, therefore, evident that through the waters of the universal flood he carried out something like a universal judgment and justice upon the whole human race, when he considered that only eight human beings should be spared from such a flood and destruction.[57] He punished the crimes of five cities by a rain of fire and sulphur.[58] The judgments are very well known that the most high carried out against the Egyptians and their gods through little beasts, namely, frogs and gnats, through fire and hail, through turning the water into blood, through the darkening of that part of Egypt in which the Egyptians were and the illumination of that part in which the Hebrews dwelled, and finally through the drowning of the king of Egypt and his whole army in the Red Sea.[59] Most certain histories tell that the creator many times also brought punishment upon the Hebrews through fire and at times through the earth swallowing some of them by its opening.[60] Moreover, plagues and famines, sterility and dryness, lack of rain are very familiar, which there is no doubt were brought about by

---

57 See Gn 7.

58 See Gn 19.

59 See Ex 7–12 and 14.

60 See Num 16:31–35.

the judgment and justice of the creator on account of the sins of human beings, since he alone has power over them and their contraries.[61]

For those who read the histories it is also evident that bears and other beasts, namely, locusts and mice, were sent as punishment on unjust nations. But it is not necessary that I speak to you about the storms of sea and land, that is, of floods and earthquakes, the submerging and burning of cities and regions. But in making a careful consideration of them one by one, you will find that none lacks the justice of the creator, since you will find that whales and almost every kind of animal practices some justice and defends its rights. /771a/ Notice how a mother bear punishes the seizure or killing of her cubs. Similarly, notice how a lion fights for his mates, for nests, for food, and for young or offspring. Notice the great justice by which the males and females mutually endure their labors so that, while the female remains in the nest or cave, the male goes out to seek food and to bring it back for his female and their young.

Even in my own time, as if convicted of adultery by the smell of a male, after a multitude of storks had gathered and a male somehow accused her and revealed her crime, a stork was stripped of her feathers and lacerated by the whole multitude, as if she were judged guilty of adultery by the council and judgment of them all. The story is also told about a horse that in ignorance had intercourse with his mother. After he found out about this, he cut away for himself his own genitals by his own teeth, as if punishing the incest that he thought he had committed, although in ignorance, because his mother was concealed from him by a covering when he mounted her. You can also read in books of histories, especially of the people of the Hebrews and of the people of the Christians—and no wise person doubts that the histories of these peoples should be believed—that angels, both holy one and bad ones, were often sent for the punishment of crimes. But in the narratives of the Christians and their miracles, the inspection of which is still salutary and very pleasant, you will find countless cases of angelic consolation, magnificent punishments, and wicked princes carried off and miserably tortured by demons.

But if someone wonders about barbarian nations, which seem to be entirely outside the laws and outside every kingdom, know that there is no nation so barbarous that it does not have its elders whom it obeys and by whom it is ruled in some way and that similarly does not have its gods and sacred words, which should rather be called curses, and some rites and ceremonies, not so much impious as ridiculous. Their barbaric wildness or ferocity also helps the governance of them. By it they repress and chastise one another, and one

---

61   See, for example, 2 Sam 24 for David's sin that was punished by a plague; also see 1 Kgs 17 for the drought that Elijah predicted; and see Dt 28:19 for the promise of famine for those who transgress the law.

barbarian is not permitted, to vent his rage upon another without the sort of vengeance that the victim is himself able to impose, and on this account they calm one another down somewhat by a fear of one another. Barbarity itself and their wildness and unbelief are most just punishments of such nations as a result of their most just abandonment by the creator, who as yet has given them neither leaders, nor rulers, nor teachers by which they might be trained and constituted like nations that live as human beings.

And since you have learned elsewhere that one justice is natural and that another is positive and instituted by human beings, but that a third is divine instituted by the creator, and this is concerned with the ordering of human morals toward perfection and with the worship that of itself is most pleasing to him and most holy, and which alone he considers worthy of the reward of eternal happiness, go about and investigate the whole sublunar world, and you will clearly find that nothing is lacking these three kinds of justice. You will find that each thing is governed by one of these three kinds or by two or by all three. Because, therefore, all these kinds of justice or laws come from the creator and through him, it is evident that there is nothing in the sublunar world that is not ruled by some law or laws of the creator. But whatever is ruled by a law or laws of anyone is undoubtedly ruled by the providence of the same. There is no human being or animal, therefore, in the sublunar world that is not ruled by the care and providence of the creator.

/771b/ CHAPTER 9

That Those Living a Life of Delights Produce in Themselves the Punishment of God, And That Favorable Events Often Become the Cause of Salvation

But I shall return to where I was and say that human beings who are seen to live here voluptuously and according to their desire and who misuse the benefits of the creator for their pride, avarice, dissoluteness, and other such plagues, make these benefits penal for themselves and instruments of divine justice against themselves, and by misusing the gifts of the creator in that way, they execute divine justice against themselves, though without knowing it, and they punish in the fiercest way their own souls, when they inebriate and blind them by delights. But who would measure or count the evils of pride, avarice, and the other vices, which all the wisdom of the philosophers and of other wise persons calls diseases and wounds, servitude and chains? Who would compare bodily riches to the treasures of moral goodness and the riches of the virtues? If the taking away of money, therefore, is a bodily punishment, and if the one who takes it away punishes the one who loses it, for how much better reason is the taking away of the previously mentioned riches a punishment? And for how much better reason does the one who takes them away punish the one who loses them? And this is more bitter to the extent that those spiritual riches are more excellent. In this way, if those who bring bodily evils—either diseases or wounds, prisons and chains—are truly punishing officers of those on whom they impose them, how much more are those who bring spiritual diseases, wounds, and the other evils of this sort to be considered enemies and punishing officers of those who suffer them, since these evils are worse than bodily evils to the extent that human souls are more excellent than bodies?

The statement I made, therefore, is true that they make the benefits of the creator instruments of punishments for themselves and make themselves executors of divine justice, although without knowing it, when they so fiercely take vengeance upon their souls and often upon their bodies for the injuries and insults to the creator, as I touched upon for you. Hence, by a most just judgment of the creator and by his justice, which is to be praised in every respect, they serve for the execution of justice against themselves, who, showing themselves ungrateful for his benefits, refuse to be willing servants of the same justice.

But you ought to know that at times the beneficence of divine generosity benefits impious and very evil persons and turns them away from their evils, that is, from vices and sins, as happened in my own time with regard to a certain rich and great man. Although his life was most ungrateful for such great benefits of the creator and befouled with dissoluteness, he was nonetheless chosen for the priestly honor and dignity, and when the election was offered to him, he immediately said, "You have conquered me, most kind and sweet God, with your untiring goodness and beneficence, because you never ceased always to bestow on me your benefits, while I never ceased to return evils. But now you have brought it about to call me, who am unworthy of every good and worthy of every condemnation and death, to the honor of such great loftiness. You have imprisoned me, and I hand myself, so imprisoned, over to your goodness, hereafter renouncing this honor and the temporal goods that I misused so ungratefully and so damnably." Going off, then, and having left all things, he gave himself to the strictest religion in order to live in it perpetually for the creator.

You know too that liberation from the perils of storms and from prisons and the gaining of victories turns countless persons away from their vices and sins, and it has brought them to the emendation of their life and the ordering of their morals. So too, other benefits of the creator have led many, even about whom it is not known, to the love for /772a/ and obedience to the creator.

But after this the fourth question can be easily settled,[62] namely, concerning those people who are exposed to scourges, tribulations, and all the woes of the body. For I say that they suffer these for the sake of justice and from impious people, that is, when they want to preserve and not to abandon justice or to consent to iniquity. And then it is evident that this does not fall outside the care and providence of the creator because there is nothing more just, nothing more in harmony with the law of the creator, nothing more acceptable to him or more worthy of reward in his eyes. But if they suffer this for their own sins and crimes, this too is most just, not only by the divine care and providence, but by the most worthy procurement of it.

Moreover, when they do not in this way come to their senses and do not return from their evils, it is also evident that they are worthy of greater punishments. Therefore, those that they suffer are justly inflicted on them, and this is mercifully subtracted from the punishments they merited.

Moreover, when such great scourges do not turn aside their malice, how great would it be and to what lengths would it go if it were not repressed and reined in by scourges?

It is, therefore, evident that they are not abandoned by the creator when he shows concern for their malice so that it is at least somewhat repressed by scourges. In this way other human beings are also beneficially provided for because, when such great malice is repressed by frequent scourges, it is not allowed to attack them. Understand, therefore, my words about the penal evils and culpable evils with care and examination, and notice that evils that are penal and entirely lacking guilt are properly and truly goods, but the folly of human beings and the corruption of the palate of the human heart have imposed the name of evil on it. The folly of human beings, of course, makes people flee from them and also makes them seem to be things that they should flee from, as you see in a skittish horse who flees from what he should not flee from, and because of the same vice[63] of skittishness he sees danger where there is only safety. In the same way, to those who have a corrupt palate of the heart, such goods taste bad, and they also call evils good and goods evil, saying that *good is evil and evil is good* and *holding that light is darkness and darkness light* (Is 5:20), as the prophetic words say. These names then are given in the same way as if persons suffering from fever imposed names on tastes, and owls on light and darkness. For it is not doubtful that sweet things taste bitter and bitter things taste sweet to those suffering from fever and that light seems dark

---

62   Perhaps another reference to the fourth question proposed in ch. 6, fol. 767b.

63   I have conjectured "*vitio*" instead of "*visio*."

and darkness light to owls and bats, and similarly, night seems day and day night.

Notice too that they for whom only punishment is seen to be evil or for whom pleasure alone is seen to be most good undoubtedly fall into the error of Epicurus.[64] The reason for this is that it is necessary that for them only pleasure is seen to be good or most good. From this you see clearly that, since both of these goods are gifts of the creator and are not given by him save knowingly and willingly, they are not outside his care and providence, even if penal evils are inflicted upon their sufferers by wicked and perverse actions.

But if someone asks how evil persons can be said to be efficient causes through their evil actions and the creator himself <can be> along with them, I have already determined for you that the creator is the cause of them, since through a most correct intention he not only brings it about that they exist, but also that they are good, salutary, and beneficial in many ways.

An example of this is seen in an impious man who wounded another with a sword, where it is evident that the wound proceeded from him through an evil will, through the power that was, nonetheless, given to him and to the sword by the creator and also through the possibility, that is, through the wounded man's potency for receiving the wound. The impious man, therefore, intended to harm the wounded man by the wound, but /772b/ by the same wound the creator intended the opposite, namely, to benefit him. The impious man, therefore, elicited from a good power an evil, namely, the evil action, but the creator elicited a good suffering. Heaven forbid, however, that the wound inflicted should be attributed only to the malice of the one inflicting it, since both the power to strike and the will, that is, the ability to will, the sword, and the possibility, as I said, of being acted upon are good gifts of the creator. The malice of the man striking, therefore, against the striker's will, serves and benefits both the wounded man and the creator, and for this reason it is permitted or allowed. Since, therefore, so many gifts of God assist and, from the intention of the creator, cooperate in producing the very being of the wound or of the pain from the wound, and since the being of the wound and of the pain is pleasing to the creator, its being is not without reason to be attributed to the creator. But this malice should in no way be attributed to him, especially since many think that the very fact that willing evil and doing evil exist comes from the creator. But its disorder and turning away from due rectitude, which is the malice and depravity, of both the doing and of the willing it, comes from the one who acts evilly and wills evilly.

---

64 Epicurus (341–271 BC), a Greek philosopher of the Hellenistic period, taught a doctrine of ethical hedonism, that is, that bodily pleasure and the absence of pain were the only goods.

But this is their view according to my understanding of them.[65] It is as if it were said that the killing of this man is the same according to essence and truth when he is killed through judgment and justice and when he is killed through iniquity and impiety. The being of it, therefore, is the same in each case. Hence, if its being comes from the creator when it comes about through judgment and justice, it will also be from the creator when it comes about through iniquity and impiety, especially since iniquity and impiety do not seem to be able to give being either to the one or to the other.

Moreover, the disorder and depravity I mentioned are accidental to the being, the willing, and the doing. They do not, therefore, constitute their being or give being to them. But all the other things from which the willing or doing evil proceeds are gifts of the creator. Willing, therefore, and doing anything come only from the gifts of God most high, both that it is and insofar as it is, and for this reason all acting and all willing, both that it exists and insofar as it exists, is only good. It is, therefore, not surprising if doing evils and willing evils are what they are from the creator and through his care and providence and if the sufferings that come from them are good.

But an example of this is seen in the motion of a ship, which can only be said to be from the wind or water or from both together, but that it is not straight but crooked can be either from the poor condition of the sail or from the poor condition of the rudder. It is evident, however, that neither the condition of the sail nor the condition of the rudder is the cause of the motion, that is, of the being or the essence of the motion, but they can undoubtedly make the motion to be straight or crooked. Just as the crooked motion of the ship is motion from one cause and crooked from another, so too a crooked or depraved action is <an action> from one cause and is crooked or depraved from another. And just as the crookedness of the motion of the ship[66] is not to be attributed to the wind or to the water, but only its motion, so the crookedness or depravity of our actions or wills are not to be attributed to the creator, but their being <is to be attributed to him,> by which they are or by which they are actions or wills. According to these people, therefore, since all things are from the creator, not only substances, but also actions and the willing of them, it is easy to see that all things fall under the care and providence of the creator since all of them are his works, and it is necessary that he produce all of them knowingly, willingly, and wisely. Nor is it possible for him to do something wisely and not providently.

---

65 That is, the understanding of those who claim that the creator is the efficient cause of the evil action.

66 I have conjectured "*navis*" instead of "*maris*."

But perhaps someone might say that actions and willing are totally from the powers, just as the whole running of a horse is from its power to move and not from the spurs or reins and not from the goads of the spurs or of the reins. In that way an action of ours does not come from the willing in act or actual willing, /773a/ because the willing is like the prick of the spurs and like a passion in the soul of the agent and because an external suggestion either of one who commands, warns, or deters is only like a spur. But many of the philosophers have already said that willing or refusing, fearing and hoping, and the others of the sort are only passions. And for this reason according to this account, just as spurs do not make horses run and are not—and are not said to be—the cause of the motion of horses, but the pricks of the spurs only incite the horses to run, so the previously mentioned passions of our souls incite them and their powers to their actions and are not their causes. Whatever, therefore, malice is called, it will not, according to this, be a cause of an action. Let these things, therefore, be for you matter for the exercise of your mind, because the explanation of these matters requires a more lengthy treatment and examination.

CHAPTER 10
That the Wisdom of the Creator Knows Great Things No Less than Small Ones, Where He Teaches What Care and Caring Are

But whether hunting by human beings and by animals falls under divine care and providence as well as voluntary actions, which seem entirely indifferent and to make no difference whether they are done or not done, involves a question that some consider ridiculous rather than fruitful or worthy of investigation. Of this sort are the questions whether under the care and providence of the creator this fish falls into the net of the fisherman rather than another and whether others escape through the providence of the creator, as if he spares them from being caught and eaten. And there is the same question concerning rabbits, goats, and other catches of hunters. In the hunting by animals there is a similar question about wild donkeys and lions, namely, whether a wild donkey is caught and devoured by one lion through divine care and providence rather than another, and whether one mouse is captured by a cat rather than another. There is the same question about spiders and flies and about swallows and insects, and these questions will come down to dogs and bones, to vultures and dead bodies, to chickens and seeds, and to other birds that feed on seeds. But there are similar questions in voluntary matters, for example, whether through the care and providence of the creator this man eats this piece of bread rather than another and this piece before another. It is the same with vegetables whether through the care and providence of the creator he eats this kernel before another and this bean before another and whether through the care and providence of the creator they are equal or unequal.

I say, therefore, to this that the wisdom of the creator in no way extends to the smallest things less than to the greatest or those in between, and on the other hand, he knows the uses, although they are very small, of the smallest no less than those of the greatest, although they are the greatest. And both these things and those things come from him and through him wisely, providently, and willingly, and as he has care that the individuals exist, as I already told you, so he has care to order individuals to their ends and uses. Nor do hunters or fishermen hesitate to say, "God gave me this fish today or this wild animal," and when they do not catch anything, they likewise say openly, "Today God did not give me anything to catch." In this difference or change between catching on one day and not catching on another, there is one obvious benefit of, belief in, and admiration for divine providence and goodness, and similarly the incitement to fear and love of the creator as well to gratitude toward him, so that when he gives, we give him thanks, and when he does not, /773b/ we fear having offended him and await from his gift what is sought.

But you ought to know that, insofar as it pertains to the present topic, "to care" or "not to care" is said in two ways or intentions. And one of these pertains in us to the internal moving mobile power, and in accord with this way "not to care" means not to have something at heart so that one neither rejoices if it occurs nor is offended if it does not, or the converse. And according to this way, the creator is said among the common folk not to care about everything by which he is neither offended nor pleased. But this is to say: for what he neither imposes punishment nor gives a reward. And in this way the creator cares about neither the number of flies that are captured by spiders or are eaten by swallows, and similarly not about the number of beans that someone eats nor about the order by which he eats this one first and that one later. And this intention perhaps agrees with the etymology of the term by which someone said that care (*cura*) is said as if derived from burning the heart (*cor urens*).[67] Hence, those things are properly said to be cared about whose occurrences or non-occurrences burn our hearts, that is, move them with some passion, such as anger or placation, sorrow or joy, and this intention does not pertain to the creator except metaphorically, for you know that he is in the ultimate degree of impassivity and immutability.

---

67 See Joannes Murmellius and Rodulphus Agricola, *Commentary on the Consolation of Philosophy* (*In libros de consolatione philosophiae*) I, poetry 2; PL 63: 895.

But this is the figure by which he is said to be angry when he acts in the manner of someone angry, that is, when he inflicts punishment, and is said to rejoice when he gives a reward for any deed and similarly is said to be placated when he stops punishing, and these intentions are more clearly designated by other words, for example, when it is said that, when such nouns or verbs are used among us, they are understood to be said in terms of affect, that is, because they signify our affections or the passions of our souls. But when they refer to the creator, they are said in terms of effect, that is, they signify his effects that I have named.[68] But this is because such passions in no way touch the supereminent purity of the creator. One of the wiser teachers of the Christians, therefore, said with utter correctness that it is not the affections of a disturbance, but the effects of punishing that make God to be said to be angry.[69]

In this way or intention the creator does not care about such a catch or escape of game or fish except when the fish or game is sought either for the necessity of the one who catches it or of another who needs it or when either love, obedience, honor, or piety toward the creator induces men to seek and hunt and to fish and catch. For no one who knows the goodness of the creator doubts that he is present in such intentions and operations as a helper, since he who knows all things sees that it contributes to or is befitting his glory.

Nor is it surprising since he has also multiplied in their time grains and vegetables by his omnipotent power and generosity, even in the barns themselves, in time of famine a hundred times and more than that, at the same time satisfying the pious desires of the religious, when the people were in danger of famine, and showing compassion for the necessities of the needy. You will also read in the stories and miracles of Christians, to whose reading I have often urged you and still urge you, that gold pieces were multiplied in the chests of holy men. It is admitted that in my own time fishes that were already cooked were multiplied at the table of a certain holy man by the kindness and generosity of the creator. For, although scarcely six of those dining could have been served from those on one platter, the whole multitude of those dining festively were served by individual plates <from those> on three platters. And the remnants of the fishes that were left over were far greater than the fishes prepared and

68 See Lactantius, *The Anger of Dei* (*De ira Dei*) 5; PL 7: 91, where in the notes it says: "Many passages of scripture testify that God is angry. But it should be noted that anger is not a violent passion in God, but the will to punish, and is attributed to God in term of effect, not in term of affect, as they say. That is, God does what angry persons do, but is not for this reason affected by a similar disturbance of the mind, as angry human beings are."

69 See, for example, Augustine, *Homilies on the Psalms* 2.4; PL 36: 70.

set /774a/ on the tables. It should not be surprising, therefore, if with certain care and providence the creator gives fishes and game already created to hunters and fishermen or to those for whom the hunting and fishing is carried out, since at times he marvelously multiplies fishes already cooked and prepared for eating on the very tables.

In the second way or intention "to care" is said "to be to pay attention to or to think about," and in this way it pertains to our noble apprehensive power and to the creator in accord with the excellence of his nobility. Nor is there anything in created things or their events that the creator does not care for in this way and intention. For there is nothing from all such things that he does not see and pay attention to—not only the thing itself, but its ends and benefits that he foreknows and foresees will come about by his arranging them. In this way, then, he cares for the number of insects that are captured by spiders and little flies devoured by swallows and for the whole order of their being captured and devoured. For he sees all things by his fixed and most lucid gaze, along with their uses and ends. For the eating of one little fly is part of the feeding of one swallow, and the little fly is part of the totality of its food.

But if someone asks with what benefit or fruit he sees these things, I respond: with the whole benefit or fruit that comes from it. I also say that, if the intellect of the ruler of each ship were of such power and brilliance that he was able to see at the same time not only the rudder, sails, and oars, but also the individual planks, nails, and ropes, he would gaze upon all these things at the same time. For how much better reason, then, can the most high ruler of the universe allow nothing to be outside his sight! I also say that it is something essentially due to all things, changes, and events that each and every one of them falls under the most lucid gaze of the creator, and because it is not possible for him to see something in ignorance or without knowledge, it is necessary that he attentively sees all things and that his intention falls upon each and every thing. For he does not see as we do, who do not see the whole thing at the same time and fully. Rather many of the conditions of things become known to us one after the other, but all of them are known to him at the same time, and the whole of them and equally.

Moreover, many items in a single thing are known to us suddenly and unintentionally, though with him it is just the opposite. But if you ask what the benefit is of the order in the eating of beans or grains, I respond that the creator sees it, whether we know it or not, although there is something in the soul of the eater that inclines or moves the eater to eat this one first or to eat it rather than the other. There is also seen in this the goodness of freedom in the eater, who perhaps without any thought or consideration of a benefit arranged his eating so that he ate this one before that one or rather than that one, wanting only to eat freely and so freely that it is as if he did it without being persuaded or enticed, but by the pure and most free command of the will, which I know has happened to me many times.

CHAPTER 11
That the Things That Seem To Come about by Chance Fall under the
Providence of God,
Where the Author Deals with the Ruling Power Given to Things by God
For their Conservation

But just as <one responds> in those things that seem to come about by chance, such as in the unforeseen encounters of human beings and in other things that come about apart from our intention and thought, so one should respond <to the question> concerning the catch of fishes in nets and of wild animals in /774b/ snares, namely, why it is this fish rather than that one or this animal rather than that one that falls into it. In the same way, what is the reason that such a man met this man in the forum, although he was not looking for him and did not even think of him? For it is evident that those walking at the same time on the same road in opposite directions necessarily meet, and they could have had different reasons for walking. For it is possible that the reason for such walking was for one man business, for another recovery of a debt, for a third the exaction of fines, for a fourth the collection of taxes, and for a fifth the search for thieves or other evildoers. The oneness of the road or the forum, therefore, for those traveling on it brought about the encounter or meeting of such men.

Thus, when a fish was perhaps going after food by one route, it happened that it was pulled in by a net along that same route, or perhaps it was fleeing from the noise and uproar that the companions of those men pulling the net were making. The fish and the net, therefore, met each other, but the meeting was clearly the cause of the fish's being caught. Another fish, however, did not go for food at the same time or by the same route, or perhaps the fear of the fishermen did not reach it so that it fled, or perhaps it fled into deeper hiding places or by another route, and thus did not encounter a net or that net, and on this account it was not caught by it. But the cause of the earlier capture is evident: at times its nearness to the net or the greater speed of its swimming or the earlier coming of the fear upon it. But there can be many causes of its escape, that is, of its not being caught, which it is easy for you to see for yourself, such as a later time or slower swimming. But this is because the nets were pulled in before it could fall into them. Or it perhaps fled by another route, or perhaps it fled backward when the net was stretched in front of it. Or it broke the net or made a hole in it for itself by which it escaped, or it leapt up and passed above the net, or it dived and burrowed into the sand or mud below the net and thus passed under it, or it passed over it when it was being pulled along. And the wisdom of the creator sees each and every one of these and orders them to the most suitable ends and uses that are perfectly known only to him.

But do not doubt that, just as for all the fishes or all wild animals to be caught at the same time would mean the universal destruction for the fishes and wild animals, so for some fish or wild animals to be caught and eaten now and then would mean the destruction of the particular nature in them in terms of one body of water or one region. For example, when there are few fishes in a river or some pond, for those few to be caught or eaten means the devastation and destruction of that kind in that place. It is not surprising, then, if by his care and providence the creator and preserver of natures watches out for particular natures, as he does for them all so that they are not totally destroyed and do not perish, until their use or usefulness has to cease, about which you have heard in the preceding chapters.[70] But if the princes of lands and their lesser lords at times forbid hunting and fishing in waters and lands under their jurisdiction, intending by this to look after only their own greed, not to provide for the conservation of nature, for how much better reason does the goodness of the creator not disdain to look after the conservation of the natures he created for such great benefits so that they do not perish completely?

And it is known to you from the law of the Hebrews how he commanded that the kinds of animals be preserved against the waters of the flood in pairs and in sevens in that most famous ark.[71] You also see the great cleverness in escaping the ambushes of fishermen and the great powers that the blessed creator gave to fishes, and similarly you see how many hiding places and refuges against hunters and also against wild animals hostile to them he gave to wild animals. /775a/ For who taught deer to show themselves on a well-traveled road to avoid the attacks of wolves? Who taught them that wolves are afraid of and avoid well-traveled roads? Who taught wild donkeys to endure the great ardor of thirst until lions have returned after drinking water lest they should meet the lions and be devoured by them if they go to the water at the time when the lions go or return? Who made them know that lions lie in wait for them? Thus for their preservation the creator also gave to hares swiftness of

---

70 See *The Universe* IIa–Iae, ch. 39; Paris-Orléans ed., I, 741b–743a, where William explains that usefulness of animals and plants will cease once human beings have entered heaven.

71 See Gn 6:14–21.

foot and to rabbits deep holes, which are almost inaccessible to other animals; so he also gave speed of flight to swallows and to many other birds, and many think that this is the reason why a swallow never falls prey to any bird of prey. I think, nonetheless, that the acquisition of its food is wholly through flight because only through it does it hunt little flies in flight. And just as many of the animals—those that walk and fly as well as swim—are not for our food, but we rather abominate them and utterly refuse to eat them, so I do not consider it surprising if for a similar reason swallows are not eaten by birds of prey.

I also remember that I saw a cat absolutely refuse the meat of the bird, which the common folk call a plover, since that meat is so sweet and savory that it is counted among the delicacies of royal foods. But I said this in passing lest you readily believe men of little experience in things of nature and in order to raise and elevate your intellect and your thought to the consideration of the wonders of the creator in natural things and the radiance of his wisdom, by which all animals are illumined for governing themselves and their life, even if by small lights, although the animals themselves are large. And they rightly ought to be held in our admiration and seen in comparison with the darkening and obscurity of human souls, which the human intellect suffers as a result of the original corruption and the added darkness from vices and sins. By this comparison we would, of course, regard as prophetic splendor in human souls the sagacity, sense of nature, or whatever else you might want to call the power in dogs of searching out and apprehending thieves. And it would be the same, if the providence of ants, about which I told you,[72] were found in human beings without a teacher and without looking at books, just as there are countless other lights of this sort, which we would not hesitate to call prophetic splendors in human beings if they were found without teaching and learning. And as these are found in animals, there is also found in inanimate bodies a regulative power by which they avoid harmful things and seek things salutary for themselves by natural motions.

But there is seen in all the kinds of magnetic stone a power that closely approximates sensation. For it seems almost to sense iron, and I have seen with my own eyes that a magnet attracted iron through the thickness of a bronze basin put between them. For there are three kinds of magnet stones, if Mercury is believed.[73] The first is that which attracts iron; this is the best known. But the second kind repels it from itself, while the third kind attracts it from one side and repels it from the other. And there is another amazing thing about a magnet, namely, that in the presence of true adamantine it ceases from such operations of attraction, as if it perceived it to be more noble and more pow-

---

72   See above Ch. 3; 758b.

73   William at times refers to Hermes Trismegistos by his Latin name, Mercury.

erful than itself, as if deferring to it out of reverence. And something similar is said concerning a male and a female palm tree, because when the branch of one touches a branch of the other, they cling to each other as in a mutual embrace,[74] in which its vital power seems to possess some sprinkling from the luminosity of the sensible power, and perhaps this is the reason why Aristotle said /775b/ that it is the most noble of the plants. Concerning the plant that is called a hazel shrub those who speak[75] say something similar, namely, that, when it has been divided lengthwise through the middle, the parts in the recent division draw close to each other and are rejoined, which deceivers, themselves deceived, attribute to the power of certain words, although this comes from the power and sense of nature.

CHAPTER 12
Why God Permits Evil Human Beings to Flourish in This Life
And Have Dominion over Good People,
And What Goods He Elicits from This

Concerning the flourishing and domination by evil and perverse human beings, it is evident that it offers great benefits for the good people who are oppressed and afflicted by them in this life in many ways, and also for the evil people it produces a great admiration for the divine goodness and generosity as well as a great challenge and even a love for and obedience to the creator, since they obtain the gifts that they consider so magnificent, namely, of riches and delights and the such like, not only undeservedly and unworthily, but contrary to their most evil deserts. It also has the element of salutary education for the good and true worshipers of the creator. For in that way they recognize that those gifts are most worthless and are scarcely to be considered among the gifts of the creator, because they are offered to such worthless human beings. And they also learn from this that the creator considers those the very least goods, which he offers even to his enemies, and they are taught patiently to do without such worthless gifts, although at times he gives such gifts even to his worshipers as a consolation of them or of other good people lest they suppose that they have been deserted or abandoned by the creator. The goodness of the creator also offers such goods to his friends and good servants for sharing with, helping, and defending the needy and

---

74 See Aristotle, *On Plants* 1.821a13–28.

75 William perhaps is referring to the Mutakallimum, those Islamic thinkers to whom St. Thomas referred as "those speaking in the law of Moors: *loquentes in lege Maurorum.*" See *Summa contra Gentiles* 3.69.11.

good people against wicked oppressors. For when the abundance of riches is obtained by good people, it nourishes and supports the needy and especially the good ones. But power defends them from unjust oppressors.

CHAPTER 13
That It Is a Most Pernicious Error to Deny the Providence of God,
And Belief in It is Most Useful

Bacause I believe that you have been satisfied on the basis of what has gone before that the care and providence of the creator extends to all things and to each of them, and I have amassed for you so great a multitude of arguments and examples on this account, namely, in order to strengthen in you this very salutary belief and to destroy the most pernicious error by which some of the foolish have thought that the creator does not have care for these lower things or even for human beings or human affairs and that everything happens by chance and accident. For what more comforting consolation can human beings have in their oppressions and afflictions than a firm belief concerning the care and providence of the creator for them and their affairs, by which they believe that the wisdom and goodness of the creator has care for them in all things? For who would not see that all the things that are done regarding them are done with his knowledge on account of his wisdom and are done beneficially, insofar as it is up to him, on account of his goodness, and are also done by his omnipotent power, with him willing or permitting and also ordering them to their due end? Therefore, human beings who have a settled view concerning the care and providence of the creator concerning themselves know as a consequence that everything in their regard is done well or beneficially, unless it is brought to a stop through them, /776a/ and this belief invites and summons them in no small way to a love for and obedience to the creator. For who would believe that the most magnificent creator cares for him and for everything about him as if he had care for him alone and would hold back his love and obedience? This opinion also arouses most holy fears and feelings of shame in them, and they feel that he observes them and their actions and sufferings, both interior and exterior ones, so watchfully and so constantly. This belief also calls forth, fosters, strengthens, and increases many other virtues in us, as I have told you concerning patience, and you will find concerning many others with a slight consideration.

But the contrary error is so harmful and so pernicious for human beings that it eliminates from human beings by their roots all concern for moral goodness, all the honor of the virtues, and all hope of future happiness. For what is left for human beings who have been blinded and deranged by the darkness of this error and who believe that no reward has been established for the saints and worshipers of God and no punishment for the evil and the wicked, and that God does not or will not judge in the future, but to precipitate themselves into every outrage and crime and to prostitute themselves to every turpitude of the vices and sins without any restraint. For since, according to this error, the creator is neither good nor just to the point that he cares what the good or the evil do or what they suffer—and no one else does on his behalf or on his side—there is nothing in human affairs but disturbance and perversity and every sort of disorder and confusion. For only the creator could set human affairs in order, and according to them he does not care or even will that they be set in order and directed, but rather has left them to be cast down and overwhelmed by chance and accident. You clearly see, therefore, how salutary is the teaching and how beneficial the wisdom by which so pernicious an error is destroyed and so necessary a belief is made stable, as something fruitful.

CHAPTER 14
Here the Author Subtly Resolves by Examples the Question of the Foolish Who Are Surprised That Concern for the Multitude of Things and of Mortals Pertains to Divine Providence

And so, following up and determining questions about these matters comes after this. The first is the question of the stupid and foolish who ask how it is possible for the creator to rule and care for so great a multitude and diversity of things. To this question Apuleius, the disciple of Plato, responds in this way.[76] Just as, he says, one king or leader rules an army of countless warriors, and at one sounding of a trumpet some run to arms, others to horses, and still others to machines, and with regard to each of these so many and such varied works are done, so one slight sign from the creator rules the whole multitude of creatures in the same manner, as if the individual natures hear or perceive him. Each thing carries out its roles, knowing the law given it by the creator, just as in an army, however great, each of those who are in it knows what pertains to him from his office and carries that out when the signal is given or at sounding of the trumpet, as I said, or at some other sign. The armor-bearers, of course, know that it pertains to them to prepare the arms for the soldiers. The soldiers themselves know that it is necessary for them to become armed and prepare themselves to fight. The keepers of the horses know that it pertains to them to saddle, to prepare the belts, to

76 See Lucius Apuleius, *The Universe (De mundo)* 30.

bridle the horses, and to provide for the bridling through others. And in this way notice that, by one royal act of will, which the sounding of a trumpet or some other sign makes known, so great a multitude and so great a variety of functionaries /776b/ are so quickly roused for so many and such diverse tasks and move so easily to what each one knows pertains to his office. Why, then, is it surprising if the king and lord of the ages, the blessed creator, by his omnipotent and most imperious will, moves and rouses the universe of creatures and also individuals among them and makes them undertake the operations pertaining to each of them and to carry out as zealously and as dutifully as possible the laws that he imposed or rather issued for them and the functions that he assigned to them?

But if someone says that warriors as rational beings understand by means of the sounding of trumpets or by other signs,[77] but how do natures, especially those without sensation, know the will of the creator? Although a reply has been given to this question in the preceding chapters through the examples of animals and artifacts,[78] I shall, nonetheless, add for you a clearer explanation of this, and I say that a knowledge of the divine will is naturally given to each nature, and each of them is born with it, and I have called[79] such knowledge small lights from the radiation and sprinkling of the luminosity of the wisdom of the creator.

And a most suitable and evident example of such knowledge is present in the spiritual and abstract substances that were created with the perfection of natural knowledge and similarly of natural moral goodness, and this is with inscriptions of natural moral goodness on their intellective power and with impressions or seals of the beauty of the natural virtues on their moving or affective power, and this is the will in them. Hence, it is evident that each of them is created with its law and as if with a book in which it reads what it should naturally either do or avoid. Similarly each is created as with a lamp or light showing it the paths by which it should walk and the path that it is necessary to avoid. And that this was also present in the first human beings, who were made and formed in a similar perfection in accord with their limits, is not doubted by those who believe that it is wicked not to believe the prophetic words and divine oracles.[80]

---

77 I have conjectured "*signa*" instead of "*ligna*."

78 See above ch. 3.

79 I have conjectured "*vocavi*" instead of "*vocabuli*."

80 See, for example, Gn 3:19–20 and Sir 17:1–9. On the basis of such text Catholic theology holds that Adam and Eve had infused knowledge.

It is, therefore, evident to you that in this way a spider is born with such a law, book, and lamp, which is a law for it that it cannot transgress, and it is a book in which it somehow reads how it is also to live well, and by what art or skills its limit is to be sought, and it is a lamp showing it the path by which it ought to walk naturally. It is, however, evident to you that every law is a word or sign of the will of the one who is commanding or imposing it. Because, then, every nature of the noble abstract substances, of human beings, of the other animals, and even of plants is of necessity born with an indication and sign of the will and good pleasure of the creator, because <it is born> with its law, each of necessity has in itself and with itself not only where it may naturally know the will of the creator, but also the natural knowledge of the same, and this is seen from the previously stated definition of law.

One of the wiser and holy teachers of the Christians gave a second response to this,[81] saying that, when a king commands that a city be built for him, from one will and one command of his concerning the building of the city, there proceed so many and such varied tasks of workmen and of many horses, mules, and other beasts of burden. You will see there some in stone quarries clearing away, others cutting, still others carving, and others polishing. You will see some carrying the same stones, others handing them to masons, still others setting them in the structure of the walls. You will see /777a/ there wagons and wagon drivers, some wagons being loaded, other loaded ones coming to the site of the building. You will see metal workers fashioning many tools necessary for that building. You will also see wood-workers, who are called carpenters by the common people, producing the works of their arts. And there are countless other functions and works that you can think up for yourself.

Because of one royal will or command, therefore, you see that so many motions of human beings and animals, of wagons and other carriers are produced; you see that so many kinds of craftsmen and workers are occupied in various kinds of crafts, with all the workers and ministers knowing what art or work pertains to each of them, and you see that at one royal command, which they recognize by the slightest sign, the individuals undertake and carry out their tasks. And I have already mentioned to you on the basis of the statement of Aristotle that the powers of seeds are similar to skills and, therefore, the seeds are similar to artisans.[82] You will see, then, from this consideration how without labor or concern the creator most high moves and rules by the least sign of his will so great a multitude and variety of creatures, since a king, who is in no way and in no respect comparable to him in magnificence and glory, moves, rules, directs, and unites for the end of his intention so great a multitude of

81 See Augustine, *The Trinity* (*De trinitate*) 3.4.9; PL 42: 873.

82 See above note 13.

animals and human beings, of artisans and workers, and of countless instruments, while he is seated most peacefully on his throne.

But if you want to make a consideration of the whole kingdom, you will not[83] find a more explicit likeness and more suitable example than of king to king, of kingdom to kingdom, of governance to governance, of providence to providence, of care to care, of justice to justice, and of judgments to judgments, especially if you imagine him so glorious that his kingdom is fully and totally subject to him without any rebellion or resistence and imagine him endowed with wisdom so that, illumined as if by prophetic brilliance, he knows and sees everything that is done in the same kingdom, and that he has such goodness and rectitude and zeal for rectitude that he prosecutes with his entire desire and strength all wickedness and injustice.[84] This king, then, will establish and order from the beginning—or rather he will adorn—his whole kingdom with the wisest and most obedient magistrates, train them with commands of truth and justice, and promulgate the most just and salutary laws through all his territories.

But he will also provide most wisely concerning all the other things that they do for the peace, tranquility, and defense of the realm against enemies. This king, then, will move by the least sign of his will his attendants, then the leading men, the rulers of his provinces, and guardians of his territories, magistrates of cities, and judges of all ranks. You will see under him a well-organized and armed militia, first of all, the leaders of legions, the commanders of thousands, of five hundred, of one hundred, of ten, and down to the last or single warrior, and the whole armed militia most properly ordered. You will see this king ruling from his throne each and every person in his kingdom. In a time of peace you will, of course, see him ruling over the tribunals so that no injustice or unjust judgment comes from them, ruling over individual private citizens and by his laws holding them back from inflicting any injury or fraud upon one another, and to put it in a word, I shall say that all kinds of human beings are ruled under him by their proper laws—slaves, freemen, and peasants. Similarly, you will see that warriors live by their proper laws, and in this way it is with the others. But he is seated most peacefully on the throne of his kingdom.

For, just as I told you concerning seeds in the natural kingdom of natural things and concerning craftsmen in the building of a city, so understand here concerning /777b/ the public offices by which the republic is governed and defended and concerning the crafts by which each of the private citizens gains a living, such as the crafts of carpenters, silversmiths, wood-workers, and even

---

83   I have conjectured the addition of "*non*," which the sense seems to require.

84   I have conjectured "*injustitiam*" instead of "*justitiam*."

farmers, which are necessary not only for those who practice them, but serve the public utility in many ways. For the arts of metalworking, woodworking, and masonry serve the defense of the republic, because the metalworking art produces breast plates, spears, swords, and helmets, but the woodworking art produces bows, missile launchers, and lances, and constructs machines of all sorts. But the art of masonry builds towers, and walls, and all sorts of stone fortifications. By the least sign of his will alone, in a time of peace he rules through judgment and justice each and every one of his subjects, and in a time of war he rules through the knowledge of warfare the armed militia from the greatest warrior to the least. But he defends his kingdom and the inhabitants of his kingdom by the armed militia and vessels or instruments of war, and you have no doubt that through his providence and care all the good things come about for his kingdom, both in a time of peace and in a time of war, and that all evils are eliminated by him from the same kingdom, and <he does> this through judgment. But the good things in a time of peace are the peace and tranquility of the subjects and the protection of their possessions. But the good things of a time of war are defense, victory, and the other things that usually come from victory, such as the spoils of the enemy and the subjection of them, either in terms of servitude or taxation or common judiciary.[85]

In this way the creator is in his kingdom, which is the kingdom of all ages. Why is it surprising if he arranges the whole series of the ages by his least sign and by the good pleasure of his will and arranges the individual things that are in them, either by their natural laws or by laws issued by the prophets or by himself—and these laws are rightly called divine—or by laws issued by human princes, which are called human laws, which the creator himself wills to be obeyed insofar as they are in harmony with the divine laws or at least do not contradict them. For, when they contradict them, they should not be regarded as laws, but as blasphemies, not as justice, but as injustice to the creator, and for this reason they are to be wiped out by fire and sword and to be removed from our midst.

But if any nations are said to be ruled by such disordered laws, the most just judgment of God and his justice, which should be praised in every respect, permits that it comes about on account of their crimes and abominable obscenities. But they should not be said to be ruled by such laws, but rather to be oppressed by them because they did not allow themselves to be subject to the laws of voluntary equity. Hence, they are not ruled by a just government and a gentle yoke, but by oppression and violence like wild animals or untamed beasts that are more to be restrained by a chain and beaten by constant whipping than trained by the disciplines and laws. Because, therefore, whatever

---

85 I have conjectured "*judiciaria*" instead of "*indiciaria*."

good, whatever equity, whatever justice human laws contain, the most high wills it all, approves it all, taught and does not cease to teach it all, either by himself or by human beings or by their books or by things themselves, which Aristotle says, do not know how to lie,[86] such laws were rightly established and issued through his care and providence to that extent. Hence, it is evident to you that the whole governance of the human race pertains to the care and providence of the creator and that unjust laws, as I said, pertain to his care and providence on account of injustice and the most just oppression and affliction of wild and disorderly human beings.

But if you want to have another example of the governance and care of the creator, consider a royal palace that is well-ordered in all respects and first the elders, that is, the wise men standing beside the king, secondly /778a/ the judges, thirdly, the treasurers, fourthly, the dispensers of the royal wealth, then the chamberlains. After these there are the stewards; then the cooks; then those assigned to carry messages or legal documents, and after them cupbearers, bread-makers, and various table servants. Lastly, the keepers of the horses, whose task it is to prepare the horses whenever the king has to ride. And you will see in the whole royal palace that all the previously mentioned functions are carried out at the least sign of the royal will alone. Since, therefore, the whole world is like the home of the creator and his royal court, in which he dwells with his whole family and wealth, why is it surprising if at the least sign of his omnipotent will each and every thing is carried out in it? I mean of his will that commands or prohibits or that permits and orders each of the sorts of evil that are done, whom it benefits, whom it harms—orders, I mean, by a law that is most equitable. And the previously mentioned wise man of the Christians expressed this in his words, when he said, Nothing is done in the whole universe of things, as in the universal republic, that does not proceed from the intelligible court of the supreme emperor, either by his willing and commanding or by his allowing or permitting,[87] who, as was disclosed to you from the preceding, does not allow or permit anything to be done apart from his care and providence, nor does he allow or leave those who act in an evil way apart from his care and providence. Rather, he orders those who act evilly, as I said, so that they carry out against themselves the judgment and justice of the creator, and their evil actions are the weapons of the creator and his most just punishments, which offer to those who suffer them, if they are willing, the helps of multiple benefits. You have similar examples concerning a ship and its captain, concerning the ministers and instruments of government, and concerning a race and charioteer.

86   See perhaps Aristotle, *Categories* 2a6–10.

87   See Augustine, *The Trinity* 3.4.9; PL 42: 873.

· CHAPTER 15

*Whether the Providence or Foreknowledge of the Creator
Imposes Necessity on Things and Events*

After this I shall pursue that ancient question that has troubled many from antiquity and still entangles many even in my time, that is, whether the providence and care of the creator imposes necessity upon things and events, and there is almost the same question about his knowledge and foreknowledge.

I shall, therefore, first state those things that have led many into this error. The first of these, however, is that because, they say, it is impossible that divine providence be deceived, it is necessary that whatever he has foreseen come about. But whatever necessarily comes about is necessary; whatever the creator has foreseen is, therefore, necessary. But he has foreseen everything that will be or will come about. Everything, therefore, that will be or will come about is necessary. Everything that will be, therefore, is immutable and unavoidable.

Moreover, they say: Either it is possible that one of the things that God has foreseen not come about, or it is not possible. If it is possible, then, nothing impossible will happen, if it is granted. Let it, therefore, be granted. It will, therefore, be true that one of the things that God has foreseen will come about will not come about. He, therefore, erred in foreseeing, and it is true that his providence is deceived. But it is certain for all people that this is impossible, namely, that God errs or that his providence is deceived on some point. It is impossible, therefore, that one of the things that God has foreseen will come about will not come about. But there is nothing that will be that he has not foreseen. There is, therefore, nothing that will be that will not come about necessarily. Because, therefore, God has foreseen that everything that will come about will come about, it is necessary that everything that will come about come about. Hence, all things will come about necessarily. /778b/

I do not want you to be held back any longer by these and other such arguments, which should be laughed at as sophistical snares and childish subtleties by the intelligent and those trained in such matters. Recall, therefore, that "It is necessary that whatever will come about will come about" and "It is necessary that whatever God foresees will come about will come about" have two intentions and two interpretations, because the necessity can refer to individuals or to the whole, and almost the same thing is said in other words "compositely" or "separately." The first is as if it were said: "It is necessary that this event and that event which God has foreseen come about," and thus it is about individual events. Many such individual events, however, are undoubtedly contingent and can fail to come about. But if necessity refers to the whole, this is what is signified by this locution: "Whatever God has foreseen will come about," about which no one doubts that it is true and necessary, as its contradictory is also impossible, which is: "He has foreseen something that will not come about."

And the Italian or Latin sophists say that this is a duplicity of locution, because it can be understood, as they say, about a thing (*de re*) or about a proposition (*de dicto*),[88] and their intention is that the proposition that is expressed by that locution: "Whatever God has foreseen will come about" is necessary or something necessary, just as this locution is also necessary and its contradictory clearly impossible. But they call the interpretation "about a thing" what I called that about individuals, and they do so with a childish and vague intention. For in the explanation of such duplicity they lacked and still lack not only words, but also a clear and pure understanding. But you will see this clearly through what I will say, first, because a thing is expressed by every locution. But this is because every locution says what it signifies. But that which every locution signifies is its thing; even if it is words or any other sign, it will be said to be a thing in relation to the words or locution signifying it. Something expressed by a locution, therefore, is a thing.[89] Hence, an interpretation "about a proposition" is necessarily an interpretation "about a thing."

Moreover, consider the predicate, and you will see that it is nothing other than the necessity of coming about. But this can in no way truly be said about a proposition because a proposition does not come about and will not come about. It is not about the future because it is true and necessary from the beginning of the ages and now as well. Because, therefore, this predicate is said only about things and natures, that locution can only be understood about things. The truth and the true distinction, therefore, is that this necessity can be predicated of things or attributed to things, either in the universal or universally—and it is in accord with the truth when "about the proposition" is understood according to them—or it can be understood in the singular and separately, and they call this interpretation "about a thing." This then is what produces the duplicity in the thing, namely, universality and singularity. For "It is necessary that whatever God has foreseen will come about will come about" is in no way true of individuals singularly and separately. It is, none-

---

88   See my "William of Auvergne on *De re* and *De dicto* Necessity," *The Modern Schoolman* 69 (1992): 111–121. The distinction seems to have been explicitly formulated for the first time in the writings of Peter Abelard. See Abelard's *Dialectica*, ed. L. M. De Rijk (Assen: Van Gorcum, 1956), pp. 195 and 206.

89   See Augustine, *Christian Doctrine* (*De doctrina christiana*) 1.2.2; PL 34: 19–20, where Augustine argues that whatever is signified by a sign, even if it is a sign itself, is a thing.

theless, true in the universal and compositely. Even if each future event were contingent and were possible not to come about, this would still be true and necessary, and the reason is that it is universality to which necessity belongs, but not to singularity, just as when you say of two contradictory contingent propositions it is necessary that one of these two be true. For in both of them there is contingency and in neither necessity, and just as if you say, "One of them will always be true," the everlastingness of the truth is not attributed separately or singly to one, but in common or in the universal. In the same way also understand there: "It is necessary that whatever God has foreseen will come about will come about." It is the same as if someone says that it is necessary that every man be alive, although it is true of each man singularly and separately that it is not necessary that he be alive, since it is possible for him to die, nor is the locution, "Every man is living," always /779a/ true for the same men, and it is also not said of the same men. For this reason the everlastingness of the truth rests on its universality and the universality of human beings, which is not changed with the change of individuals, just as the species is not changed in its character of species.

Moreover, such an expression, "Whatever God has foreseen," is different when the speaking refers to individuals separately and determinately. For, when the speaking refers to individuals singularly and determinately, it is the same as if individuals were spoken of as individuals. But this is as if it were said, "It is necessary that this event that God foresees come about, and that one and another," and thus <it would be said> of individuals. But when one remains in the universal, as I said, the individuals are not spoken of singly and determinately, and for this reason the signification of the locution remains the same, whether the things foreseen remain the same or other things are foreseen. In the same way, this locution too, "Every human being is alive," does not change what it signifies or what is said because of a change of the individuals of the species, unless one intends it in the previously mentioned way about individuals separately. For then it is the same as if the individuals were said as individuals, that is, this one and that one is alive, and thus <it would be> about individuals.

This is, therefore, the duplicity of the previously mentioned locutions, and this is the deceptive or sophistical change in them. For, when it has been granted by way of universality and conjunction, "It is necessary that whatever God has foreseen will come about will come about," you know in what way it is granted. But when it assumes that whatever necessarily comes about is necessary, it is transferred to individuals separately. For by this locution, "Everything that is going to come about is necessary or immutable or unavoidable," the necessity and immutability is attributed to individuals separately, and in that way it is the same as if it were said, "That this will come about and that will come about is necessary and immutable," and so on about other individuals.

And one does not solve this sophism except with reference to a particular person,[90] if one says that a change of both subject and predicate is made in such argumentation. Because in this locution, "It is necessary that whatever God has foreseen will come about will come about," an infinitive is the subject, and necessity is predicated of the thing of the infinite.[91] In the conclusion, however, which is this: "Whatever God has foreseen will come about is necessary," this whole, "Whatever God has foreseen will come about" is the subject, and necessity is the predicate. A change of the predicate, therefore, was made since the necessity that was predicated of the thing of the infinitive, which is "to come about," is predicated in the conclusion of the thing of such a circumlocution, "Whatever God has foreseen will come about." This thing, however, is the universality of those that God has seen will come about. A change of the subject was also made, because before the subject was the infinitive, but in the conclusion the previously mentioned circumlocution <is the subject>. But this is the reason why a man will not explain himself who says when he is asked whether the predicated necessity belongs to every thing of the infinitive, insofar as it is made the subject there, that is, whether it belongs or does not belong to every future event foreseen by God. And because it is evident that it does not belong, since not every such coming about is a necessity or necessary, he will be forced, despite that change, to admit that the first proposition is false in every way, that is, this one: "It is necessary that whatever God has foreseen to come about comes about." It is also evident that it is true in some way. He does not, therefore, free himself from such a sophistical snare or knot.

But concerning these locutions, "If God has foreseen this, it will necessarily come about, or it is necessary that it come about," although in my time children knew the duplicities of them, I still see many miserably entangled later. For who would not see that necessity can be put on the condition, and then the necessity of the condition or of the consequence is said and asserted by that conditional locution, and in that way /779b/ it is the same as if it were said, "This condition or consequence by which it is said, 'If God has foreseen this, it will come about,' is necessary," which is undoubtedly true. But the other interpretation of it is that by which the necessity is transferred to the consequent precisely and absolutely, and it is the same as if it were said, "If it

---

90   William uses the expression "*ad hominem*: in relation to a particular person."

91   The Latin says literally, "Whatever God has foreseen will come about, to come about is necessary," where one can see that the infinitive "to come about" is the subject and "is necessary" the predicate. In the translation I have used a more normal English word order.

is true that God has foreseen this, this is necessary, that is, that it come about," which means that, if the antecedent is true, the consequent is necessary, as if it were said that the necessity of the consequent follows upon the truth of the antecedent. But this is undoubtedly false.

But know that others make this same distinction in other words when they say that the conditional utterance,[92] "If God foresaw this, it is necessary that it come about," can be called the necessity of the consequent, and this is what I said, namely, that the necessity can refer to the consequent, or it can be called the necessity of consequence, and this is what I said, namely, that the necessity refers to the consequence. But because these things are childish, and because ignorance of these is not tolerable in children, I pass on to the root of this question. I say, therefore, that ignorance of the knowledge or cognition of the creator and of the manner by which he foresees or knows has given rise to this question, and this is also the reason on account of which they have thought that, if he has foreseen or known something, he cannot not have foreseen or not have known or not have cognized it.

Another certain root of the truth led them <into error>, which is the following, namely, that it is impossible that divine providence be deceived or err or not be true, which is undoubtedly most true. Another <root> was the ignorance of the disposition or condition of certain truths and falsities, which are able to have either, that is, either the truth alone or falsity alone, still not so fixedly that they are necessarily in one or the other. And singular contingent propositions on those things that are about the future or are dependent on these contingent things that are future are of such a condition or disposition. And examples of these are that you will eat only once tomorrow, and its contradictory.

It is evident to you that this is either true or false. But if it is true, it is not of necessity fixed in its truth; in fact, it can be false, and the converse. It also happens in such propositions that, if it is true, it was always true, and it is the same way with falsity, and hence it is that none of such propositions can change from truth to falsity, or the converse. For to change is to have one disposition after another or to have had one disposition before another. But this is not possible in such propositions because, if one of them is true, it was never in the contrary disposition, and it is the same way with falsity, and for this reason it does not follow: "This is true, and it can be false. Therefore, it can change from truth to falsity." The contrary argument is likewise not valid. But the reason for this is that the verb for changing expresses two dispositions, one before, the other after. But such truths are not receptive of truth and falsity at the same time, as you know, nor at diverse times, that is, so that it has the one first, but the other later. But divine providence is this way because, if it has

---

92 I have conjectured the nominative instead of the ablative here.

foreseen something, it has foreseen it from eternity. If it knows something, it has known it from eternity, and if it does not foresee or know it now, he has not foreseen it or known it from eternity.

It is, nonetheless, true that he knows something of this sort and can still not know it, and what seems surprising to the foolish, if he has known or foreseen something from eternity, it is still possible that he either did not foresee or did not know it. The explanation of this, however, is evident because, if it is true that you will eat only once tomorrow, this was also true from eternity. But everything true, insofar as it is /780a/ true and as long as it is true, both is known and was known by the creator. Hence, if this is true, God has known it from eternity, but it is not the case that, if it is true, it is for this reason also necessary. Hence, although it is true, it is, nonetheless, possible that it not be true, and if it were not true, it would not now be known by the creator, nor would it ever have been known by him. For the truth in each of the things that can be said and the knowledge of the creator always accompany each other so that, if it is true, it is known by the creator, and if it is not true, it is not known by him, and if it was true, whenever it was true, it was known, and the converse.

Because, therefore, it turns out in the example given, that, though it is true, that is, that you will eat once tomorrow, it is possible that it not be true, and also although it was always true, it is still possible that it never was true. Consequently, it is true on account of the previously mentioned concomitance that, although it is known by the creator now, it is not known[93] afterward, and although it was known by the creator from eternity, it is possible that it was not known by him, just as it is possible that it was never true. For you do not doubt that it is only possible that knowledge, providence, or foresight fall upon what is true. From this, then, the likeness that I mentioned is apparent to you. For, it is not the case that, if God has foreseen something, and if it is not possible that it not come about, therefore, it is possible that he be deceived or err, and this is on account of the previously mentioned concomitance, namely, of divine knowledge and of truth in what is foreseen or antecedently seen.

---

93 I have conjectured "*sciatur*" instead of "*sciat.*"

CHAPTER 16
How It Is True That the Creator Has Known or Foreseen Something
Which It Is Still Possible for Him Not to Have Known or Foreseen

But with regard to how and for what reason it is true that God has foreseen or known something that it is still possible he neither knew nor foresaw, I say that this is through the perfection and luminosity of the creator, to whom nothing accrues or comes from the side of things by which he might know. Similarly nothing withdraws or is taken from him in any way, by which, that is, through whose withdrawal, he might become not knowing, and for this reason when he is knowing something, without any sort of change and apart from something withdrawing from him or ceasing to be in him, he can become not knowing of it. But there is another marvelous thing in the knowledge of the creator because by that knowledge and by a vision the same in every way by which he knows or sees one of two contradictories when it is true, he will know the other when it is true. But it is far different with us. For all our knowledge, also all our thought is something new and adventitious and an addition to the essences of our souls, and for this reason without some change of our souls we do not come to know those things that we previously did not know or were not knowers of. Nor can we know one contradictory by one and the same knowledge by which we know the other. But the reason for this is that, since such knowledge in us is taken from the things themselves, it follows the diversity of things as its cause, and for this reason there is not numerically one actual knowledge in us of an affirmation and a negation or of any other two things. One knowledge as a habit and one discipline is perhaps of contradictories, and I say this because Aristotle swallowed this statement without the chewing of scrutiny.[94] For, since each of any two contradictories has its proper and separate modifications and perhaps has contrary /780b/ modifications and dispositions from the dispositions and modifications of the other, it does not seem that there would essentially be the same knowledge of both, but perhaps accidentally. And as a consequence that statement of Aristotle is to be understood in the sense that one who knows essentially and properly on the basis of proper modifications, dispositions, and also reasons, knows accidentally and consequently concerning the rest.

But if our knowledge came from natural lights such as is naturally in the angels or came from a more noble irradiation such as are the prophetic splendors, just as the things known are not their causes, so it does not follow that they imitate them in their unity or multiplicity nor in their identity or diversity. Yet

---

94   See Aristotle, *Metaphysics* 6.4.1027b17–29.

in whatever way actual or even habitual knowledge comes to be in us, it still does not come to be in us without a new change of our souls, unless someone would want to take a stand on the natural and habitual sorts of knowledge that, according to Plato, are created along with out souls.[95]

It is, therefore, evident from all this how and for what reason it is true that the creator knew something from eternity, and it is still possible that he never knew it and how and for what reason he knows something now, and it is still possible that he never knows it afterwards, and both of these without any sorts of change, and why it does not follow that, if he foresaw something would come about, which it is possible not to come about, it is possible for him to be deceived or to err, because the word "to be deceived" and the word "error" notes a twofold state and discrepancy or separation among the occurrences of things or things themselves and the providence or knowledge of the creator, although between them and it there is always an inseparable concomitance, as you have heard.

It has, therefore, been explained to you by this why and how the providence of the creator is not necessary in such a way that, if something is foreseen by him, it is for this reason necessary that it was foreseen by him. In fact, it is possible, as I showed you, that it never was known or foreseen by him. It is, nonetheless, undoubtedly true that <his providence> is infallible and immutable—infallible on account of the necessary concomitance of it and of things, by which it is not possible that it be discordant or in disagreement with things. This, however, is to say that it is not possible that he foresees something otherwise than it comes about, and the converse, and it is not possible that he foresee that something will come about, and it does not come about, although of itself it is possible regarding any of the many events foreseen that it not come about, and it is similarly most true that it is possible regarding any of them that it was not foreseen. But the concomitance of prevision and discovery is separable in no kind of thing, because they follow upon each other, so that, if it was foreseen regarding each of them that it would come about and if it did not come about, it would follow that it was not foreseen that it would come about. The providence of the creator is also immutable on account of the duplicity of states and conditions that I told you about. It is the same way with regard to his knowledge, because it is immutable, that is, not receptive of that duplicity that I told you about and, for this reason, of newness. For it is not possible for it to be truly said of the creator that he

---

95 Since William's direct knowledge of Plato was limited to part of the *Timaeus* in Latin translation, he probably got this from Cicero, perhaps from *Tusculan Disputations* 1.24.57–59, where Cicero reports the argument from the *Meno* about the slave boy and his recollection of geometry.

either knows or foresees something newly, because, if he knows something, he has always known it, and if he has foreseen something, he has foreseen it from eternity. Newness is, therefore, far from him in this respect. But this is on account of the two states or two conditions that the understanding and intention of newness has, just as the intention of change and being changed also has. But these are the two states of newness, namely, to be and not to have been, but <the two states> of change are to be otherwise than before or to behave otherwise. But both of these diversities are far from the knowledge and providence /781a/ of the creator. For the same reason it cannot be said of him either that he learns or that he comes to be a knower, because the intention of learning or of one who learns falls into two states, namely, in knowledge and ignorance—I mean present knowledge and past ignorance. It is the same way also with his coming to be a knower because there is a similar duplicity of intention in it since one is said to become a knower only of what he did not know before. And I have gathered all these examples for you in order that in predications made about the creator you might avoid such words lest such a duplicity be referred to the creator by them. But I say this because, if they are not referred to the creator or to that which is identical with the creator, that is, to his knowledge or providence, they do not have such danger, as when he is said to create something newly or to change unbelievers into just persons, this newness is not referred to him, nor is it poured back onto him, but onto that to which it truly belongs, namely, to that which is created. For that is truly new. For it exists although it previously did not, and the change in this example is not referred to the creator, but to those to whom it truly belongs. These are those from whom the malice, which they previously had, is taken away, and to whom justice, which they previously did not have, is given. But concerning the creation by which the creator is said to create something and concerning all the other things that are said of him by way of acting, I have satisfied you in the first treatise of this teaching, which treatise is about the first principle, about what is signified and in whom what is signified ought or ought not to be.[96]

---

96 See William, *The Trinity*, ch. 10; ed. Switalski, pp. 66–73.

CHAPTER 17
Cautions against the Subtleties of Words about God
And on the Difference between Divine Knowledge and Ours

One must also similarly avoid the often mentioned duplicities in things that are said about the future or depend on the future, about which I told you, because they[97] are not receptive of two such dispositions or conditions, and you need to be circumspect regarding the intentions of words that somehow signify such duplicities, as I said to you about the word "newness," whose intention is only explained from the signification of two states or conditions, which are present existence and past non-existence, nor should you shrink back if you call non-existence or some other privation a condition or state. For poverty is usually said to be a state, and nudity another state. Even Aristotle himself in *Physics from Hearing* was not afraid to call a lack a natural principle,[98] nor should you place any force in such <a privation>, since it is often necessary to make up words either on account of a lack of words or for the sake of a clearer explanation of things. But such words are: "to begin," "to cease," and likewise: "first to exist at some point." It does not follow, therefore, if it is true and could be false that you will eat tomorrow only once, it could then either cease to be true or begin to be false or first begin to be false at some time. But this is on account of the previously stated reason that, if it is true, it was always true, and if it is false, it was always false. But if it began to be true or false, it would be true although it was previously false, or it would be false although it was previously true. In him, however, this diversity and duplicity has no place.

In the same way you must avoid all those terms that signify addition or lessening or increase. For if someone says that the creator can foresee many things that he has /781b/ not foreseen and that he is able not to foresee or also was able not to have foreseen many things <that he has foreseen>, therefore, an addition and subtraction can be made in the number of things foreseen by the creator, or the number of things foreseen by him can increase or decrease, know that the conclusion is impossible. For, if it were possible, nothing impossible would result if it is granted. Let something be added, then, to the number of things foreseen. I say, therefore, that it was not previously among the number of things foreseen; it was, therefore, not foreseen. But it is added to the number of things foreseen; it is, therefore, among the number of

---

97 William is referring to God or things identical with God, such as his knowledge and providence. See the end of ch. 16.

98 See Aristotle, *Physics* 1.7.190b28–34.

things foreseen, although it was previously not among that number. Hence, it is foreseen although it was not foreseen. It has already been shown to you, however, that, if something is foreseen by the creator, it was foreseen by him from eternity. It is evident, then, that the previous conclusion is impossible. In this way you will explain that it is impossible that something be subtracted from the number of things foreseen by the creator. For, if it were possible, it would follow that what was subtracted from the number of the things foreseen became not foreseen, although it was previously foreseen, and such an impossibility has already been shown to you, because it is impossible that the number of things foreseen by the creator increase or decrease from them. For it is most certain that it is impossible that the number increase or decrease save through addition or subtraction. Because, therefore, it is evident to you that both addition and subtraction are impossible in him, it is evident that both increase and decrease are impossible in him. For that of which the cause is impossible is necessarily impossible itself. But the cause of increase and of decrease is addition and subtraction.

In another way this impossibility, that is, of increase and of decrease, can nonetheless be explained to you, because, if something were added to the number of things foreseen, its contrary[99] would be subtracted from the same, and thus as much would be subtracted from it as was added, and thus as it would increase from the addition of the one, it would decrease from the subtraction of its contrary. It would, therefore, remain in the same amount. Pay careful attention, therefore, to these examples lest you become entangled in the snares of the sophists and reveal yourself as deserving to be mocked by children who know these things.

And the diversity and difference between the knowledge that comes to us from things and from outside and the knowledge of the creator and between our ways of knowing and his are already evident to you, because his knowledge is essential to him and in no way adventitious and one in every way and unable to be multiplied in any way. For it does not follow upon the diversity and multitude of the things of which it is knowledge, and <his knowledge> is one and the same numerically and is the same of one of the contradictories, if it is true, as it would be of the other, if it were true. In our knowledge, however, it is just the opposite in every respect, and from this there is consequently explained to you something that is both a source of wonder to you and incredible for the foolish. But this is on account of their ignorance of such differences. For, they say, the knowledge or providence of the creator is incomparably more immutable and determinate, but it is necessary that, if a human being either knows or knew something, it is always necessary after this that he knew it, nor

---

99   I have conjectured "*contrarium*" in place of "*contractum*."

could he in any way not have known it. How, then, is it possible with regard to something that the creator knows now or knew that he did not know it, and how can he hereafter not have known it?

Pay attention to these things that I have said because this is apart from all change in the creator so that from the fact that he knows or knew something, it is not understood that something came or accrued to him, and if he does not know or did not know something, it is not understood that he lost something or something withdrew from him. But in us it is just the opposite in every way, and the reason is that knowledge comes to us through teaching or discipline, or /782a/ through personal experience or investigation, and it cannot happen that we are not knowing except through its withdrawal from us or through the loss of it, which is forgetfulness or a disposition opposed to knowledge, such as doubt. For it is possible for someone to know something even by the path of demonstration and afterwards through some sophistical argumentation doubt it or opine or believe the opposite. But you see that these three dispositions, namely, doubt about what was known, an opinion contrary to it, and the belief of its contrary are dispositions opposed to knowledge in that way, that is, so that they expel it from our souls and do not permit it to be in them along with itself. For forgetfulness is a privation of knowledge and an erasure of it from the memory or understanding, like the erasure of writing or its obliteration from a book or tablet. It is then evident to you that one who is or was knowing among us cannot be not knowing without one of these manners of change and without the loss of knowledge, which occurs through forgetfulness or the acquisition of one of the dispositions contrary to it, which I listed for you. But forgetfulness and the acquisition of such dispositions and the loss of knowledge are changes that have the duplicity about which I have often spoken to you. For it is only possible for someone to lose knowledge who at one time had it, and someone who at some time has it among us cannot not have it unless he loses it. But in the creator it is otherwise because the creator now has knowledge of many things that are future; yet he is able not to have it, that is, not to know them without a change of his knowledge.

Watch out, however, that you understand this correctly because the creator cannot really not have some knowledge that he ever has or had, but <is able not to have> a comparison of his knowledge by which he is said to be knowing something and which can in some way be called the falling of his knowledge upon it or a relation of his knowledge to something else. And although the creator has both such a falling and such a relation, he is able not to have them without a loss of something that is in him, and this is not surprising in the creator, since in us things are the same way in comparisons and relations and respects. For that which is equal or similar to something else can be not equal and not similar to it without any change of itself and without a loss of something that is in it. But an example of this is found in two equal things, one of which is increased or diminished, which for the sake of clarity I want to be called **B**. But the other remains unchanged in quantity, and let it be called **A**. You see, therefore, that, although **A** was previously equal to **B**, it is now not equal or is unequal, and this is without any change of it or loss of something that was in it. It is this way with two similar things, one of which is altered, while the other remains unchanged in quality. Whatever change, therefore, takes place in things upon which divine providence or foresight falls, no change takes place on this account in the divine knowledge or providence, and nothing is added or subtracted on this account, but if these two were really both possible, namely, that the creator would know something now and would not know it afterwards, it would be necessary that some change take place with regard to his knowledge or providence. But you have already heard in the preceding chapters that such duplicities are not able to be joined, that is, to be predicated together of the creator, either in accord with the same time or in accord with diverse times. For he is immutable in every way.

But if someone asks about something false, which /782b/ can nonetheless be true—let it, for example, be called A—whether the creator now has knowledge of **A**, and proceeds in this way: The creator does not now know **A**; therefore, he does not now have knowledge of **A**. Moreover, **A** is now not knowable, since it is false. Therefore, there is not knowledge of it or about it now. Neither the creator, therefore, nor anyone else now has knowledge of it, and he can have knowledge of it. On the other hand, he will have knowledge of it when it is true. Therefore, he can have and is going to have knowledge that he does not have.

This deception is obvious. For, if he can have knowledge of that of which he does not now have knowledge, it does not follow that he can have knowledge that he does not have. In the same way, if someone is born in his kingdom or someone else newly becomes his subject, over whom he did not previously have power, a king has power over someone over whom he did not previously have power by the royal power by which he is king and lord of all his subjects, but he does not nonetheless have power that he previously did not have, because he has power over him or is lord of him on the basis of the power he previously had. He has lordship over him over whom he did not have lordship, but he does not nonetheless have another lordship, just as he is king of him of whom he was previously not king, but he does not nonetheless have a kingship that he did not have. For the question is about universal lordship, and my intention here is not concerning the individual lordship, which he perhaps does not have over him.

But if he goes further and says that the creator now has such knowledge, which is now true, and at first he did not have knowledge of this, recognize in this part the ambushes of the sophists, and know that they draw a distinction here, granting that he previously had knowledge of this, and yet they do not concede that he previously had knowledge of this, because in the previously mentioned comparison, when the verb of the past time, namely, "had," precedes, it freely refers, as they say, to the present or past time, but when that verb follows, it refers only to the time of that verb, that is, to past time, and then, according to this position, the divine knowledge did not fall upon it, since it was false.

But if someone says that the creator now has such knowledge and previously did not have such knowledge; therefore, he now has such knowledge and previously did not have it, watch out for yourself in this, because when it is said "The creator did not previously have such knowledge," it is not denied that he had this knowledge without qualification, but in relation to this, or rather the relation to this, because they accept it on account of relation that is understood to be denied there. But when it is said, "He had it or did not have it," knowledge or the habit of knowledge is unqualifiedly denied or unqualifiedly affirmed of the creator.

CHAPTER 18
A Reply to Certain Errors concerning Words and Stateables, And That the Providence of God Does Not Impose Necessity upon Things

Do not, however, forget the opinion of those who say that all truths are of this sort so that concerning those matters or over those matters these duplicities do not occur, namely, change from truth to falsity, or the opposite; likewise, beginning to be true and the contrary ceasing. They think it horrendous—and not incorrectly—that the creator now first knows something, whatever it might be, and begins or ceases to know it. It, of course, seems very much to express an injury and insult to the wisdom of the creator, and they cannot escape these, who hold that truths and falsities alter and change in that way. For, since nothing can be known by the creator save when it is true and as long as it is true, it is necessary /783a/ that the creator begins to know it when it begins to be true and consequently that he ceases to know it when it ceases to be true, and that he first knows something when it is first true. It seems to follow that, if he begins to know something or ceases to know something, he learns it or forgets it, and that, if he now first knows something that he previously did not know, he is either taught it by someone else, or newly discovers it by himself, or it newly comes to his knowledge in some other way. But you ought to know that the whole human race should not only avoid true blasphemies against the creator, which signify true injuries or insults of the creator, but should also wipe them out with all fire and every sword.

But another most stupid opinion and one most insulting to the creator gave cause and occasion to this error—that by which they held that stateables (*enunciabilia*), that is, all truths and falsities, existed from eternity and have their manner of existing by themselves apart from creatures and from all works of God and were not made or created by the creator, but are eternal and existed from eternity and, for this reason, owe nothing to the creator in terms of their being or their well-being.[100] But how were such <stateables> composed of subjects and predicates, which are certainly temporal and for the most part began in time? And how did they precede their parts not only in time, but by eternity, especially since they were composed—and not <composed> by the creator nor by themselves? Who were their composers or who was their composer, or how were they composed with no composer? I pass over the destruction of this error that an unimaginable feebleness of intellect dreamed up.

I shall, therefore, return to that point at which I was, and I say that by affirmations and negations one affirms and denies only the[101] things that are signified by the predicates and only about things that <are signified> by subjects, and I say that only from these, that is, from the things that are subjects and predicates, can something one be composed by a natural composition. In fact, such compositions do <not>[102] belong to reason and intellect, in whose power it lies to compose intelligibly or rationally those things that are not able to be composed in the manner of nature, and similarly to divide in their way those things that cannot be divided in the manner of nature. And these intellectual or rational compositions and divisions are only affirmations and negations, concerning each of which there are found true and false ones, possible and impossible ones, necessary and contingent ones. And on this account, that a

---

100 See N. Lewis, "William of Auvergne's Account of the Enuntiable: Its Relations to Nominalism and the Doctrine of Eternal Truths," *Vivarium* 33: 113–136, where Lewis points to various thinkers whom William may have had in mind, such as John of Salisbury, Nicolas of Amiens, and the anonymous author of the *Ars meliduna*. I have followed Lewis in translating "enuntiabilia" as "stateables."

101 Instead of "*tres*," I have conjectured "*res*," which is also found, according to Lewis, in the earlier edition of the *De universo* (Nuremburg: Georg Stuchs, 1496).

102 I have followed Lewis' conjecture in adding the negative.

grammarian[103] is musical, about which you have heard in the logic of Aristotle,[104] was neither caused nor eternal, because neither an affirmation nor a negation causes what is affirmed or denied, because it does not give it being, and intelligible composition joins things only in the intellect, and on account of it they are not less in their division or their contrariety in themselves. Likewise, on account of negation they are not less in their conjunction. For, if you say that the east is the west, or the converse, the east is not less far from the west on account of this conjunction, and if you say of that which is in the east that it is in the west, or the converse, it has not withdrawn from the east nor drawn closer to the west. It is the same with the converse.

And he is not far from such an error who set forth the three predicaments and three kinds of things, namely, natural, moral or civil, and rational. And concerning rational ones, if they called only words rational things, their opinion had nothing of danger or dangerous error, unless perhaps they fell into that insanity so that they were crazy enough to say of words what those previously mentioned erroneous people and their errors said about true and false things, that is, that they said that words have existed from /783b/ eternity and were eternal and other things of the falsest insanity about these matters. On this you see how great was their ignorance in natural matters and how great was their feebleness of intellect in these things in which they supposed that they were trained and of whose wisdom they boasted. But the destruction of these matters is quite easy for you from other things.

I shall, therefore, return to the point at which I was, and I shall say that utterances about the past and the future do not differ by these three times in their significations or in what is signified, just as those verbs do not. For "is" and "was" and "will be" signify one thing, namely, being or entity, and "disputes" and "disputed" and "will dispute" signify only disputation, although in various ways, just as the disputation is not other or something else when it is present and when it is future and when it is past. But things are those that are known indubitably and those that are signified and those that are apprehended. For in all the sciences one deals with the things of those sciences, and in all <the sciences> there is sought either the being of things or their proper dispositions or modifications. All the sciences, therefore, are about things, and the creator is also said to know, as he also really does, past things, present things, and future things, and these are only things. For those things that they call stateables (*enunciabilia*), things that can be affirmed or denied, can be true or

---

103 Here too I have read "*grammaticum*" instead of "*grammaticam*," following Neil
    Lewis's transcription of the Nuremberg text.

104 See Aristotle, *Topics* 1.104b19-104b28, p. 174: "for a musician who is a grammarian is so without ever having come to be so, or being so eternally."

false, always existed, according to their error, and therefore, those that remain perpetually are not past, nor are they future, since they always have been, according to them, nor are they present since the present time does not limit or measure their being.

But I shall reply next to those points that are seen to favor such an error and to have given it occasion. I shall say, therefore, not only what the truth has here and what has been explained to you by me elsewhere, namely, in the first part of the treatise, *On the Universe*,[105] and also in the first part of such sapiential knowledge,[106] namely, that he also is both eternal and from eternity,[107] and he knows from eternity and saw and sees by his most vigilant gaze, as I said to you in the preceding chapters,[108] all the things, those that have already passed, those that are future, and those that are present, and this is the common and true statement of the faith, which has already been explained to you, and as you have heard, his knowledge and providence are an outpouring to which the whole series of ages is subject, and the course of the whole of them is immutable.

And the previously mentioned duplicity of states in no way has a place in him, and you see from this how and why he knew something, which he nonetheless could have not known, and how in us it is not possible, because there is not in us a numerically one actual and essential knowledge of two contradictories, one after the other, and because that someone knows something that he could not know is only possible in us through some change, as I said, and for this reason none of us can with such knowledge know something that it is possible for him afterwards not to have known, on account of the changes that I said and the duality of the knowledge of the two contradictories. But in the creator it is just the opposite on account of his previously mentioned immutability, unity, singularity of his knowledge.

But in order that you may clearly see what I am setting forth for you about things that exist among us, let it be granted between you and me that a man is going to speak to me before all the others and that his name is **A**. I say, therefore, that **A** is the name of a certain man, namely, of that one who is going to speak to me first. It is still possible that **A** was never the name of that man,

---

105 See *The Universe* IIa–Iae, chs. 1–4; Paris-Orléans ed., fol. 683a–688b, and also see my "William of Auvergne on Time and Eternity," *Traditio* 55 (2000): 125–141.

106 See *The Trinity*, ch. 11; ed. Switalski, p. 73.

107 "Eternal" refers to God's timeless being, while "from eternity" means that he has no beginning. See N. Lewis, "William of Auvergne's Account of the Enuntiable," here p. 128.

108 See above ch. 16.

and this is so because it is possible that another man should speak to me first, and if that were the case, that is, that another man first spoke to me, **A** would be the name of that one, but not of the first one.

In the same way, if I pointed him out to the intellect and said /784a/ that this man will speak to me first, it will in the same way be possible that I did not point him out, because, if someone else is going to speak to me first—which of course is possible—it is evident that I pointed out that man, namely, the second one. It is, therefore, evident to you that in these two acts of mine, which are naming and pointing out, there occurs what I was saying, because I named and pointed out a man, and it is possible that I neither named nor pointed him out. The reason is that which man the naming or pointing out falls upon is connected to and accompanies a future act or state of that man. In the same way the falling of the creator's knowledge or providence accompanies the truth or the occurrence of the thing to which it refers so that, if the truth or the occurrence is not under it, it does not fall on it. And the fact that it does not fall upon something upon which it has not fallen from eternity depends on the truth or occurrence in some way, not only so that the creator's knowledge falls or does not fall over it, but also so that it will have fallen or will not have fallen over it, just as which man the previously mentioned naming and pointing out fall or do not fall upon depends on a future act for this, that is, on the speaking that will be had with me first. Similarly, one of them depends upon which it shall have fallen or not fallen upon, even after each has happened, and for this reason, upon whichever of them one of them shall have fallen, it is able not to have fallen upon him, just as to whomever that act will belong, it is able not to be going to belong to him and to be going to belong to the other.

But the explanation of this is evident because the providence of the creator does not impose necessity upon things, nor does necessity in things follow upon it. For, if it did, nothing would be contingent and possible not to come about, since it cannot be doubted that all things that are future and whatever were in the future fall under and have fallen under the providence of God from eternity. For it has also been explained to you by me in the first treatise of this sapiential and divine teaching that all things present, past, and future were completely known by the creator from eternity and were not less known when they were future than when they were present, nor less known after they are past than when they are present.[109] And you heard the reason for this, namely, because neither things nor their dispositions nor the times of things, that is to say, neither the futurity, nor pastness, nor presentness of things in any way

---

109 See *The Trinity* ch. 9; ed. Switalski, pp. 61–62.

adds something to the knowledge or providence of the creator, and similarly does not lessen anything in him.

All things, therefore, would come about of necessity, and nothing would be contingent about the future, but it would be necessary that each event come about, or it would be impossible for it to come about.[110] You have, however, learned the destruction of such a position from the books of the Italian philosophers,[111] and you will hear another destruction from me in the following.

Moreover, if the necessity of future events followed from the providence of the creator, either it would follow from it as from a cause, and then it is necessary that <providence> be a conjoined cause of such things, that is, one, given which, things would consequently exist of necessity, and then good things and evil ones, that is, future adulteries, murders, and other such blameworthy evils, will equally fall under the knowledge and providence of the creator, just as they fall under his knowledge. It would be necessary that divine knowledge or providence be the cause of each and every one of such evils. But this is wicked to hold concerning the creator or concerning his knowledge or providence. Not only would it be necessary that it be the cause of such evils, but even the agent and efficient cause, and on this account it would be necessary that the creator be the author of all such evils and also on this account be not only evil, but the very worst.

But if the previously mentioned necessity in things does not follow from the providence /784b/ of the creator as from a cause, what then will be the cause of this consequence? For it is impossible that there be such a concomitance or consequence of two things, neither of which is the cause of the other, and which do not have a common cause or a relative connection to each other. But it is that way between divine providence and the things we mentioned, that is, blameworthy evils.

But if he says that this is the cause of that consequence, namely, that, if the creator knows or knew that something will come about, it will come about, and this condition or consequence is necessary, this error is destroyed in two ways: first, because, just as this consequence is necessary, so is the converse, namely, that if this is going to come about, the creator knows or knew that it will come about. Therefore, things will be imposing necessity upon the providence of the creator no less than the providence of the creator upon things. <It is destroyed,> secondly, because a similar condition or consequence is necessary with regard to you, each human being. For, if you know that something will

---

110 The sentence needs a conditional clause, such as: "If the necessity of future events followed upon the providence of the creator, all things. ..."

111 See Boethius, *On the Consolation of Philosophy* (*De consolatione philosophiae*) 5, Prose 3 and 4; PL 63: 838–850.

come about, it will come about. Still, on this account your vision does not make it come about or that it is necessary that it come about. Therefore, the knowledge of the creator also does not make things come about in the way in which it is knowledge or cognition. Otherwise, the knowledge by which you know that the sun is in the sky or over the earth would make that sun to be there or that it be necessary that it be there. But it is evident to you that each of them is impossible, namely, that, because you know that sun is in the sky or over the earth, it is necessary that it be in one of those two places.

Moreover, divine knowledge or providence is so separated from such things and also from all temporal things that it preceded them by the whole of eternity in which it existed, although none of them as yet existed. It, therefore, existed without the things, but they cannot exist unless it has preceded. But precedence, in the way in which it is precedence, puts no necessity upon what follows. For, although the setting of the sun could not occur unless its rising preceded; still its rising does not make it necessary that its setting follow, or the converse, especially since, as you learned elsewhere, one of two relative things is not a more worthy cause of the other, nor the converse. Nor likewise is one of two contraries <a more worthy cause of the other>. Rising, therefore, is not a more worthy cause of setting than the converse, nor is precedence a more worthy cause of the consequence,[112] or the converse. Therefore, divine knowledge, in the way in which it is knowledge, also does not impose necessity on what is known, and just as your vision by which you see the sun in the sky does not impose necessity on the sun's being in the sky. And the providence of the creator does not impose necessity on things, neither as a cause nor in the way it is knowledge or vision, just as your vision does not, nor is there a necessary concomitance between it and things by reason of the fact that it is their cause, since there are countless things of which it is not the cause, namely, all blame-worthy evils, all vices and sins, nor <is there such a necessary concomitance> by reason of the fact it has a cause in common with things, since it does not have a cause in any way. Nor is it necessary in that comparison about which I already told you; that is to say that its falling over certain things is possible and contingent, that is, over contingent things, for which it is possible to come about and not to come about.

And I already told you and gave you a most suitable example for this, because it falls upon many things from eternity; still, it is possible that it never fell upon any of them, and the reason is that it is possible that none of them come about, and if any of them ever came about, the providence of the creator would have fallen upon one of them. I also explained to you how the knowledge of the creator is one and how it is not multiplied by the multiplication of things nor

---

112 I have conjectured "*consequentiae*" instead of "*conversionis.*"

diversified by their diversification, and for this reason, while remaining one and the same in every way, it falls upon one /785a/ contradictories and can fall upon the other without any diversification and change that takes place in it. I have also explained to you how it is just the opposite in knowledge that either comes from things or is acquired by us through them. Pay careful attention, then, to this, and you will not be entangled in the errors that there are about this, nor will the puerile subtleties of the sophists disturb you in any way.

CHAPTER 19
Concerning Four Things That Move the Misguided to Suppose
That All Things Come About of Necessity and
That Nothing Comes About Freely

But because it seemed to some misguided people that, by other ways than by the providence of the creator, all things are also produced or come about in this world of necessity and that nothing at all is freely in our power, but that we are rather impelled by necessity to do all the things we do and that it is impossible that we are prevented from doing all the things we do, I think that it is most suitable that we deal for a little while with these things and attend to the destruction of these errors that you see are most pernicious.

Know, therefore, that there are four things that led them into such an error: first, there was divine providence by its concomitance about which you have heard or by the mutual concomitance between it[113] and things that will or will not be, and the ridiculousness of the subtleties, which I have resolved for you in the preceding chapters,[114] contributed to their deception. And it is not necessary that we repeat the things that were said about this or that we add others to them since they ought to be enough for you.

The second was the motion and configuration of the heavens and the other dispositions of the stars and lights from which astronomers were accustomed to consider all events and all actions and changes that take place in the lower world, and especially among humans and human affairs. The third was *hei-marmene*,[115] which some of the philosophers called the interconnected and

---

113 I have conjectured "*ipsam*" instead of "*ipsas*."

114 That is, in chs. 15 to 18.

115 "*Heimarmene*" is a Greek word for fate or destiny. It literally means "ordained of fated," although William treats it as a distinct source of error from fate. In *The Nature of the Gods* (*De natura deorum*) 1.55, Cicero refers to *heimarmene* as "that fatal necessity, which you call *heimarmene*, such that whatever happens, you say that it has flowed from the eternal truth and continuation of causes."

incessantly running series of causes and the necessary dependence of one upon another. The fourth was fate or being fated. Concerning the latter three, then, I shall try to satisfy you through my usual way of proofs, and I shall satisfy you if God wills.

CHAPTER 20
He Argues against Those Who Hold That Necessity Is Caused in Things From the Motion of the Heaven and the Disposition of the Stars

If between the heavenly motions and the previously mentioned things[116] there is such causality, which produces a necessary consequence in things—since of any two, one of which follows upon the other, or one of which follows from the other, if the antecedent is necessary, it is necessary that the consequent also be necessary—it will not be possible to escape <the conclusion> that, as the heavenly motions are necessary and immutable and so far apart and remote from our power that we can do nothing at all regarding them to prevent them from running their course exactly as they do, it will follow of necessity that we can also do nothing about the course of the previously mentioned things. Hence, nothing is to be imputed to us concerning their course. In all the things, therefore, that happen in human affairs, we will be entirely blameless. For what is not to be imputed to someone is not blameworthy in him, nor likewise is he to be praised on its account. Hence, no one will act well or badly. For no one acts badly unless he acts in a blameworthy and reprehensible manner, and likewise no one acts well unless he acts in a praiseworthy manner. There will, therefore, be no vice or /785b/ sin, and nothing will be done viciously, and it will be impossible for any one to sin. But to punish those who do not sin is wicked and unjust. The justice, therefore, by which the guilty are punished will be either wicked or injustice, and all the judgments by which it is decided that the guilty should be punished will be wicked and most unjust, since it is necessary that all human beings be innocent, since it is impossible for any of them to be guilty or to sin in any way. This error, therefore, destroys justice and judgment, which are so necessary and so salutary both for human beings and for human affairs, and it subverts the whole order and entire peace and tranquility of human affairs.

Moreover, correction will be nothing, and discipline will be nothing, since correction is nothing but a turning away from culpable evil and a turning toward its contrary. Each of them, however, is impossible according to this error. For necessity is unavoidable and inevitable, and impossibility is irrevers-

---

116 That is, all the things that are produced or come about in this world.

ible. For it is impossible according to this error that anyone be turned away from that to which the necessity of the heavenly motions impels him, and it is no less impossible for one to turn toward that from which the impossibility contrary to the previously mentioned necessity keeps him. Against this error, therefore, we must not so much argue by reason as fight with fire and sword. For they say that all the vices and sins come down from there and that all of them are blameless and should in no way be imputed to those who have them or cause them, and for this reason neither those persons nor those deeds are worthy of any penalty or punishment. But <this error> defends and fosters the nurse of all the vices and sins, namely, impunity, to the point that it wipes out all penalties and does not allow that any be imposed or that any should be imposed, where it is in no way to be doubted that people need penalties very greatly and can be taught by them alone. For if they are scourged from every side, treated with insults, and deprived of their property, it is surprising if their stubbornness is so great and so misguided that they would complain about none of the men who impose these on them and if they would say that no one is doing them an injustice or even can do them an injustice. For they necessarily have to admit this or come back to their senses from this error, and this is one of the three ways by which philosophy takes care of errors, as you have also heard elsewhere.[117]

And pleas and admonitions will be useless or superfluous among human beings. A certain friend of mine beautifully[118] mocked one of these misguided people. For the latter constantly asserted that all the events that come about come about of necessity and that all the events that do not come about are prevented from coming about by impossibility, and he boasted that he could defend this by irrefragable proofs, and my friend could not turn him away from this stubbornness. Rather, that misguided fellow asked him to go with him to someone who was considered a leader among the wise men and teachers, and he promised that he would force that wise man by most solid proofs to grant this. My friend replied to this misguided man, saying: "You believe that all the things that come about come about or will come about[119] of necessity and that it is impossible for those events that do not come about or will not come about to come about. You, therefore, are very foolish to ask me to go with you since it is either impossible for me to do what you ask, if I am not going to do it—and then your pleas are useless—or it is necessary that I do it, if I am going to do it—and then your petitions are superfluous, since whether

---

117 See *The Universe* Ia–Iae, ch. 1; Paris-Orléans ed., I, 594a.

118 I have conjectured "*pulchre*" instead of "*pulchras*."

119 I have conjectured "*evenient*" instead of "*eveniant*."

you ask me or you do not ask me, I am going to do it from necessity." In that way, then, having been mocked and laughed at, he recognized his error and ceased from his pleas.

Moreover, according to this error, the flight of a single fly cannot be prevented by any force or power, just as its cause, that is, the heavenly motion, cannot be, and all attempts at any works among human beings will be in vain, that is, either superfluous or useless. It will be vain, therefore, to labor in order that any /786a/ good things be done or that any evils be avoided, since the avoidance of approaching or imminent evils is impossible, and the attainment of good things that are not coming is impossible. But you must be careful not to be deceived and err in the response that one of the Italian philosophers made, when he said: "When asked about a sick person whether he will recover or not from the sickness from which he is suffering, if someone says that he will, it was objected to him that the medicines are, therefore, superfluous. But if he said that he will not recover, it was objected to him that the medicines are, therefore, useless."[120] I reply that he does not argue well who says: "He is going to recover; therefore, medicines are superfluous," because the medicines are the means by which he is going to recover. And it is as if he said: "This is going to be; therefore, that is superfluous by means of which it is going to be," or as if he said: "This house is going to exist; therefore, the building of it is superfluous," or if he said: "You will attain or have this knowledge; therefore, it is superfluous for you to make the effort to have it, or study is superfluous by means of which you are acquiring it, or the examination of books or listening to teachers or anything else is superfluous by means of which you will acquire that knowledge." No intelligent person doubts that such subtleties are more worthy of derision than resolution.

Perhaps someone will try to reply to the aforementioned illusion and others that I introduced on this in the preceding chapters in a likeness to this response and say: Although something will be or will be done from necessity, still pleas are neither superfluous nor useless with the person who does it, and the reason is that it will be obtained from him by the pleas that he does it, just as I said about medicines and future health. It is the same way with correction as well, because, although he is of necessity going to be turned away from his error and laziness, a reproof and penalty from one giving them is not superfluous because such correction of him will come about through the reproof and penalty. In the same way it seems that one can reply to other similar arguments.

Pay attention, therefore, to the fact that these examples and causes are very remote, that is, because of the great dissimilarity of the heavenly motions in relation to human and voluntary affairs, and the reason is that the cause of

120 See Cicero, *On Fate* (*De fato* 28–29).

knowledge that is acquired is in us, or we ourselves are the cause, and the acquisition comes from us, and on this account we are free to acquire it and not to acquire it. But the heavenly motion, according to the position of these people, is outside us, and we can essentially do nothing to it, neither with respect to its being nor with respect to its being otherwise. The dissimilarity, therefore, of the previously mentioned causes in their causalities is evident to you. But I shall make you know that in voluntary matters, that is, in things that are either done or acquired by our will, the heavenly motion can do nothing naturally and essentially.

But the first explanation of this is through the freedom of our will. I say, therefore, as you have also heard me say elsewhere,[121] that such freedom is so great that it does not tolerate being forced to its act, which is willing, or being kept from it against its will, that is to say, if one wills the act. Let it be that it is forced against its will, and that its unwilling subject wills something, and let that be called **A**. According to this position, therefore, he wills it unwillingly and willingly, because the subject is willing **A** unwillingly and willing the willing, and this on account of **A**. He is willing **A** more, because that on account of which each thing is such is even more such.[122] He, therefore, is willing **A**; he is not, therefore, unwilling with regard to it. He, therefore, does not will **A** under coercion or unwillingly.

Likewise, I say that he cannot be kept from willing **A** if he wills to will **A**. For let it be that he is kept, if it is possible. I say that he wills to will **A** first, since willing without qualification is only able to be willed on account of **A**, and no other willing /786b/ can be willed except on account of that onto which or over which it falls or passes. Hence, willing **A** is not willed by the subject except on account of **A**. Hence, **A** will not only be willed, but will be willed more. He, therefore, wills **A**. Hence, he is not kept from willing **A**. But it was supposed that he was kept <from willing **A**>.

I have, therefore, made it evident to you that it is not possible for someone to be forced to will something when he is unwilling to will it, nor is it possible for someone to be kept from willing something when he wills to will it. And this intention of mine in this discussion is about the will by which someone truthfully says, "I will (*volo*)," which no one says truthfully who does not do

---

121 See William, *The Virtues*, ch. 9; Paris-Orléans ed., I, 120–122, and my "William of Auvergne on Freedom of the Will." In *Moral and Political Philosophies in the Middle Ages*. Proceedings of The Ninth International Conference on Medieval Philosophy. 3 vols. Ed. B. Carlos Bazán, et al. New York: Legas, 1996. Vol. 2, pp. 932–938. Although William also discusses freedom at length in *On the Soul*, that work is most probably later than this one.

122 See Aristotle, *Posterior Analytics* 1.2.72a29–32.

what he can. My intention in this discussion is not about the will by which someone says, "I would like to (*vellem*)."[123] For this latter will is rather a desire than a will, because it is more optative than imperative. But the former will is imperative by which someone who wills that something be done commands those whose obedience is necessary for doing it so that each one does his own part, as you see in the work of writing. For, if someone wills to write, he commands such a will and the motions necessary for writing both to the eyes and to the hand and commands the sharpening of the pen and other things necessary for this.

It has, therefore, already been explained to you by this that our will, in accord with the intention I state, is not subject to the necessity of the heavenly motion, nor to any other necessity. Hence, neither are those things that are subject to the will or those things that come from it or through it. For, if the will is free through itself, it is necessary that those things that are subject to its command and are from it and through it be free, as long as they are under its command. I say this because the motions of our members are at times not subject to the command of the will, as is apparent in those whose hands or feet are bound. With regard to these people it is evident that they are not released by the heavenly motion nor bound by it; rather, <they are bound or released> by the will of the one who has the power for this. In these and such <motions> that cannot be subject to the command of our will, our will and we ourselves can suffer force, violence, and necessity, but in its proper and immediate operation, which is to will, it is most free, as I said. And similarly <it is also most free> in itself. For it is impossible that it will under coercion or unwillingly, when it wills something.

It is, therefore, evident to you that neither the will nor voluntary things are subject to some necessity, but to our will or to another's or partially so. For, by being acted upon or by helping, we ourselves can impede our wills from external works, which are produced in the body and through the body, while their freedom is entirely preserved with regard to the first and immediate operation of them, where it is evident that the prevention of such works is only voluntary or due to our will, as I said, or another's or partially so. For someone can tie his own hands or feet by some help or artifice or can help someone who ties them. It is, therefore, evident to you in this way that there is no necessity in voluntary matters from the heavenly motion, since they depend entirely on human wills, as I said.

Moreover, the human will is not inclined toward something by violence or necessity, as I said, but by counsel and persuasion, fear and hope, and the

123 Thus in English we distinguish between willing something and having a mere velleity.

other passions, and it is also inclined only of its own accord, and on this account by either one or more apprehension. But apprehensions do not come to it from the heavenly motions, but rather from things, unless perhaps one thinks about those motions. But <our will> has no apprehensions of voluntary things from them. Hence, our wills have no inclinations from such motions. But our voluntary things, that is, our actions, come from inclinations, and those things that follow from them or through them are caused through them. /787a/ None of such things, therefore, pertains to the heavenly motions.

Moreover, all apprehensions with regard to voluntary matters either are likenesses of such things or are produced through likenesses of them. But apprehensions, as you learned elsewhere, are causes that generate affections or impress them in another way. Because, therefore, the heavenly motions are not causes of apprehensions, they will not be the causes of the affections caused by them, and on this account, they will consequently not be causes of the works, of which <the apprehensions> are the causes. For, if there is not a cause for the source from which both intermediate and the last things come by way of affection, there will not be a cause for any of the intermediate things and much less for the last. But there are many very suitable and very clear examples of this sort. One of these is found in the motion of the sun and in the day and solar year. For, if what envelopes the sun did not give the cause for its motion or was not the cause of its motion, it would not be the cause of the day or year, and it is this way with other things. And what is not the efficient cause of fire—either for its being or for its being hot—will not be the efficient cause of the heating or burning that comes from it.

Do not let the words of the common folk and of those who do not understand the nature of causality disturb you, for they say that the cause of burning is either the one who applies wood to the fire or fire to the wood or to other combustible material. Likewise, uneducated men say that one who removes a column from a building or undermines its foundation is the cause of its collapse. And he is really a cause, but not the efficient cause. Rather, the weight of the building is the efficient cause of its falling, which is its natural downward motion, of which its weight is the natural and efficient principle. Some people call such a cause a cause without which the collapse of the building would not take place.[124] And it is not really a cause in some kind of the causes, which you have heard about elsewhere, but it is among those things that help causes either by removing an impediment that prevents them from

---

124 "Such a cause" refers to someone who removes a column that supports the building. William uses the expression "*sine qua non.*" He is explaining the distinction between an efficient cause and an accidental cause. See Aristotle, *Physics* 8.4.255b32–256a3.

their operation or by providing something that the cause needs in order that it may be operative in act, as you see in the example of the column that was just given and in the example of the foundation in the building. It really adds nothing new to the weight, which is the efficient cause of its collapse, but it removes an impediment that was preventing the operation of the weight of the building, that is, the downfall or collapse of the building. For the column or the foundation prevented the downward motion of the building and held it up contrary to the nature of the building. Similarly, the foundation was doing the same thing. But someone who applies either wood to the fire or fire to the wood, until they touch one another, undoubtedly gives a new help both to the fire with regard to the action of burning and to the wood with regard to its being acted upon, namely, contiguity, contact, or nearness, without one of which such strong and powerful actions would not be carried out.

But in the heavenly motion it is not even possible to imagine such helps for our voluntary actions or modifications, unless someone perhaps might say that by its luminosity the sun helps our voluntary actions, and especially those in which the act of seeing is required, or that Saturn helps the sellers of wood in their sales because of the prolongation of the cold and its increase. For, according to the positions of the astronomers, it makes wood to be sold more easily, at a higher price, and in greater abundance. Similarly, <some one might say that> Mercury helps those sailing because it is the lord of the wind, according to them, and at times, according to them, it impedes them no less. Similarly, <someone might say that> it also helps those winnowing on the threshing floor, and it is this way with other things, according to their opinion. And they have filled many books of this sort, namely, all the books of astronomical predictions. But it is evident /787b/ to you that such helps are not sufficient that they should make the planets the efficient causes of our voluntary affairs, namely, those of which our wills are the effective principles.

Moreover, if, by their motions and other dispositions, the lights and stars of heaven are causes of our voluntary affairs, which I mentioned, this will be either through their intention and will or apart from their intention and will. But if it is through their own intention and will, since vices and sins are voluntary in us—otherwise, they would not be vices or sins, or in any way imputable to anyone and not to the previously mentioned causes—<the stars> will alone be defiled by all the human vices and sins, especially since, according to this error, it is not possible for human beings to resist such causes, which operate through their natural dispositions and necessary motions. For their natural dispositions cannot be increased or diminished or changed in any way by us. Hence, those things that follow from these naturally and by way of efficiency cannot.

Moreover, it follows from this that the malice of stars is innate to the lights and heavens and that they are naturally evil and ablaze for the evils of man. Hence, they are not only evil, but worse than human beings, for whom they are the agents of all acts of malice.

But I have destroyed this for you in another chapter on the same matter, namely, the predictions of astronomy.[125] But if our voluntary affairs are apart from their intention and will, they are from chance or matters of chance in relation to them. But there is no order or permanence or even frequency of matters of chance. Hence, there is also no knowledge, and astronomy ought not to be believed on such matters, nor should its possessors be consulted. And this is what I intended, namely, to explain that the heavenly motions are not in any way causes of necessity in human affairs.

CHAPTER 21
He Attacks Heimarmene or the Connected Necessitating Series of Causes

B ut because I have written and said much for you on this, I shall proceed to the destruction of *heimarmene*, as these misguided people held it. They said that it was the intertwined series of causes, according to what Mercury understood and expressed in his book, *On the God of Gods.*[126] They must first be asked whether they understand this series of causes to be intertwined and continuously flowing from the first cause to the last so that some first effect flows from the first cause, who is the blessed creator—I mean flows immediately and through necessity—and something else from it likewise immediately, and this until it gets to the last effect, or whether it runs to infinity, or it is not so.[127] If they say that from the first cause there first and immediately flowed one effect from necessity, then it is necessary that it flow

---

125 See perhaps *The Universe* Ia-Ia, ch. 22; Paris-Orléans ed., I, 616a.

126 See Hermes Trismegistos, *Book of the God of Gods* (*Liber de deo deorum*). In *History of Medieval Philosophy*, Maurice De Wulf says, "A dialogue entitled *Asclepius* was also widely attributed to [Apuleius of Madaura]. It was, however, regarded by the better informed as one of the "hermetic" or occult writings, and identified, under the title of *Liber de Deo Deorum*, as the work of an Egyptian philosopher, Mercurius Trismegistus." Hermes is the Greek name for Mercury.

127 See Augustine, *The City of God* (*De civitate Dei*) 5, 8; PL 41, 148, on fate as "the connected series of causes responsible for anything that happens." Although such a connected series of causes was usually understood to be a series extending into the past, William understands the series as extending to the first cause or God, perhaps because he rejected the possibility of an endless regress in past time. See

from it in the manner of nature or through will. And concerning the manner of nature you already know how far it is from the nobility and glory of the creator, for, as you learned in Aristotle, nature operates in the manner of a servant and for this reason operates servilely.[128]

Moreover, a nature is not free not to do what it does naturally, nor does it have power or freedom or choice about doing and not doing. Hence, the manner of the operation of nature is in no way suited to the creator, just as servitude or servility is not, nor does anything befit his magnificence and excellence more than freedom. The causation, therefore, of the first comes from /788a/ works of the creator through his most free will. Hence, it does not come through necessity. This continuous connection of causes through the whole series of causes and effects is not continuous, that is, I say, having continuous necessity.

Moreover, if the first work of the creator is an intelligent substance, it will be possible to show the same thing concerning it, since every intelligent substance operates only through choice and will. Otherwise, it could act neither well nor badly and could neither act rightly nor sin. Nor would anything be imputed to it for merit or for blame, for praise or for censure. For on this account those beings that do not have power over acting and not acting, but are borne by necessity to those things that they desire and are turned away by necessity from those that they fear, and that do not with freedom apply themselves to them or turn away from their contraries, are said to act neither well nor badly, nor to be able to do anything culpably nor praiseworthily. Hence, if such a substance were borne toward some things or recoiled from them by a similar necessity, neither would be imputable to it, that is, neither the turning toward or application to them nor the recoiling from them.

Moreover, the intellect would be superfluous and utterly useless in such a substance—I mean the intellect by which it would know what it should do and what it should avoid, since this knowledge would be of no use or benefit in such a substance.

Moreover, those things that pertain to virtue would not have to be done by such a substance, nor would those that pertain to the vices have to be avoided, nor would any law have to be imposed on it, nor would one have to do anything concerning morals with it, just as we do not with brute animals and stones. For necessity has no law, nor can it be subject to law. Hence, there would not

---

my "William of Auvergne on the 'Newness of the World,'" *Mediaevalia: Textos e Estudios* 7-8 (1995): 287–302.

128 See above note 13 on Avicenna, who said that nature acts in the manner of a servant.

be present in it an understanding of the virtues or vices, nor knowledge of intelligible good and evil, save in vain.

But if someone said that these are present for acquiring sensible goods and evils, this is not true since the senses along with the estimative power[129] could suffice for this and they would be owing to it.

Moreover, such understanding, that is, of what is to be done and avoided, which they call practical, exists only for this purpose, namely, to do things that are intelligibly good and to avoid intelligible evils. But this is impossible <in such a substance>. Hence, such an understanding would exist for an impossible end, and it would be in vain. For every power and every potency whose operation is impossible exists in vain, and this problem recurs through the whole order and series of the noble abstract substances. In that whole order, therefore, the necessary, inevitable, and immutable connection of causes will not be present on account of the previously mentioned problem, that is, neither in the whole order of intelligences that Aristotle and his followers held,[130] nor in the nine orders of holy angels that Christian doctrine holds.[131] And my intention in this discussion is about the necessity by which a nature operates naturally, as I have already told you, and this is the necessity of servitude or servility.

But in causes that operate through wisdom or foresight and choice, there is freedom over operating and not operating, and no necessity impelling or forcing them to operate unless someone perhaps says that the will or command of the creator forces such causes to fulfill or carry out his commands or good pleasure, where you should avoid the term "coercion" and its intention. For, properly speaking, the intention of this term does not occur in those causes that operate voluntarily, although a vulgar and quite certain usage has these things so that someone who is subject and bound to the one giving the command by a very strong love says that he is compelled by his love for the one giving the command. In this way someone is said to do under the compulsion of love something that is offered most voluntarily, most willingly, and joyfully. But the reason behind such words is that, just as /788b/ the violence of one who coerces has the powers or forces of the one coerced wholly subject to himself

---

129 See above note 9.

130 William again is thinking of Avicenna and the cascade of the nine intelligences from the First rather than of Aristotle. See my "William of Auvergne's Rejection of the Agent Intelligence." In *Greek and Medieval Studies in Honor of Leo Sweeney, S.J.* Ed. William J. Carroll and John J. Furlong, pp. 211–235. (New York: Peter Lang, 1995).

131 Catholic theology distinguishes nine choirs of angels, namely, Seraphim, Cherubim, Thrones, Dominions, Virtues, Powers, Principalities, Archangels, and ordinary Angels.

so that they can do nothing against him, that is, resist his violence in no way, so in someone who loves strongly, love occupies and possesses the whole will of the same person so that he wills nothing opposed to the will of the one who commands, and if the love were very strong and firm, he could not even want to. Such is the love for the creator in the choirs of most holy angels, where there is no doubt that, just as that love cannot be lessened or in any way grow cold in them, so the will to fulfill whatever the goodness of the creator deigns to command them cannot, and the strength and immutability of such a will comes from the strength and immutability of the love for the creator.

But since you are certain that all coercion comes from the weakness and defect of the one who suffers it and who is unable on this account to resist the greater power of the one who is coercing, the difference between the proper intention of coercion or violence and the common and improper intention is evident to you. For the former, that is, the proper intention arises from the weakness of the power that endures it, but the latter arises from its strength, and therefore the one who coerces in the latter way does not impede the power of the one coerced and does not impel it to the contrary operation by his own power. But in the one who loves in that way the will of the one who commands in no way impedes his power, that is, his love and obedience, but rather increases it and strengthens it, if it finds it susceptible of increase and strengthening. For it is the certain joy of those who love truly and perfectly not only to come to the aid of the needs of those whom they love, but also to obey their good pleasure and commands.

You ought to know that, just as the goodness of the creator is not only not less free by reason of the fact that it can neither decrease nor change and, for this reason, can only do good, but it in fact has this from the ultimate degree and supereminence of freedom. In that way with those excellent and noble substances, the fact that they cannot either not love or not want what they know that he wants or that they cannot not do what they understand that he commands them to do does not in any way come from a weakness, lowering, or injury to freedom. To act in any evil way, therefore, is either servitude or comes from servitude or is even to become a slave, as you learned elsewhere.[132] Just as, then, the fact that someone cannot become a slave or serve or do the work of servitude belongs to him from the perfection of freedom, that is, from its greatness and strength, so it is in the creator and in the previously mentioned substances. For all these things come from remoteness or are remoteness itself from servitude. But it is impossible that freedom be impeded or harmed in any way because of remoteness from servitude.

---

132 See, for example, William, *On the Soul*, ch. 3, pt. 7; Paris-Orléans ed., p. 95a.

It is, therefore, now evident to you from this that the interweaving of causes in the course of natural causality and of such necessity is not found in the abstract intelligible substances nor in any other substances with regard to the actions of will, and that the necessity of voluntary obedience does not contradict freedom or harm it in any way, but rather perfects it, and the fact that the previously mentioned noble substances cannot not obey the commands of the creator does not come from weakness or impotence or a defect of power, but rather from the strength, abundance, and perfection of it.

But someone might say that things run their course, as they do, in spite of these factors and that they do not make it have to be not the case that this course of causes is necessary, that is, impossible to be or to occur otherwise. I say to this that the will of the lofty or blessed creator is not over such a course of causes so that it is always that way and not otherwise, just as it is not over the powers that move the heavens so that they always move them in that way /789a/ nor over the motion of the heavens and of the other heavenly bodies so that it either is always or is always that way. Rather such motions are going to cease, and the powers that move them, if the powers moving them are intelligent and move them voluntarily—as Aristotle and his followers held[133]—will cease at the end of the current ages, since they understand the will of the creator on this. Thus I say also concerning the most holy angels who serve the most lordly creator for many benefits to human beings. But when such benefits cease, the ministries that they carry out on their account will also cease. Hence, there is also found in them not only the possibility of being otherwise, but also that they will[134] many times be otherwise, because what the holy angels now do regarding human beings they will not do at some other time. It is, therefore, evident that such a previously mentioned fulfillment <of their ministries> is neither necessary, nor does everlastingness or perpetuity have any place <in them>. It has also been made clear to you in the preceding chapters[135] that necessity or intertwining <of causes> has no place in voluntary affairs that take place among human beings, since the freedom of the human will is so great that it cannot be forced to its first and proper operation, which is to will, or be kept from it unwillingly. But in those voluntary actions that come from willing and after it, namely, bodily actions, the previously mentioned prevention and coercion have a place insofar as they are motions of the body or of its members or the opposite of motion. For, in the state of this misery the body

---

133 William most probably refers to Avicenna who held that the intelligences moved the heavens by will; see, for example, his *Metaphysics* 9.2, ed. Van Reit, p. 461.

134 I have omitted "*non*" here, which does not seem to fit the sense.

135 See above ch. 20.

and members of each human being can be moved against his will or kept from motion by ropes or other impediments.

CHAPTER 22
Whether an Effect Follows of Necessity From the Aggregate of the Efficient Cause and of All the Things That Help It

B ut you should know that I said, "insofar as they are motions of the body or of the members,"[136] and did not want to say, "insofar as they are voluntary actions," because incense can be put in the hand of someone when he is completely unwilling and utterly opposed, and such an offering can be moved to the feet of an idol, and the incense can be placed before the idol by his hand. But this placement will not be the offering of incense or a voluntary act with regard to that man, nor even an act of the will, but will be violent. Yet it will perhaps be the offering of incense and veneration of the idol on the part of the one who inflicts such violence, and this is the case if his intention in this was that the idol be venerated in that way.

But perhaps someone will say that this intertwining is in accord with the words that one of the Italian philosophers spoke, when he said, "We are the sowers of our occupations."[137] An example of this, however, is that, when the will to write, the opportunity, and everything else requisite for this action occur together in someone so that the power to write may go into act, it will necessarily go into act. It is the same with the things of which the cause is the act of writing as with other things, since they follow from the act of writing along with other things, and this by a necessity similar to that by which the act of writing followed from its cause and other helps, and so on to infinity or up to the last effect. For this reason either the existence or the occurrence of every single thing will be necessary, and this argument once led me in my youth to think that no single contingent event had such a cause, whether one cause or many gathered together—I mean a conjoined cause, given which <the event> is necessarily given. You will hear /789b/ other things from me on this in this present chapter.

Know, therefore, that it is perhaps true that, given such an aggregate, namely, of an efficient cause and of things that help it to act, it is necessary that there be the beginning of the operation or work, but not the work itself or its completion. And I say this about these things that are generated or come to be through a succession of time, and the reason is that it is possible that the

---

136 See the end of the preceding chapter.

137 See Seneca, *Moral Letters* 8.72.1.

consummation or completion of such a work not exist, or that the efficient cause not exist at all, or that one of the things from the aggregate that help it does not exist. You see in the building of a house whose efficient cause is the will of the builder or of the one who causes it to be built. It is possible that this will change to the opposite will before this house is completed and completely cease to exist. Similarly, it is possible that material be taken from him or removed by theft. It is also possible that he be prevented from building it and that many other impediments come about by which the completion of the house would be impeded. It is the same way with writing or the act of writing, that is, because the completion of such things or of such events depends upon the aggregate of many possible things, of which, if one is missing, its completion is impeded. It is necessary, therefore, as I said, that when the efficient cause and all the things that help it come together or are gathered together, the work or operation begins or starts, and because for its completion or consummation the stability of the whole of such an aggregate is necessary, if they occur together, the consummation will follow. But because this stability is not, so to speak, stable with a necessary stability—in fact, it is possible that it not exist—it is not necessary that the consummation follow as necessary from the aforementioned aggregate. And for this reason it is generally not true in such things that the consummation follows from the oft mentioned aggregate, unless the permanence of the whole aggregate is understood in it. Similarly it is not necessary that in this way, that is, with the stability included, the consummation or completion follow as necessary unless that permanence is understood to be with a solid necessity, and it is this way in all causes that operate in time or through succession. In the same way it is apparent in the brightness of the day that, although it is produced as a result of the revolution of the sun over the earth as by its efficient cause, it is still not necessary that <light> come from it, although it is necessary that it exist, because the solar light can be impeded in terms of its operation by a haze, clouds, an eclipse of the sun, or the arrival of a swarm of locusts, as often happens in the land of Palestine and in parts of Egypt. The solar light, therefore, is not necessary or stable with necessity.

CHAPTER 23

That Many Changes Depend upon Those Who Acted upon,
And How It Can Be Said That Something Is in Our Power

You should also know that many and even countless actions are dependent upon those who are acted upon, because many times they are not done contrary to the will of the one who suffers them, but are in fact done in accord with it, as you see in the illumination of human beings by the sun and their being warmed by it. For it is possible for many human beings to turn away from the light and its warmth, and many do this, hiding themselves from it in forests, in caves, in subterranean places, or in others built and suited for this purpose, as you could have heard about the Ethiopians and in Lybia.

And if you attend to this, it will be easy for you /790a/ to solve the question that once seemed to me difficult to resolve. But this is that question: If the cause is not in our power, I mean the cause, given which the effect is given, the effect will not be in our power. And my intention in these words, "to be or not to be in our power," is that a cause is said to be in our power when we can bring it about that it is or that it operates or can prevent that it is or operates. Hence, it seems to follow that, when the cause is not in our power, either in terms of being or in terms of operating, the effect is also not in our power.

An example of this is found in the sun and the daylight, from which it is evident that the daylight is not in our power, because the sun also is not, either in terms of its being or in terms of its operation, by which it produces the daylight, and its operation is its shining above the earth. For we cannot prevent the being of the sun or its shining above the earth or turn it away at all or impede it in any way, and for this reason it is evident that it is not in our power that there be no daylight. In the same way, it is not in our power that there be daylight, because, when the sun is beneath the earth, we cannot bring it about that it is or shines above the earth. It is evident, therefore, that, if such a cause is not in our power, neither is its effect. Hence, if the effect is in our power, the cause is also. Hence, the cause of the cause is <in our power>, since each of the causes up to the first is the effect of some cause. Hence, if any cause is in our power, the first cause will be in our power. Because, therefore, it is not in our power, there follows by the destruction of the consequent that nothing at all is in our power. Hence, none of the things that are or come to be are in our power either that it should be or that it should not be. We cannot, therefore, avert or prevent any of those things that are or come to be so that they are not or do not come to be or cause or procure that they are or come about. Hence, all things will be or will come to be or will come about of necessity in relation to us. We, therefore, have no freedom, no power whatever.

Know, therefore, on this that you should not only avoid saying or holding something false about the blessed creator, but that we should speak of him devoutly and reverently and with circumspect and well-examined words that have no appearance or suspicion of error. Because, therefore, that the first cause is in our power implies the subjection of him who, it is agreed, is not only most free, but the most dominant lord of all the ages, such words undoubtedly sound bad, having the appearance of the worst error. It is, nonetheless, evident and without any doubt that, just as we cannot bring it about that a ray of the sun enters through a window, we still can keep it from entering. We can also do something else by which, once it has been done, it will enter, such as opening a window or removing some other obstacle. And for this reason it is at times said to be in our power that our houses are illumined by the sun, that is, because the solar light is present as well as a good disposition of the air, if there occurs along with them the removal of an obstacle that prevents it. For no external action is totally in our power, that is, neither to eat, nor to drink, nor to walk, and this is because our life and our continued existence is required for each of these. But it is not in our power that it continue to exist for eating one mouthful or for quaffing a sip of wine or until we complete one step. It is the same way with the health of the members and the power to walk. For we are not able to preserve the soundness of our feet until we take even half a step. A path is also required. Regarding these things /790b/ what we can do and what we cannot do is evident to you. Hence, it is evident to you concerning all such things that none of them is totally in our power, that is, with all their helps and hindrances.

Pay attention also to the works of the creator that he works in us, such as the gifts of the graces and of the virtues. I say, therefore, that it is in our power to turn ourselves away from his generosity and beneficence with regard to such gifts, just as it is in the power of someone holding a vessel to turn it aside and, when the rain is falling from above, either to block its mouth or to turn its bottom to the rain. Foolish and evil human beings act in this way when they turn their hearts, which are vessels of the virtues and receptacles of graces, to vices and sins. For they turn such vessels away from the generosity and beneficence of the creator, which is ready to descend like rain falling from the most overflowing fountain, which is the goodness of the creator. And as you see human beings turning aside their bodily eyes, so they often turn the eyes of their hearts away from the first light, which is God most high, when they direct and turn their noble apprehensive powers to think of and seek out other things.

You have, then, been shown by these and such examples that there are many operations of the first cause that we are able to turn aside or prevent so that they do not take place in us, not, nonetheless, contrary to the will of the creator, that is, if he is unwilling, and for this reason it is not surprising that, if you consider this more closely and carefully, it is not properly and totally in our power, since even this turning away or disorder is in the power of the creator to the point that he may certainly take it away from us when he wills and can give us the contrary dispositions and preparations for receiving his gifts, whenever the divine goodness deigns. When he allows or permits it in that way, we turn our hands or the vessels of our hearts away from his gifts, and on this account we do not receive them, and we do this on the basis of our natural forces or powers that he has given us. We do not, therefore, act in so disorderly a way because of some power by which we can resist him. You see, therefore, that he against whom we can do nothing should not properly be said to be in our power through the abuse of the powers given to us by him. Still, when he permits it, not unjustly, but by his just judgment, we do not impede the creator himself, but we grievously injure ourselves, when we repel from us his finest gifts. In the same way, if someone tears out his eyes, he does not do this against the sun, whose light he drives from himself, nor to its harm or detriment, but to his own personal injury.

You, therefore, will see from all these things that have already been said, when you have carefully considered them, that the intention "to be in the power of" is not said properly, without qualification, and in terms of the whole, except concerning the creator, because there is in his power each of the things that exists, either that it exists or that it does not exist, that it comes to be or does not come to be, and it is in his power to destroy and wipe out vices and sins entirely because this is proper to his excellent and most dominant power. To cause or to procure their coming about is not in any way in his power because this is a mark of weakness and servitude most vile.

Whether, therefore, something is in our power has now been determined for you because properly and truly we ourselves are not in our own power, and on this account nothing is truly and properly in our power because we are not sufficient either to do or to be anything, or to cause or procure that it is, as has been shown to you in the acts that seem most of all to be in our power, such as the acts of eating, drinking, and walking, and the reason for this is that for each of such acts to be or to take place, there is required /791a/ a considerable aggregate of helps that contribute toward its being or coming about.

But by that intention by which something is at times said to be in our power, namely, in a certain respect or because we can do something by which, when it is done, that other thing will be done or will not done, necessity or impossibility does not in any way result regarding us, nor any injury to our freedom. And it also does not follow that, if we can do something regarding an effect of the creator or of some other cause, we can do something with regard to him or with regard to it. For it is evident that we can do something about the illumination that takes place in us or regarding us from the sun, and we still cannot on this account do something to the sun or in opposition to it.

CHAPTER 24
That Fate Is Understood in Different Ways

After this I shall pass to the investigation of fate and fating and of those persons who are commonly said to be fated and to have the power of fating, whether they do or not, and what this fating is according to the intention of those who held it.

Know, then, that according to one intention fate is good fortune or ill fortune, adversity or prosperity, a raising up or a lowering that has been preordained, predestined, or prepared for someone from his birth or before, and this is the intention according to which the astronomers called the knowledge of their judgments prophetic (*fatidicas*), and it is called fate in a loose sense from the verb "I speak, you speak" (*for, faris*), as if the constellation at birth, conception, or even at some other time preceding conception and birth spoke (*fata fuerit*) or uttered these things by being a sign of or signifying them in advance.

In another way and in another intention the worshipers of a multitude of gods understood fate as what was preordained and foretold by the gods whom they worshiped, I mean foretold by announcement. For they thought that the gods spoke in three ways: by advising, by threatening, and by announcing. But they said that those things that they spoke by threatening or by advising could be averted so that they do not come about. But the things announced necessarily come about like decrees and statutes of the gods. Hence, they called them fates, like statements and predictions of the gods who, they believed, could not lie. Fate according to this intention is a statement or assertion of the gods, when they speak or say things expressed and announced to mortals concerning great successes of someone. For "fate" is not used of daily and modest events. Many stories and statements of men, and especially of women, that they have heard the gods speaking of those successes at the births of men and women, have given rise to this opinion. But even up to today such an opinion exists among many nations and perhaps among all or many outstanding soldiers, whom they say were fated in that way, that is, that their great successes were foretold by the gods or goddesses before they came about.

Certain people explained that it was goddesses who foretold or predicted such things, especially at the births of human beings, perhaps on the basis of similar narratives and statements of people who said that they heard goddesses conversing about the successes of those being born, or perhaps they thought it more suitable that goddesses rather than gods attend those giving birth and at the births of human beings. And although this seems to be said superstitiously and almost in the manner of old wives, because it is said in rumor and myths, it is still commonly said, and many of the ancients were fated, and a certain person even of this age not far distant from the land of my birth <was also said to be fated>. /791b/

We should not pass this over without seeking the truth, if God wills, or probability, and without testing whether it can be found by me. You should, however, know that it was one of the Italian philosophers whose eloquence the whole Latin world not undeservedly admires right up to today, and among the Italians I think and judge that his wisdom must be admired, who said that fate or *heimarmene* are the same and did not distinguish between them except only by their names, saying that fate is causes tied together by which things connected to other things arise or come to be in a series.[138] And again he said in other words that fate "is everlasting truth flowing from all eternity."[139] Although he thought that he explained the truth to you by these words, he, nonetheless, passed over the meaning and explanation of the naming, and it is not clear to us, nor does he bring us to know why fate was so named.

Recall, therefore, those things that you heard in a preceding chapter, that is, in the first part of this treatise, which is on *The Universe*, and in the first part of the whole *Sapiential and Divine Teaching* about the first or firstborn Word, by which the first Father and first speaker spoke himself eternally before all times and before he created anything. And by the same word he said that whatever he was going to make and whatever was going to be, whether in things or concerning things, in such a way that there is no event or thing or human being that he did not say in that word and through it.[140] Similarly, no order or limit in the whole series of ages was passed over or not spoken by it. Hence, he spoke (*fatus*) then and said whatever was then going to be, and for this reason what was then spoken (*fatum*) or said is such. From this, therefore, the firstborn word can be seen to have been called fate because he was spoken by the first speaker and first father. For you know that not only is a thing said to be spoken or said (*fatum*), but also the saying or speaking by which the thing is spoken or said or going to be said. This then seems to be the meaning of the name or of the naming of fate, and it seems to fit only the word of the creator

138 See Cicero, *On Divination* (*De divinatione*) 1.55.125.

139 Ibid.

140 See *The Universe* Ia–Iae, chs. 19–22; Paris-Orléans ed., I, 613b–627b, and *The Trinity*, chs. 8 and 19; ed. Switalski, pp. 49 and 107-111.

in which and by which he established and ordered within himself before the ages the whole series of ages and every effect and all the events of human beings, which are called good fortune or ill fortune, and all the goods of nature and of grace and of future glory, and also temporal and bodily ones. Among their number there are penalties and afflictions, impoverishment, insults, and poverty itself, all torments of this sort, and even death, all of which common foolishness calls evils, and it flees from them as evils and repels them as best it can. But he said and foresaw within himself that blameworthy evils, which are called vices and sins, would exist, and he did not will that they come about because of him or from him or through him, because it does not befit his glory and goodness that he be the cause of such things. He decided, therefore, within himself in his most omnipotent word and through it not to prevent, but to limit, order, and moderate them. He decided to limit them so that they did not burst forth wherever evil human beings or evil demons wanted or suggested. He decided to moderate them by many means of repression and resistence, and only his wisdom knew all of them totally. He decided to order them so that they did not come to be before or earlier than he might elicit the benefits from them, on account of which he chose to permit them rather to avert or prevent them.

/792a/ CHAPTER 25
If Fate Is Taken for the Word of God, That Term Should be Used Carefully, And concerning the Error That Says That All Things Are True by the First Truth

After we have determined these points, carefully beware of the understanding and intention of common speech by which human beings very carelessly say, "This has come about by fate or through fate," because if fate is understood there to be the Word of God most high, it will be able to be said only of goods of nature, grace, glory, the body, or fortune. By the term "fortune" I understand the previously mentioned goods, which the mob of foolish people call misfortunes, although no wise person doubts that they are good gifts of God beneficial and inestimably precious in many ways for those who use them well.

It was, of course, explained to you in the first part of this treatise[141] that by the Word of the God and through him, all things have been made, and that there are being made whatever the creator is making, and that there will be made whatever he is going to make, and the authoritative usage of the words of the prophets of the Hebrew people has this. For one of them says, *The heavens*

141 See *The Universe* Ia–Iae, I, chs. 17–22; Paris-Orléans ed., I, 611b–617b.

were established by the word of God (Ps 32:6). But the law and teaching of the Christians abound with such language. This is, however, because this Word was made known especially to them, and they hold with undoubting faith that he is their lawgiver, author, teacher, and preacher, and they venerate him with an equal honor of worship with his father in the unity of the godhead with total devotion and zeal.

And such words, namely, "This happened by fate or through fate," are not accepted among those who are learned among the people of the Christians, because such an intention that I mentioned, namely, by which the name "fate" signifies the Word of God, is not found among them, and even if it were, they would not accept it without an explicit distinction and explanation. For they not incorrectly avoid for themselves, not only the errors of any impiety, but also the appearance or suspicion of them in their words and discussions. Hence it is that they abhor the name "fate" as if smacking of idolatry, which they greatly detest or mock, like the raving of the folly of an old wife or crone.

And if you remember similar subtleties, which you heard in the preceding chapters on the providence of the creator, the subtleties of the sophists will not be able to disturb you, or they should not be able to, when they say, "Since the creator eternally said all the events that would be, and since his Word is immutable in every way, and since every speaking or assertion <of his> is necessary, and since it is absolutely impossible that he lied, it is necessary that whatever he said come about or be true." For you ought to react in a similar way in all the things that are objected against the word or speaking of God, just as you did in all the things that were said against his providence, and you ought to beware for yourself of the expressions that explicitly signify or imply the duplicity or duplicities, about which you have heard, or a discrepancy or unlikeness between the word of God and[142] what is said, such as the words "lying" or "speaking falsities," for example, the falsity of the word of God or a false word of God.

For they say that there is a discrepancy between the word of God and the things said, and such a discrepancy is undoubtedly impossible. For it is impossible that it be otherwise in things or for things to be otherwise than God has spoken. And just as it is not necessary with regard to each of the things that God foresaw that he foresaw it—in fact, he foresaw many things, each of which it is possible that he did not foresee, and it is the same way with his knowledge—so also with regard to his word or speaking, it is very true that he said many things from eternity, concerning each one of which /792b/ it is possible that he did not say it.

---

142 I have conjectured "*et*" instead of "*vel.*"

Also, just as I said that you must beware of universality and particularity, composition and division, the expressions "about the thing" (*de re*) and "about the proposition" (*de dicto*), in accord with the language of those who speak about the providence of the creator, so you should beware of similar words concerning his word or speaking.

And in order that what you have heard about the word and providence of the creator might be made clearer for you, pay careful attention to the example that I propose for you. If someone says concerning two contingent contradictories, of which it is necessary that one always be true, "This is true," after the one that is true has been pointed out, and if he has confirmed his intention on this in such a way that he did not point out the other, it is evident that he cannot lie by this utterance, "This is true," in this intention that I mentioned. For it is possible for that about which he said that it is true not to be true, because it is possible concerning each of them that it is not true. Since, according to this position, each is contingent, for how much stronger reason ought it not to be surprising that God cannot lie by his word, although it is possible that any one of the many things that he says or has said not be true!

But the reason for this is that, just as the intention or pointing out of it falls only upon that one of the two that is true, similarly this speaking and this word of his, which is, "This is true," cannot be false, although that which is signified by it could be false. But if it were false, it would not be signified by that speaking or by that word. For how much stronger reason can the word of God not be false, although many things fall under it, for which it is possible to be false. But it will be more evident in events, if I say concerning the death or life of someone, "It will be so concerning him tomorrow," after what will be concerning his death or life has been pointed out, I still do not know what will be, that is, whether he will die or live, after what will be has been pointed out. You see here clearly that I cannot lie, and my word is true, whatever happens concerning his death or life.

In the same way the word of God falls upon only those things that are true or are truly future or past, as you heard concerning his providence, and just as I would say it by these same words, namely, "This will be," if something else were going to be concerning his life or death, so it is concerning the word of God insofar as it is permissible to state or to find a likeness in things so far distant from each other, because by the same word in every way, by which the blessed creator said that this event, which was really going to be, was going to be, he would have said that it was not going to be if it were in truth not going to be, and by that only word all the things were said that can be said by all the things we can say.

But now the error about which I already told you concerning what can be said and stated seems to take its occasion from the claim that stateables (*enunciabilia*) have existed from eternity,[143] and this in the ways that I shall show you. For either they were true by the truth that existed and was in them, or they were not. If they were, then their truth existed and was in them. The <stateables> themselves existed, since neither the truth nor anything else could be in non-beings. But if their truth did not exist and was not in them, how then were they true by that truth that did not exist and was not in them? For this seems to be said as if one were to say that something was white by a whiteness that did not exist and was not in it.

And the statement by which those things that are about the future are said to be true involves perhaps no less difficulty, whether those things are necessary or contingent. For how is it true that the sun will rise tomorrow, if its truth does not exist? It seems to be no otherwise than if it were be said, "Socrates is a philosopher or is wise with a wisdom or a philosophy that does not exist." And if he says that this truth is future, this is as if it were said that Socrates is wise with a wisdom that is not yet, but that will be. But if he /793a/ says that this truth exists, where then is it? It cannot be said that it is in the sun, because, even if the sun did not exist, provided that it was going to rise tomorrow, the statement would be true by which it would be said that it was going to rise.

But if he wants to cavil and say that the sun exists, and on this account the truth of that proposition has a subject in which it is and by which it is supported, he errs with great feebleness of intellect. For this solution will abandon him if you say to him, "A particular day is past, which no longer is," or "A particular day will be, which is not yet." It is evident to you that neither of these statements has a subject that exists; hence, it does not have a subject in which the truth exists, since the subject of neither exists.

Disturbed by these and similar arguments and failing because of the weakness of their intellect to discover the truth and not finding the door to it, like blind persons wandering about, they said that it is the first truth by which all such propositions are true. This error, however, will be destroyed in the ways I shall show you. The first of these is this: They understand that all such things are true by the first truth either formally or effectively. This is to say that either they understand that the first truth, which is none other than the blessed creator, is predicated by this term "true," and then they hold that it is necessarily in everything true, or they understand that some effect of the first truth that falls upon everything true is predicated by this term "true," like the light from the sun sprinkled upon everything that is illumined by it. And for those with understanding, it is evident that such truth is the intelligible light

---

143 See above ch. 18.

for our intellective power, just as bodily light is <light> for our power of sight, and on this account everything true and only what is true is knowable for us, just as only the bright in act or the illuminated is visible. They necessarily, therefore, have to hold, in accord with this intention, that the essence of the first truth is in things that do not exist at all, because countless substances, both bodily ones and spiritual ones, such as human souls, and their modifications and habits are going to exist and do not yet exist. It is, nonetheless,[144] true of each of them that this thing will be, whichever of them is pointed out, or perhaps nothing exists because the subject of such a statement does not exist, nor does the predicate. For "will be" does not predicate "is," nor does "will not be."

But the composition of the subject and predicate also does not exist. For those non-beings are in no way joined by a real conjunction and according to the truth; in fact, they are really divided since this thing really does not exist or does not yet exist. Hence, that this thing will be is about non-beings, but it is true that this thing will be according to the stated intention of this term, "true," by which one says that the first truth is in that about which it is predicated. Hence, the first essence will be in this non-being and in every similar truth and, on this account, similarly in a non-being.

But who would understand that being is in non-being? For a liquid does not exist in a vessel that does not exist, nor does a soul exist in a body that does not yet exist, nor does knowledge exist in a soul that does not exist, nor can any kind of thing be thought to exist in something else that does not exist.

Moreover, it is evident that many and countless things are now true that can be false, and the converse. And if this occurred, the essence of the first truth would withdraw from them, and the opposite of them would enter, as if its changing place or dwelling will follow upon it.

Moreover, a greater problem will follow from this because, when falsity or something else expels it, <the first truth> will be driven away from something true, in which it was, as if unable to remain there. For truth cannot remain where falsity inheres.

Moreover, whether falsity is something or nothing, it is impossible that it expel the first truth. For, if it is /793b/ something, it is impossible that it be comparable to it in strength. How then would it be expelled by it if falsity is nothing? Far less will it be able to do something against the first power or truth. In accord with this, you will also find other problems not so much impossible as worthy of derision.

---

144 I have again followed Lewis' transcription of the Nuremberg text with "*tamen*" instead of "*tunc.*"

But if he says that this truth by which the stateables are true or what they signify is true is like light sprinkled by the first truth over all such truths, he does not escape without necessarily having to grant and to admit that this light is sprinkled over non-beings and that they are illumined by it and that infinite non-beings are bright because of it. But neither the imagination nor the intellect accepts this claim. For, if that light is an accident, how is it in a subject that does not exist?

Moreover, this accident will be eternal and immortal and universally incorruptible, something also impossible in things that are true. For it is impossible that none of the contingent things that can be said (*dicibilium*) is true. After all, it is necessary that one of any two of those contradictorily opposed be true.

Moreover, if two such contradictories are in the same proximity to the truth, how would this light not fall equally over both? In the same way, if two objects that can be illumined are or stand in the same proximity and other dispositions in relation to the sun and are equally able to be illumined, they will be equally illumined, and either both will be illumined, or neither will be.

Moreover, how does the light of the truth withdraw from one of them? Either the first truth pulls back its ray to itself, and this does not happen in any kind of natural operations, or that which was true withdraws from that light, and this is not possible unless it is moved. But who would understand that things that can be said are moved? How would anyone understand that an statement or that which is stated is moved, since it is not possible that it be moved either voluntarily or naturally?

Moreover, such light will be either divisible into parts or indivisible into parts in everything that is stated. If divisible, then a part of it will be in the subject and a part in the predicate. Hence, if one or the other of them is destroyed, that part will be destroyed. But this is evidently impossible, and I will set forth an example for this, namely, that Socrates disputes or does not dispute. For this is always true, whether Socrates exists or not, and it is equally true if Socrates is destroyed. But if part of this truth were in Socrates, that part of the truth would be destroyed if Socrates were destroyed. But if a part is destroyed, the whole would not remain entire and would not continue to be. But its entire truth remains, which is that Socrates disputes or does not dispute. That also remains no less true in any way than it was when Socrates remained. Hence, it is evident that neither the whole truth of it nor a part is in Socrates. Hence, it is in the predicate, which is "disputes" or "does not dispute." Because in "does not dispute" there is neither the truth nor anything else, nor can there be, since it is also non-being and nothing, like a pure negation, the whole truth will of necessity be in "disputes." Hence, if it is destroyed, the truth will be destroyed. Since, therefore, Socrates' disputing will not exist, there will not be truth in that whole "Socrates disputes or does not dispute." Therefore, if Socrates does not dispute, it will not be true that Socrates disputes or does not dispute.

Moreover, this outpouring of such a light descending from the first truth scattered over all things that are true is either natural or voluntary for the first truth. But if it is natural, as I indicated earlier, it will be servile or pertaining to servitude.[145] But the nobility of the first truth does not admit that, as you have heard many times. But if it is voluntary, then all these true things will be true through his will. Hence, that this person plunders, that another steals, that still another blasphemes, and that yet another denies God will be true through his will, and since he makes them to be true, his /794a/ will, therefore, will be the cause of all thieving and plundering. For whatever causes it to be true that this man steals, causes him to steal.

Moreover, this outpouring is neither the essence of the creator nor essential to the creator. Hence, it can be separated from him in act or at least by the intellect. Let us, then, separate it from him by the intellect, that is, understand that it does not pour forth or sprinkle. Since this light has no other cause, it will not exist at all, since it will not be from the creator. Hence, there will be no truth, and for this reason nothing will be true. It will, therefore, be true, namely, that there is no truth, and this other one that there is nothing true, and countless others of this sort.

Moreover, since such truth is neither a part of that upon which it falls nor the whole of it, it is separable from it, at least in intention or by the intellect.

Moreover, it can be lost and non-recoverable in many things, that is, many things are true, which can be not true and many are not true which can be true. But "true" is said univocally of all things of this sort; it is, therefore, accidental to all things of this sort.

Moreover, that Socrates disputes does not admit truth in its meaning or essence. For, if truth were essential to it, it could in no way admit falsity. For nothing is able to receive something that is its contrary or a privation either of its whole essence or of something essential to it. But it is able to admit falsity. Therefore, truth is not essential to it.

Moreover, that Socrates disputes is not something else or of another character if it is true than if it is false. But it would be something else or of another character if truth were essential to it. It is evident, therefore, according to this intention, that, since there is an outpouring from the luminosity of the first truth descending over all true things and since it is univocally said of all of them, it will be separable, at least by the intellect, from each of them, and this is undoubtedly so. Thus it stands with everything that is not the whole essence of that in which it is, nor a part of it, but received over the whole and complete

---

145 See above note 14.

essence. Hence, this truth will be separable in act or at least by reason from each of such things. But this is evidently impossible in countless <statements>, of which one is that Socrates disputes or does not dispute. For no intellect can separate truth from it, and it is the same way in all similar ones, that is, ones that are contradictory disjuncts. It is the same way with "Something is true," or "There is some truth." For no intellect admits that it is not true that something is true, nor that it is true that there is nothing true. Similarly no intellect admits that there is no truth.

Moreover, it is evident that there have been from eternity many diverse and varied truths that are completely independent in relation to one another. I mean many contingent truths about the future. But nothing existed from eternity except the creator. That truth, therefore, was not poured forth when the creator was not, or rather, when the light <was not> sprinkled by him over all truths, according to this position. Therefore, either there were no truths, or they were true by a truth that did not exist. But if he says that this truth existed as soon as the most luminous truth, which is the spiritual sun of the intellect and of all intelligent substances, in the same way that, as soon as the sun or its luminosity existed, there existed the brightness shining from it and sprinkled through the whole world receptive of it, I say that, even if the whole last heaven were luminous like the sun, no light would fall or be sprinkled by it outside of it, and the reason is that outside the heaven there is nothing else receptive of either the light or of its outpouring, unless someone is so insane as to say that non-being or nothing is receptive of some impression or outpouring. But this is, as I told you, as if someone would say that a vessel that does not exist receives /794b/ some liquid, that air that does not exist is illumined by the sun, and that a non-existent subject supports some accident. And if he says that the brightness from the sky is sprinkled over the void or vacuum, you have already heard Aristotle and his expositors about this, who think that they have destroyed a void or vacuum.[146]

CHAPTER 26
That Truth Is Understood in Six Ways
And in What the Truth of Statements about Non-Beings Consists

You must know in these matters that truth is said in accord with many intentions, and in one intention <it is> a sign or signification, and in that way falsity and truth are opposed. And in this way truth is only the thing signified itself. In the second way truth is opposed to the falsity that

---

146 See Aristotle, *Physics* 4.6–10.213a11–217b28.

is the appearance of something that is not there. And in this way human beings are called false who pretend to be exteriorly the opposite of what they are interiorly, and to call this by its common and familiar name, it is usually called pretense. In the third way truth is purity from adulteration, as silver that is pure is said to be true, and it is truer, the purer it is. Impurity is opposed to this truth, whether as its contrary or, as seems truer, as its privation.

In the fourth way <it is> the very being of each thing, that is, the residue from the whole variety and clothing of accidents, and this is the being that the definition explains, into which no accident enters, but only what is the essence or substance of the thing. Hence, an account of the substance is called a true definition because it is an entire and pure explanation of its substance without any admission or admixture of one of the accidents. And it is called substance because it stands under that whole variety and clothing of accidents and sustains it. Otherwise, they would fall into non-being. On this account an accident is also named as if falling upon (*ad cadens*) a substance, trying to rest upon it and to be sustained by it, as unable to subsist by itself. Or it is called an accident as falling into non-being, insofar as it is considered in itself, that is, as considered in the nature of accidentality, as unable to subsist by itself, that is, by its proper, that is, natural strength.

In the fifth way truth is said to be the being of the creator or the creator himself, and everything else in comparison with him is falsity, as Aristotle says in the book of the *Metaphysics*, when he says that there is one alone of which there is no cause, and that is the truth.[147] But all other being is possible being, and it is falsity or vanity, and this intention is to some extent like one of the preceding intentions. But the reason for this is that silver that is silver only externally is said not to be true, nor is an ape said to be a man because he is a man only externally, but is a brute interiorly. In the same way each of those things that are apart from the creator are only externally and as having being from outside and as adventitious, since, as was explained to you in the first part of the whole *Sapiential and Divine Teaching*, the being that is predicated by this word "is," which is the being by which each thing is—this being, I say, is said accidentally of each of the other things or according to participation.[148] But it is said essentially or according to essence or according to substance only of the creator. It is separable from everything else in act or by reason or intellect. But it is in no way separable from the creator; otherwise, it would be acquired by him or adventitious. But such an impossibility is evident, because, if it were acquired by him, /795a/ it would be acquired by him either from himself or from another, and he would thus either be the cause of himself or have another

147 See Aristotle, *Metaphysics* 2.1.933b19–30.

148 See William, *The Trinity*, ch. 2; ed. Switalski, pp. 20–25.

cause, and in that way he would not be the first nor the principle, and it is not necessary for me to pursue here the destruction of this error, about which you have the fullest certitude in that previously mentioned treatise.

Because, therefore, everything other than the creator is only externally, that is, accidentally, by an external and adventitious being, and only the creator is internally or rather intimately, every other being is rightly called false or falsity. But only the creator is true being or truly being and true and the truth. But an example of this in the illuminated or enlightened air is most appropriate. For it is to be said to be falsely bright or shining in comparison with the sun, and especially in comparison with the sunlight, which is essentially light, and its being is to shine.

But the sixth intention of true and truth is that by which those things that have been enunciated are called true or propositions are true, and this, Avicenna says, is the adequation of speech and things, that is, of affirmation and negation <and things>.[149] And it must be understood in the words of Avicenna that he calls speech both exterior speech, that is, written or vocal, and spiritual or intellectual speech. But whether you say adequation or equality or likeness does not matter in terms of the intention of Avicenna. Something true according to this intention is adequated to its affirmation or negation, and this adequation is not according to only one time, but according to every time and extends to eternity. An utterance, therefore, is true by which what is is said to be or what is not is said not to be or what was is said to have been or what was not is said not to have been, and it is the same way with the future.

You ought also to know that the statement of some stateable is not true, which asserts either something else or something more or less or otherwise in any way than the stateable has or contains, and this is the likeness or equality or adequation that Avicenna intended, whether you say agreement or concordance between the stateable and its utterance or its negation, I mean, as I explained to you before, that is, the agreement or concordance of the stateable and the statement is the truth of both, and the contrary or its privation is the falsity of both. A stateable, then, is true that does not disagree or is not discordant with its affirmation or negation. Hence, it is evident that truth and falsity according to these intentions are like relations or comparisons of compositions and divisions with their affirmations and negations, and the truth and falsity

---

149 See Avicenna, *Metaphysics* 1.6; ed. Van Reit, p. 64. This definition of truth is close to the classic definition of truth as the adequation of the intellect and reality, the source of which is disputed. Though in *De veritate* 1.1, St. Thomas attributes it to Isaac Israeli, some contemporary scholars regard it as the common opinion of the Parisian masters.

of affirmations and negations are comparisons or relations or references to the compositions and divisions of the things they signify.

Elsewhere, however, it was explained to you by me that comparisons and relations do not in themselves add or subtract from things, nor do they put something in them, nor does what is compared or related, by reason of the fact that it is compared or related, have something in itself, but it has something in relation to itself or for itself.[150] Similarly, what is said or signified, apprehended, thought of, or loved does not have something in itself by reason of the fact that it is signified, thought of, apprehended, or loved. Nor do these dispositions or comparisons require that in which they are or about which they are to exist. For often what does not exist is signified, nor is the signification by which it is signified something in it. Similarly, what does not exist is loved, and a son who does not as yet exist is desired, and gold that has not as yet been produced and never will exist is desired. A thing, therefore, is apprehended by an apprehension that is not in it, and it is loved by a love that is not in it, and a son is desired by a desire that is not in him, and it is generally true that passive denominations or predications are made about things in which /795b/ they do not exist, because they are toward them or in relation to them or about them.

But from whiteness or any of the other sensible qualities, a denomination or predication is made only about the things in which they are. For nothing is said to be white except that which has whiteness in it or in which there is whiteness. But that in which love exists not said to be loved, but that <is said to be loved> toward which[151] or about which the love exists, unless perhaps ones adds "loved by oneself." For then the same person is loving and loved, and it is this way with our significations, apprehensions, and affections, because they are predicated of things in which they do not exist and about things in which they are not.[152] But do not extend this to sensible apprehensions and similarly not to sensible affections, because, just as only that which exists senses, so only what exists is sensed. But the reason for this is that only what presently acts upon a sense, that is, upon an organ of sensation, is sensed. Similarly only that which exists sensibly causes delight, and that which does not exist is not delighted. But in imaginations and in the dispositions of our souls that are above them, the matter is as I said.

I shall return, therefore, to solving the questions and arguments set forth above, and I shall say that stateables about the future, where neither the sub-

---

150 See *The Trinity*, chs. 30 and 31; ed. Switalski, pp. 170–177.

151 The reading "*in quo*" seems incorrect, and I have conjectured "*in quem*."

152 I have conjectured the addition of the negative.

jects nor the predicates exist, are presently true with such truth, that is, with such agreement, harmony, adequation, or equality, and I say that many such agreements and many such comparisons are nothing in things and do not put anything in them and are even certain privations of them or are said according to privation. For it is usually said that all non-beings are agreeing or agree in non-being, and all impossible things agree in impossibility, and all blind persons are alike in blindness and naked ones in nakedness. And they are said to be on a par and equal in this respect.

It is, however, evident that none of them is something in terms of the truth. Similarly holes are said to be equal, and vessels alike or equal in their mouths, and men are said to be equally naked, and their nakedness equal. The image of <Caesar or of> Hercules is said to be like him although neither Caesar nor Hercules exists. Because, therefore, the agreement between an utterance and what is signified is a privation or is said according to privation, as is seen from the character of the adequation, which was set forth, that is, which does not contain, that is, assert or deny, something else or otherwise or more or less that what is stated, in accord with this, therefore, nothing prevents something from being true with a truth that does not exist, just as something is naked with a nakedness that does not exist and just as non-beings agree in an agreement that does not exist, and impossible things similarly.

You also ought to know that when stateables are said to be true, that is, agreeing with or adequate to their affirmations or negations, what is said about their affirmations and negations is not understood in terms of act, but in terms of potency, and this is to say that I do not mean: to affirmations or negations that they have at present, that is, by which they are presently or actually signified, but rather those by which it is possible for them to be affirmed or denied. Stateables, therefore, were true from eternity, that is, agreeing with or adequate to their statements, that is, by which they could be affirmed or denied. You will not, therefore, be forced by the previously mentioned arguments to say that countless truths or countless stateables existed in act from eternity.

But if someone wants to say that by the first word all the truths that can be affirmed and all the truths that can be denied were affirmed and denied from eternity and always agreeing with or adequate to it, he will speak the truth, but he does not loosen the knot of the question because he does not explain the truth about such agreement /796a/ or adequation, and the reason is that it will of necessity limp according to him, since it will not have on the side of the stateables anywhere to put its foot, since, even if stateables were things, they still would not exist in the truth of being. How, then, will he understand agreement to be a relation when it cannot have a correlation in things on account of their non-existence, unless he has recourse to what I said? Just as something is true that does not, nonetheless, exist, such as that a chimera <does not>¹⁵³ exist, of which neither the subject nor the predicate exists, so it is not surprising that something is true with a truth that does not exist, especially since such truth is rational or logical truth and the agreement of stateables, which does not demand that things exist rather than not exist, and the converse. Nor is it more in relation to beings than to non-beings. For the affirmation by which it is affirmed that a chimera <does not exist> agrees equally with what is affirmed by it and is adequate to it, as that by which it is affirmed that the creator exists agrees with what is affirmed by it or is adequate to it.

Concerning relations, however, and predications and modes of predicating I have set you and me free in a single treatise, on the occasion of the predications that are made in accord with the teaching of the Christians in divine matters or rather matters of the divinity.[154] And if you wish to recall those things that were said there by me, you will be helped no small amount toward the explanation of questions and of the explanations that were set forth, although those that you have heard here should rightly suffice for you.

CHAPTER 27

*From Where the Term "Fate" Has Come into Use
And That Fating by the Gods or Demons Is To Be Contemned,
And an Investigation of the Soul of the World according to Plato*

After this I shall return to the fates and instances of fating. Know, therefore, that both the law of the Hebrews and that of the Christians agrees on this, namely, that revelations of great events concerning men being born were made at their births or before their births, and the law of the Hebrews reports that such revelations were made by the creator and especially concerning princes and patriarchs of that people.[155] But the law of the Christians reports that such revelations were made by angels.[156] In the narratives we read that

---

153 Again I have followed Lewis's transcription of the Nuremberg edition, which adds the negative.

154 See *The Trinity*, ch. 44; ed. Switalski, pp. 225–254.

155 See, for example, Jdg 13:2–23 for the announcement of the birth of Samson.

156 See, for example, Lk 1: 8–20 for the announcement of John the Baptist's birth and see Lk 1:26–38 for the announcement of Jesus's birth.

many such revelations were made through dreams and also through prophets or through prophetic men.[157]

But the name "fate" or "the Fates" or "fating" is an object of horror and abomination among both peoples, as I already told you, and it is not read or heard in either of the laws mentioned. And because the mention of the worship of the gods and goddesses and idolatry are older than both laws, the idea of fating has remained like a remnant as a result of such worship, but especially among old wives or crones, who have not yet abandoned them because they are drawn by curiosity, female levity, or money-making, for which they are not afraid to lie.

Hence, if one believes their stories, it is a somewhat tolerable belief at the time when a multitude of gods, that is, of the worst demons, were worshiped. As they were permitted to give responses and do many other things for their worshipers, so they could be heard to converse and predict at the births of many what they thought concerning the successes of those being born and what they themselves perhaps did not know, and they suggested to human beings that their conversations were such cases of fating, that is, firm arrangements of such events and likewise that the fates are considered to be like non-retractable decrees. They did all these things, however, with a most malign and wicked intention, namely, in order to persuade their worshipers and others as well that they were true gods and that they /796b/ had it in their power to foster by their mere word or utterance great and famous successes and to raise them up with great honors so that they might draw foolish people to their worship, in which they could only intend the insult of the creator and the overthrow and perdition of their worshipers or their own most vain honor. For it is thought to be the case that they desire greatly to be called and regarded as gods and venerated with divine honors.

One ought to hold the same thing with regard to the Fates, that is, with regard to the falsest and vainest goddesses, because they are only demons when they are anything real and when they are heard in the truth of their conversation, intending to seduce those to whom they are permitted to say such things and in such a way. At times they are the fictions and inventions of old crones who want to obtain something from the foolish by such lies. For greed and adulation does not easily withdraw from old women, especially from poor ones. But they have so great a love of lying about the explanation of divinations and dreams and so great a boldness that they cannot be frightened off from them even by scourges. Other women also generally have such a great credulity about such

---

157 See Mt 1:18-25 for Joseph's being told in a dream that Mary's child will be called Emmanuel and will save his people from their sins. See Nm 12:6 where God promises to speak to his prophet in a dream.

things that they cannot cease from frequenting old crones who lie about and make up such things, although many times they prove them liars and truthful about nothing. Moreover, they are so bold as to buy such lies and fictions at great prices. But it is evident that the statements of gods of this sort have no firmness or necessity since neither a word nor a statement of the omnipotent creator introduces such necessity into contingent events, as you have often heard in the preceding chapters.[158] For how much greater reason will the statements of the false gods and most vain goddesses have no firmness or necessity!

Moreover, how often the gods and goddesses have been proven and found to be liars by their worshipers! But if you want to have certitude about their lies, read the narratives of the Christians; also read their responses, and you will find a countless multitude of lies and ambiguities in their responses, which can be interpreted for either side of a contradiction, in which it is seen that they did not know the truth and gave their responses with such shrewdness that, whatever happened, they would seem to have predicted it.

Moreover, it has already been explained to you in another treatise,[159] and it has been written for you concerning their worship that they can do or undo nothing for mortals or against them, but rather the whole of well-being, the whole of prosperity, the whole of ill-being, which is adversity, lies in the good pleasure of the omnipotent creator. If then they can benefit or harm human beings by no force or power of their own, for how much better reason can they not do so by a word or speaking or speech!

Moreover, if it is their nature or power to know the events of human beings, how much more ought they to have foreknown their own! They, therefore, foreknew the extermination of their worship. How then did they not avert that?

Moreover, if by their mere word they can give honors and powers to human beings and turn away from them every kind of misfortune, how have they allowed themselves to be dishonored, overthrown, and trampled down so that all the honor paid in their worship is exterminated from the kingdom of the Christians and the kingdom of the Saracens and at one time from the whole Roman world? Or have they fated the Roman emperors to such a great insult and fall of themselves?

Moreover, it is certain that the people of the Jews and the people of the Christians and the people of the Saracens are most hostile to their worship and persecute them on the basis of their whole law with their full zeal and might. How, then, since they can do this, do they not by their mere word render so unfortunate or unhappy each of those persons /797a/ who are born in one of

158 See above chs. 15–18.

159 See William, *The Universe* IIIa–IIae, 6; Paris-Orleans ed., I, 124bGH.

those peoples so that they can do nothing against them? But I shall set you and me free from these and other questions concerning these and others in the next treatise after this one, if God wills.[160]

But the philosophers have held many rulers in the sublunar world, and others such as Plato and his followers have held a soul of the world,[161] while still others have held the power of the same and many other occult powers and have held that demons also take care of human affairs. Hence, it is suitable to examine these views insofar as it pertains to the present treatise, and I think that I should first of all deal with the soul of the world. For the soul of a body that animates it is undoubtedly its governor, king, and emperor. But its command and dominion over it is seen from the obedience of the whole and of the members. Similarly its providence <is seen> from the seeking of those things that are necessary for the body and its members, such as shelter and clothing, food and drink. Abumasar, the astrologer,[162] also attributed the whole fabrication and formation of animal bodies to their souls or to their natures, as if the leonine soul took from the matter from which the body of a lion is generated that from which it forms teeth and claws for itself, and similarly the bear soul does. Nor is it surprising if he attributes this to souls since Aristotle seems to hold the same thing regarding the power of seeds, as I have already told you.[163] For why would the power to form flowers, leaves, and fruits and all the bodies of plants be in seeds and the power of forming human bodies not be even more in seeds,[164] since the seeds of animals and the powers of their seeds ought to be more noble to the extent that the bodies of animals are more noble than the bodies of plants.

The whole governance of the world, therefore, will stem from its soul, especially since Plato explicitly held that the world is a living being that understands the sanction of divine wisdom.[165] But there can be a doubt about what led him

---

160 That is, in *The Universe* Ia–IIae.

161 See Plato, *Timaeus* 30B and Cicero, *On the Nature of the Gods* 1, 23–24 and 2, 22.

162 Abumasar, that is, Abu Ma`shar, or Albumasar, d. 886. His work, *The Book of a Greater Introduction to the Science of the Judgments of the Stars* (*Liber introductorii maioris ad scientiam judiciorum astrorum*, has appeared in a new edition by Richard Lemay. The work was originally translated by John of Seville, Gerard of Cremona, and Herman of Carinthia; the new edition was published in Naples by the Istituto universitario orientale in 1995.

163 See above note 13.

164 I have removed "*vegetabilibus*" here because it does not make sense.

165 See perhaps *Timaeus* 36E.

to this and whether he held that the whole world, that is, the bodily universe is an animal or only the heaven, that is, that part of the bodily universe that is from the moon up and the whole part that moves in a circle, namely, that which contains the nine mobile heavens, about which you have heard in the preceding, or whether it is the whole universe, which is composed of the nine heavens and four elements. For Aristotle and his followers seem to have held that it is only the heaven,[166] that is, the part that is from the moon up, or perhaps the heaven of the first star could be a living being, and Avicenna clearly says that "the heaven is a living being obedient to God."[167]

But it does not seem to have been fitting for so great a philosopher to hold that the four elements are animated. For who would say that fire or air is animated and similarly water and earth? Life is not seen in them, nor any form of motion except local motion, unless it is violent motion, which is in no sense vital. But in all plants the motion of increase and decrease is seen, and Aristotle says that they are determined by increase and decrease.[168] But from these things that appear on the earth and in the waters, they are seen to have a certain power generative of plants and even of animals.

Both the law and doctrine of the Hebrews agree on this, and the doctrine and faith of Christians does not disagree with this. But I already gave you the reason and proof for this in the preceding chapters,[169] and I said that earth, insofar as it is earth, does not have a power generative of animals or plants. For a body can generate through its corporeality only a body of its own species, earth only earth and water only water. The fact that other bodies generate, namely, animals or also plants, comes from a power added to both of them, and /797b/ the previously mentioned laws admit this, namely, that it was given by a blessing of the creator to both of them to generate more noble things than they themselves are, and the law of the Hebrews taught in its beginning the words of the creator by which this blessing is understood, namely, by which it is said, *Let the waters bring forth* (Gn 1:20), and, *Let the earth produce* (Gn 1:25), and so on.

But you ought to know that the lack of animation of the four elements is not the reason that ought to prevent <the world> from being a living being, just as the lack of animation of the four humors in the human body does not prevent a man from being a living being, and this example is most well suited to the view of Plato, since he held a certain likeness between a man and the

---

166 Once again, William most probably is referring to Avicenna.

167 Avicenna, *Metaphysics* 9.1; ed. Van Reit, p. 446.

168 Aristotle, *On the Soul* 2.2.413a25–30.

169 See *The Universe* Ia-IIa, ch. 40; Paris-Orléans ed., I, 635a–635b.

world so that he did not hesitate to call man a microcosm.[170] You should also know according to the view of Plato that the world surrounding the four elements does not need the sublunar world, but rather just the opposite, and this is already known from others. You also know how the members of the human body and their parts are nourished by the four humors, which are likened to the four elements, and how in it there are generated from them superfluities and certain tiny[171] animals. Thus plants, metals, and liquids are generated in it from the four elements, and those things that can be nourished from such generated things are generated from the elements. The followers of Plato also said in confirmation of this opinion that effluences of the seas were the breathing and respiration of the world. Hence, they put its quasi nostrils where there were great flooding or effluences of the seas, which is in the great abyss, which Aristotle called the mother of all the waters,[172] or in those seas where such inundations appear more violent and greater.

But the error of these people is readily evident if you consider how breathing and respiration take place in animals, and first of all, because they do not take place without the motion of expansion and contraction of certain parts in them, namely, of the stomach and lungs. But nothing of the sort is seen in parts of the earth, that is, in all the depths of the earth, which is like a belly containing all the seas.

Moreover, breathing and respiration increase in animals as the result of the violence and strength of motion and are lessened from their contraries. But no motion is seen in the body of the earth. Rather, the winter and spring inundations of the seas are greater and stronger than the inundations that are produced at other times.

Moreover, western and northern seas have more violent and greater inundations than eastern or southern ones because they are seen to be nearer the vital parts of the world, as those parts that are nearer to the lungs and heart in animals are moved more forcefully by breathing and respiration than the parts more remote from them. But it is evidently clear according to Aristotle and his followers that the fountain of vital warmth is toward the east and south. They also place the powers on the basis of which they hold that there is generation

---

170 Though the idea of man as the microcosm can certainly be derived from what Plato said, the word itself does not seem to be in his writings. Man is said to be "*minor mundus*" in many of the Fathers of the Church from Jerome on.

171 I have followed the alternative reading in the margin of "*minutorum*" instead of "*inimicorum*," which is found in the text.

172 See perhaps Aristotle, *Meterology* 2.2.355b33–35, although Aristotle is merely reporting Plato's theory from the *Phaedo* 111C, which he rejects.

and the life of animals toward the south, namely, the sun and the other planets and the twelve signs.

Moreover, it is evident that the sinuosity and depth of the earth draws the waters of the sea and rejects them, or something else does, since water does not overflow like that except because of a violent motion. If he says that the earth draws them within its folds and depths, this is seen to be impossible in many ways. First, because waters cannot be drawn except to where they were not. Hence, some depth of the earth would be empty of waters, in fact so great a sinuosity and so great a profundity that would suffice to receive the returning waters. But it is clearly impossible that the place that they enter should be completely empty of a body, which is impossible, or that /798a/ it should be full of air. But air could not prevent water from entering and dividing it and casting it out of that place, especially since that place has so many folds and exits.

Moreover, bodies draw in air only by expanding the lungs and extending the belly. But nothing of the sort takes place in the depths of the earth.

Moreover, breathing and respiration are only of the wind (*spiritus*), that is, of air, from which they get their name. But it is evident that, if all the interior parts of an animal, namely, the stomach and lungs were full of water, it could not breathe, but would rather suffocate and be killed with its breath cut off and the path of respiration blocked. But it is evident that breathing and respiration are only of air, because only animals breathing and inhaling air live in it. For this reason fishes cannot live in it except for those that raise their heads into the air and carry their heads above water when they swim. But fishes that always stay under the water do not breathe, and on this account they are also said not to have lungs.

And it is not necessary for me to delay more on the destruction of this fantasy since, besides these things that I have told you, you can recall the things you learned in the knowledge of meteors where the cause of the motion of the seas was explained to you,[173] because such a motion is only a boiling. Hence, it is usually called the fervor of the sea. And you already know that the motion of boiling comes from steam released by heat that is multiplied and that rises up and drives the water by its multitude and rising, raising it up and forcing it to overflow.

---

173 See perhaps Aristotle, *On Meteors* 2.1.353a2 7–354a33.

CHAPTER 28

*Whether Plato and Men Like Him Held One Soul or More for the Nine Heavens
And How That Soul Could Act on Lower Things*

I shall return, therefore, and say that Plato and whoever held such a view either understood that there is one soul for all nine heavens, or they did not. If they did, I say that the same proofs that show that the one of the heavens is animated show that all are animated, namely, their motions. Moreover, the diversity of their motions indicates diverse movers. But no one held that their movers were anything but souls. There will not, therefore, be one soul animating all nine heavens.

But someone might say that the multitude of the heavens does not prevent one soul from animating them all. Since, after all, it is obviously seen in the human body that there is so great a multitude and diversity of members and that a single soul animates them all, for how much better reason will a single soul of such nobility not be prevented from animating bodies so alike as are the nine heavens?

But if someone says that the diversity of motion prevents this in the heavens, why does it not in the members of animals? There is, after all, such a great diversity of motions in the members of animals. For the heart does not have a motion like the motions of the other members, and they called its motion systole and diastole, that is, rising and falling, and such motion is not voluntary or commanded, and it is not in the power of or by the will of a human being or of another animal to suppress or prevent such motion. But the motion of the eyes is seen to be revolving; the motion of the arms toward within; the motion of the feet forward. But what can be said of the liver, spleen, heart, genitals, tongue, and lips, which seem so remote from one another? Yet no one as yet has held that there is a soul proper to each of them; rather, all these are vivified, governed, and ruled in common by one soul, which is the soul of the whole /798b/ body.

Moreover, if Plato held that all the heavens and the whole sublunar world were moved and ruled by diverse motions at the same time, for what purpose did he hold that it was composed, especially from the same and the other,[174] unless it was because the diversity of the world required these two natures, since it had a part that was as if the same, that is, persisting and remaining in one state, namely, the heavenly part, which contains the nine previously mentioned heavens, and the sublunar part, to which there belongs such a great mutability and such a great diversity, especially with respect to the state of the

---

174 See Plato, *Timaeus* 35AB.

lower elements and of those things that are in them, that almost nothing in them remains in the same state.

Moreover, the bodies of animals and plants are made of the elements and composed from the other, because they are composed from contraries. For the elements are contraries, as you have learned elsewhere. It is not surprising, therefore, since each soul has to fit its body as the perfection of it and the form of its proper matter—it is not surprising if someone held that part of the soul of the whole world was the same[175] and part other on account of the correspondence that I said that it ought to have to the same and the other.

Moreover, since the nine mobile heavens are individuals either of the same species or of diverse species, how did Plato hold that they have a single soul rather than that many human beings or many other animals do?

Moreover, he who held that there is one soul for diverse bodies that are able to exist by themselves or similarly that there is one form for diverse matters that are able to exist by themselves does not seem to have known the nature of the soul in the way it is soul nor the nature of form in the way it is form. I say this on account of the members of human beings and of other animals that are not able to exist by themselves, but in their wholes and from them, and for this reason the soul of the whole suffices for the whole and the parts of each one, especially since all the parts have a mediated or immediate connection to one another, as it is in all the members of animals. But the heavens do not have a connection to one another except one of contiguity. Contiguity, however, is not a connection sufficient to bring it about that one soul should suffice for many bodies. Hence, he who says that this is the reason does not say why there has to be one soul in the nine mobile heavens.

But if he says that there are other connections of those heavens that are not undeservedly unknown by human beings because of their being far distant from them, I say to this that this fellow does not know the motions of these heavens and the diversities of their motions. For their diversity is such that they have diverse centers and poles and on this account diverse regions. Moreover, the motion of each is continuous and unfailing and total, that is, in terms of every part. For no part in any of them is at rest, but in human beings and other animals it is different. For no part has its proper motion by itself from the interior except the heart, as I said. But the other parts from the interior are not moved except by the motion of the whole. The exterior parts, however, are moved by the command of the whole. And you know the cause of their motions.

---

175 I have followed the reading in the margin, namely, "*idem*," instead of "*quidam*," which is in the text.

It is evident, therefore, from these points that the heavens are not related to one another as members or parts of the higher mobile world since they are so divided from one another both by their motions and by the centers, regions, and poles of the moved, that they can in no way be considered either parts or members of it.

Moreover, they hold that the souls of the heavens produce only this in their bodies, namely, that they are moved in a circle, for they do not produce nutritive life in them, but only such motion. Because, therefore, the motions are so diverse, so diverse from one another and so appropriate to their movers, as their immediate and essential effects, it is necessary that the movers be diverse. For it is not possible that /799a/ such acts diverse in species go forth by themselves and immediately from one power by a natural operation. But these motions are natural operations, and there are only such operations of the movers in their bodies. That is, they do not have any other influence on them, unless perhaps they say that it is something else besides motion, which is not seen. For such bodies do not need the conservation or restoration that is produced by nourishment or other things since those who have had this opinion hold that they are naturally incorruptible. This argument leads them to the point that they are necessarily forced to hold many movers for the previously mentioned heavens on account of the multitude of them. And for this reason <they> also <are forced to hold> many souls, since all circular motion is a soul or comes from a soul.

But he might say that nothing prevents many powers of movement from being in the members of animals, and nothing prevents each of the mobile members from having its proper power, although the soul is one, from which, as from one star of many rays, there proceed all those powers, like many rays. And in that way, from that soul of the first of the mobile heavens eight moving powers go forth into the eight lower heavens. I say to this that these words disagree with the opinion of Plato in this respect, since he held contrariety in the motions of the heavens.[176] He held that the seven heavens of the planets move from west to east and that the motion of the eighth heaven is just the opposite. But it is impossible that contrariety come from one principle by itself and immediately.

But if he says that Plato did not hold that this soul was one properly and truly, but that he held many and contrary ones, since he held that it was composed of the same and the other, which without a doubt are contraries, I say to this that either each part of this composition is in one heaven or those two parts are in diverse heavens. But if they are in one heaven so that neither of them is

176 See Plato, *Timaeus* 38 C–E.

in the other, they ought[177] to move that heaven by two contrary motions. But this is found in none of the heavens, and it is evident that it is impossible.

But if he says that part is in one of the heavens and part in another, there will not be one soul from them, just as there is not <one body> from their bodies, that is, from the heavens in which they are. Moreover, in this way then, it is as if it were said that one soul is composed from the soul that is in the body of Socrates and the soul that is in the body of Plato.

Moreover, in one body there is one soul, I mean in an animate body that is by itself one and divided from the others. Because, therefore, according to him all the heavens are animated, this will not be by numerically one soul, but by as many souls as there are heavens, just as it is in other individuals of animated beings, both human beings and the other animals and also plants.

Moreover, the heavens that are moved from west to east in a way contrary to the first motion, as he held, do not have a diversity or contrariety in their motions, but are rather motions of the same <directions> and uniform in terms of their times, just as the first motion is. There is no reason, therefore, why the motion is diverse or their motion is otherwise than the motion of the first, unless he perhaps wants to say that this is on account of pauses and retrogressions, risings, descents, epicycles, and the motions of these and the motions of the others, which Ptolemy put there for the reason that you heard and in the way you learned elsewhere.

I respond to this and say that those who held this diversity of motions in the planets and cycles, likewise held many diversities in the fixed stars, and they placed forward and backward motion in the head of the Ram and in the head of the Libra. But if they hold that this whole soul is in the first mobile heaven, they will hold that the lower heavens are not animated. From where, then, do they have their motion? But if they[178] hold that the whole of it is in each of the mobile heavens, then the motion /799b/ ought to be the same and other in each, since those two motions have, as causes and as principles of their being, the two parts of that soul, which are the same and the other. But he might have understood the same and the other in the soul like two respects or comparisons, which that soul has, namely, one toward the same, to the creator, that is, to the unity and immutability of the creator himself, but the second toward the other, that is, toward the diversity and mutability[179] of the sublunar world, in which there is such a great variety and multitude and diversity of things through so many motions and changes. It is as if he intended the one

---

177 I have conjectured "*debent*" instead of "*debet*."

178 I have conjectured "*posuerint*" instead of "*posuerit*."

179 I have conjectured "*mutabilitatem*" instead of "*immutabilitatem*."

or being one on the side of the creator, in which and according to which it is not split or divided either in powers or operations. But it is split and divided on the side of the sublunar world by countless powers and operations, both according to Plato and according to Aristotle and his followers and all those who believed the judgments of the stars.[180] For all such people held that the whole diversity of things that can be generated and corrupted and also of all events that happen in the sublunar world are caused by the higher world or heaven, and this on account of its soul or souls. For it is impossible for a body, in the way in which it is a body, to have a power productive of such noble and such multiple operations. On account of this same and other, therefore, Plato held an angular and bifurcated form for this soul, and he did so only in a comparison according to his custom, by which, as Aristotle said, he aims at comparisons.[181] You have also learned elsewhere that no noble or intelligent soul is divisible by bodily partition or division,[182] nor does an angular or bi-furcated form fit it in any way.

It seems difficult to understand that a soul existing in one body can oper-ate on very remote bodies and that our souls are acted upon by foreign and remote bodies rather than that they make impressions on them. How then in earth and in waters and in air are so many and such noble works produced by this soul if not by intellect and will? For the body of such a soul, whether it is one or many, as I already told you, is not like an instrument of production so that the production of animals and plants takes place by touching, impress-ing, pounding, or in another way of that sort. It is, therefore, evident to you, as was shown to you elsewhere, that the operation of that soul on the things I mentioned and the <production> of them, that is, of animals and plants, is only spiritual, that is, only by a spiritual will, as you have heard in the preceding chapters concerning the operation of the creator, who by his omnipotent and most imperious word spoke and they were made and by his most dominant will he commanded and they were created.[183]

---

180 See *Timaeus* 41E–42D; for Aristotle and his followers, see Avicenna, *Metaphysics* 9.2–4; ed. Van Reit, p. 447–488; from the title of his book one can assume that William is referring to Abumasar; see above note 161.

181 See perhaps Aristotle, *Metaphysics* 12.8.1074b3–11, where in the translation in *Aristotelis metaphysicorum libri cum Averrois Cordubensis in eosdem commentariis* (Venice: Junctas, 1562), fol. 333vLM, Aristotle claims that all other accounts of the first mover are like myths (*fabulae*).

182 On the indivisibility of the human soul, see William, *On the Soul*, ch. 2, pt. 10; Paris-Orléans ed., II, 80a–80b.

183 On creation by the word of God, see *The Universe* Ia-IIae, ch. 22; Paris-Orléans ed., I, 614b–616a.

But according to this position it turns out that the motions of the heavens, the stars, and the planets, do not produce sublunar things or act upon them except in terms of four elementary and radical natures or qualities, which are heat, moistness, dryness, and cold. For that soul operates through intelligence and will alone and does not need the heavens or their motions or the stars or the planets or their motions. With them all standing still and at rest, it will produce the same operations in the sublunar world. This opinion, therefore, destroys the judgments of astronomy that rest entirely upon the previously mentioned motions of bodies and things that follow upon that motion, which are conjunctions, oppositions of appearances, configurations, risings, and settings. And for this reason astronomers consider and observe all these and from them form their judgments. Moreover, there can be no doubt that the intelligence and will of that soul depends in no way upon the previously mentioned /800a/ motions. Otherwise, it would be the most inconstant and mutable of all souls, since nothing is more mobile than such bodies and nothing more inconstant than the shapes of the constellations.

Moreover, since human souls are far closer to modifications and changes on account of the passivity of their bodies and accordingly are changeable by means of their bodies, and since their intelligences and wills do not follow the motions of bodies, but rather just the opposite, it will of necessity be impossible that the intelligence and will of that soul follow the previously mentioned motions. Hence, such operations do not follow them since they come from the soul through intelligence and will.

Moreover, who would say that it shapes the triangular or four-sided appearances or others and that it intends them, since they come about of necessity through the motions of the heavens without its intending or thinking about them? For it is evident that it is superfluous either to intend or to think about those things that still come about without their being intended.

Moreover, according to this, it will cause the pauses, retrogressions, risings, descents, and all the other configurations of the constellations, and it will cause this only through intelligence and will. Hence, it will knowingly disturb and confuse the heavenly motions through intelligence and will, although its intelligence cannot err and its will can only be correct.

Moreover, it is evident concerning our souls that by their own motions, that is, of their bodies, they do not intend one of the above mentioned configurations unless such a configuration is necessary for some other operation. For at times human beings form themselves into a circular figure, for example, for leading choruses, or for lifting a burden that has a certain figure they form themselves similarly, or they form themselves into a parallel figure or a figure of length only or also into some other, as the necessity of the operation that they intend to carry out demands.

But a triangular or quadrangular or some other appearance can in no way help an operation that comes from intelligence and will by itself and alone. Otherwise, such an operation would not come by itself through intelligence and will, as the operation of weaving or of building do not, concerning which it is evident to you that, although they are done through intelligence or imagination and will, they are not done through them alone or from them alone. Rather, they are done through instruments.

Moreover, what would happen to what Aristotle says and to what is also evident from the testimony of the senses concerning the powers of seeds, whose operations are so evident, if <these powers> were not in seeds or did not operate in them? The alternative to this is necessarily the case, if by that soul, which Plato said is the soul of the world,[184] all these things that are generated and corrupted under the sphere of the moon, namely, human beings, animals, and plants, were generated by the intelligence and will of that soul alone. For such powers in seeds would be superfluous and useless if the intelligence and will of the soul of the world were by itself sufficient for such operations.

But if someone says that the moving powers productive of the other operations are also in the members of animals, although there is one soul in each animal, and that those powers are not, nonetheless, superfluous, I say to this that this statement is destroyed in two ways: first, because according to it human beings and other animals will be members of this animal, whose soul is that soul, that is, the soul of the world. And on this account, as no member of an animal is an animal, so neither will a human being nor some other animal be an animal, but they will be members of that great and very monstrous and most horrifying animal, and consequently it will result from this that /800b/ there will be a soul in no human being or the other animals, nor will the human soul be a soul, except equivocally, since no perfection of any of the members of human beings or of the other animals is or is said to be an animal, nor will human beings be many animals or one animal, and on this account neither one human being nor many.

Such a statement is destroyed secondly by the fact that it is impossible for a soul that is outside any body to animate it or to give it life or to perfect it, since every perfection is an essential part of what is perfected and of necessity has being from it and in it. Hence, just as the soul that is in Socrates cannot animate or give life to Plato or in any other way be a perfection of him, so the soul of the heaven or the soul of the eighth heaven or of any other body cannot be the perfection of any of the human beings, animals, or plants that

---

184 See *Timaeus* 30B–D.

are among us, that is, under the lunar orbit. But because I told you in the preceding paragraphs[185] about this soul that <supposedly acts> in retrogressions, risings, descents, and other motions of this sort, such as the besetting of planets, eclipses, and all the others by which the astronomers have held their powers and operations are impeded, and because I did not state on this the complete account by which the argument or proof that I intended might be made solid, I will reinforce this proof here.

I say, therefore, that, if that soul causes those things that I have listed and named for you, it causes them knowingly or unknowingly and in ignorance and for this reason violently or unwillingly. But if it knowingly produces the impediments to the operations of the planets, how then does it move them, since all the astronomers hold that they are moved by motions and configurations of motion, and all the philosophers are in agreement with the astronomers?

Moreover, why does it make them move backward? Is it because they went forth more than is right, beyond what it commanded, or because they were moved too fast, or because it repents of having moved them so far? Hence, it is necessary that they be moved apart from its command and its will, either partially or wholly.

Moreover, how does it beset them, placing one of them between two evil ones where the astronomers have written that its power is amazingly bound? And for what reason does it frequently eclipse the sun and moon and at times others? With what benefit or use does it seek and procure so many and such great evils for such bodies, and this evil does not befall the brute soul so that it knowingly moves the body in which it is or a member or some of the members to an impediment of it or an injury to its power. For much better reason then it is not possible that it befall that most noble and most wise soul.

But if it does this unknowingly, this statement is very mistaken, because, even if this ignorance in it were natural, it would have been removed a thousand times by such a long experience and acquired knowledge contrary to it. For we see in brute animals many instances of natural ignorance are removed by experience and that they are taught in many things as if through a discipline, so that we even see that some of them talk or speak,[186] if such a mimicking of human speech should be called speech. How then has this ignorance lasted so long in the soul of the world?

Moreover, these astronomers, who were human beings and also are short-lived and far from these motions, the configurations of them, and the other things I listed and named for you, discovered by their investigations and observations

---

185 See above in this chapter.

186 I have conjectured "*dicere*" instead of "*discere*."

the operations of the heavens. How then can the soul of the world be ignorant of some of all these?

Moreover, since the motions of our bodies and members are very well known to our souls and since this is accomplished through their imagination or intelligence and will, how /801a/ will all the heavenly motions or configuratis of motions escape the notice of the soul of the world since they are produced by its intelligence and will?

But if he says that such impediments of their powers happen to the planets against its will, there is, therefore, another power moving the heavens and the planets than the soul of the world. But none of the philosophers held that any of these is moved except by a soul, and Plato himself did not. Hence, there will be another soul moving the heavens or other souls moving them apart from this soul of the world, and there will be the same question and the same difficulty about this.

It also follows upon this error in many ways that there is violence, conflict, and a sort of fight and rebellion in the heavens. But none of the philosophers have said this.

CHAPTER 29
He Explains What Plato Thought about the Soul of the World,
Where He Deals with the Error
of Those Who Say That the One Soul of the World Animates
Whatever Is Animated

With these points set forth for the sake of exercise and of explaining the truth, I say with regard to the opinion of Plato that the opinion of Plato was not in my view that the whole bodily world was one living being, but only the heaven, that is, the whole that is from the moon up or the last of the higher mobile spheres, which Plato perhaps believed to be the sphere of the fixed stars. For the ninth sphere may have escaped his attention, just as the tenth escaped his attention and that of the other philosophers. Only the Christian teaching, of course, holds the tenth heaven, which it calls the empyrean, that is, the bright or gleaming heaven,[187] and Avicenna seems to have held this and to have agreed with Plato where he said that "the heaven is

---

187 One of the propositions that William condemned on 13 January 1241 was "that glorified souls are not in the empyrean heaven with the angels, but are in the aqueous or crystalline heaven, which is the firmament," *Chartularium universitatis Parisienis* I, no. 128 (Paris: Delalain, 1889–1897), p. 170 (my translation). See *The Universe* Ia-Iae, chs. 42–44 on the production of the heavens and on the empyrean heaven as the dwelling of human souls and angels.

a" certain "living being obedient to God,"[188] and according to this, the world seems to have been called that from the excellence of its cleanliness and purity or from the ultimate degree of its nobility and velocity.

But Abusamar, the Saracen,[189] in his book on the explanation of Aristotle's *Hearing* said that God is the spirit of the heaven, which he understood about the creator, and he erred intolerably. You should also not doubt that he was blinded by a most blameworthy ignorance. For in the supereminence of his nobility and the ultimate degree of freedom, the creator is in things in such a way that he is neither united nor bound to them or to any one of them. For every spirit that is truly said to be united to a body is bound to its body by a natural chain so that it either cannot exist outside of it or can exist well only in all respects in it and with it. But I say this on account of the human souls existing in the society of the blessed angels, for those souls have well-being, but not in all respects. That is to say that their beatitude or glory is not yet complete because all their powers, through which they operated in their bodies, remain to be perfected and glorified for them. But it is evident to you from the ultimate degree of his glory how far from the creator is all incompleteness and all defect. Because so great an error should not readily be believed concerning so great a philosopher, I think that it is more likely that he understood his words by participation,[190] that is, that he considered him the spirit of the heaven on account of its nobility and its approach to the nobility and divinity of the creator, not in that intention or concept by which God is said to be the creator. In that intention nothing shares with him. In fact, that name is the proper and incommunicable name of the creator. On this account it does not have a plural, because his divinity is multiplied in no way. Therefore, "God" /801b/ and "gods" are said equivocally of every other and of all others and is in no way said in that meaning or intention. In that way, then, Abumasar should be thought to have called the spirit of the heaven god, like Jupiter or Apollo, and also in the same way some have not been afraid to call the world

188 Avicenna, *Metaphysics* 9.1; ed. Van Reit, p. 446.

189 Although William gives the name of Abumasar for this commentary on Aristotle's *Physics*, R. De Vaux says that Abumasar or Albumasar, the astronomer, did not comment on that work, and argues that it is really Alfarabi, who was at times called by the Latins Avennasar, Abunazar, or Albunasar and who composed a gloss on the *Physics*, which was translated by Gerard of Cremona. See *Notes et textes*, pp. 20–21.

190 William uses "*transumptio*," which is a translation of the Greek μετάληψις.

itself god.[191] One of the Italian philosophers mocking them said in his book on this, "What beauty can this rotund god have?"[192]

With regard to what is asked about the other heavens, whether they are animated by that same soul or each of them has its own soul, it seems that it should more suitably be said according to Plato that each of them is animated by its own soul, because he understood that the one whole aggregate of those souls is composed from the same and the diverse on account of the connection that the heavens have to one another. In the same way the same Plato held that the head, heart, and womb in human beings is a living being and that each human being is still a living being, just as the world is commonly called one whole or one universe by people. But he placed the one or the unity that he held in that soul in the heaven, which he thought to be the principal and most noble among the heavens. But he seems to have understood the other of this soul to be the aggregate of all souls of the other heavens, both on account of the multitude and diversity of them and on account of the diversity that is seen in their motions as well as the opposition to the motion of that heaven that he thought most noble and principal.

You ought also to know that Plato held that in a human being the head was the man, while the rest was like a column to support and carry the man, that is, the head, on high.[193] In that way he also held that the most noble part of the bodily universe standing above all the rest of it was the soul and that the rest was like a vehicle or support to hold or carry that animal on high. Nor would Plato deny that the members of a human being are parts of a human being on account of the common usage in naming a human being. For a human being is commonly and usually not called the head alone, but is understood to be the whole that is composed from the head and what is under it. And Plato understood that the whole was called a man from that part rising above the whole, as the whole is called a human being (*homo*) from earth (*humus*) because he is terrestrial or earthly. Although, then, it was the habit of Plato to use metaphors, this intention of his words still seems the more likely about the soul of the world.

But you ought to know that they were so blinded and so intellectually deficient that they believed that the numerically one soul of the world animated whatever is animated in the world and that the soul of Socrates was not something other than the soul of Plato in terms of essence and truth, but another soul, and this as a result of the otherness of the animation and of what

---

191 See Augustine, *City of God* 7.6; PL 41: 199–200.

192 See Cicero, *The Nature of the Gods* (*De natura deorum*) 10.24.

193 See Plato, *Timaeus* 44DE.

is animated.[194] As a result of this they necessarily had to admit that Socrates was not something other than Plato in terms of essence and truth, but other as a result of the previously mentioned otherness. Hence, according to them, there will not be generation and corruption in human beings and other things although, according to Aristotle, generation in things terminates in a substance, and corruption is an departure from it,[195] and they do not take place in terms of accidents, but rather in terms of substantial forms. For such changes, namely, those that take place according to accidents or accidental forms are alterations, not generations or corruptions.

Moreover, in terms of accidents, neither human beings nor other things are counted, nor are they said to be one person and another or one thing and another. Nor is Socrates formerly a lad and now an old man counted as one person and another person or as two human beings, although the /802a/ old man differs from himself as a lad by numerous accidents.[196] Hence, if there is not among human beings a difference of another kind than in terms of accidents, number will not be found among them, nor will there be many persons or many things, but one and the same man, like Socrates formerly a lad and now an old man. But in the destruction of this error one should not use arguments and proofs, but fire and the sword and every kind of penal destruction.

And let not the words of one from among the Italian philosophers disturb you who said that only a variety of accidents produces numerical difference,[197] because his intention in this was only to exclude specific difference or other substantial differences, or he referred the understanding of these words to us, understanding this difference as our distinction. His intention in these words, therefore, was that only a variety of accidents, that is, not a species, substantial difference, or one of the common essential characteristics produces numerical difference, that is, diversifies individuals themselves or produces for us a numerical distinction of individuals. For in a species we do not distinguish

194 The position that William is criticizing held that soul in a plurality of people is individuated by diverse accidents, while remaining the same in its essence and truth. This is close to the view that William attributed to Aristotle and his followers earlier in *De universo* Ia-Iae, ch. 26, 619bC. See my "William of Auvergne on the Individuation of Human Souls," *Traditio* 49 (1994): 77–93, where I argue that William really has Avicenna in mind.

195 See Aristotle, *Physics* 7.3.246a4–9.

196 That is, William is claiming that different accidents do not constitute numerical difference, though he admits that we recognize numerically different substances by their different accidents.

197 See Boethius, *How the Trinity is One God* (*Quomodo Trinitas unus Deus*) 1; PL 64: 1249.

individuals, but rather unite them by an essential likeness of every kind, which belongs to them in the species or, rather, which is the species itself, according to him. He himself said that a species is the substantial likeness of individuals,[198] and you ought to understand what I said, namely, substantial, that is, in terms of the whole substance. For apart from the concept of a species, nothing has a substantial individual. Know, however, that such a likeness is commonly called identity in species.

Nor should you doubt that, if our intellect were here illuminated by the illumination of its ultimate glory, it would distinguish and count <individuals> in its own species, not by an unlikeness, because they have none in the species, but by the diversity by which it would see that this one is not that one, and the converse, and it would count with complete truth and would say one thing, another thing, and a third. But in the state of such a dark misery it is illuminated to count and distinguish them only by the variety of accidents—I mean of sensible accidents— unless by prophetic splendor or by some other splendor of human irradiation coming from above, it receives the gift to be able to do this.

I also say, as you have learned elsewhere, that just as the brute soul is not perfective of a human body or of a human being, so on this account and for much better reason this heavenly soul that Plato held will not be perfective of human bodies or of other animal or vegetative bodies, since there is a much greater diversity between a heavenly body and a human body than between a human body and brute bodies. And it is necessary that it be the same way with the souls of the other heavens, if he held souls for them or that they are animated.

I shall return, therefore, and say that Plato seems to have held that this soul is only in one heaven or in the universe containing the nine mobile heavens. But with regard to what I said in the preceding chapters against such statements of Plato about the divisions and diversity of the heavens, namely, that they prevent one soul from animating all of the heavens, know that it is easy for many natures and more noble living things to have connections to one another and for them to be firmed up and strengthened through the contact of their bodies.

But one example in natures is the contact of iron and adamantine or even a magnet, which has far less power than adamantine in this respect. For, when iron touches adamantine or even a magnet, it attracts another piece of iron and that piece another, and this perhaps is endless. Hence, if a pin touches such a stone, it receives from the touch such a power of attracting and of gluing, as

---

198 Boethius, *Commentaries on the Topics of Cicero* (*In Topica Ciceronis commentariorum libri sex*) 3; PL 64: 1089.

it were, another pin to itself, and the second pin does the same with another, and the third /802b/ operates in the same way on the fourth, and the fourth on the fifth, and it has so far not been proved for me by experience whether this has an end or stops at a certain number of pins. For you will see that the first pin of those ordered in this way hangs from this stone which it touches; then that the second pin adheres to it by a similar contact, and the third, the fourth, and so on with the others. Since, therefore, the power of the adamantine by which it makes the first pin to adhere to it is transferred to all the pins, why is it surprising if the vivifying or animal power of the first heaven is transferred to the second, and from the second to the third, and so on until it comes to the last of the mobile heavens, which is the heaven of the moon, even if there is not another bond or bonding between them than contiguity or contact, as is seen in the proposed example.

Moreover, in grafting onto trees it is evident to you from sensation that vital power is transferred from the trunk to the branch inserted into it, although they clung to each other by no other connection than contact. Why, then, is it surprising if that life of the first heaven pours itself into the second, and so on with the others?

Moreover, in the opposites of life itself you will find countless transferences, as in the diseases of a human being—and this is a matter of no slight admiration for me—because, when one person suffering from epilepsy falls down, many fall down. You see, therefore, that this disease also transfers itself to those present, and especially to children, on account of the nearness of contiguity. The laxative and purgative medicine also transfers by sight alone its power and noxious humors to one who looks at it, and it empties them out. It is also very well known to you regarding the power of fire and other active powers how they transfer their operations to things near them that can be acted upon and are receptive of their operations and that contact is the path for such operations.

Hence, if that first and most noble heaven is, according to Plato, the seat of that soul and, for this reason, has in it the greatest overflow of life from the very presence of that fountain, why is it surprising if it pours life and motion and other operations of souls into the bodies of the subsequent heavens, since from their likeness to that heaven and their most noble dispositions, such bodies are naturally most apt for receiving such influxes and are receptive of them? For in that way it seems to me that, according to the intention of Plato, that heaven had in itself the source of life and of motion, as the sun has the source of light and of heat, and pours them forth by a similar generosity into things that are receptive.

But if someone says that those outpourings are souls or only animal outpourings, it makes no difference, I think, according to the opinion of Plato. That is,
it does not seem problematic to grant that they are really souls since he himself
said that certain parts of living beings are living beings, and Aristotle did not
shrink from saying that the soul of the eye is sight or the power of sight.[199]

But if someone objects that, in accord with this, there will be one soul and
another soul, this too is not problematic for many people, that is, that the
power of sight comes to be from the soul of the whole animal, whether of a
human being or of something else. Nor does anyone intelligent doubt that the
perfection of the eye by which it is a living and natural instrument of seeing, is
a perfection of the natural body only by the power of the living being or of the
being having life. Hence, it will necessarily be a soul according to this account
of Aristotle, unless Aristotle perhaps wanted to understand with regard to the
whole body that it is able to exist by itself, not in another or from another, and
someone would perhaps not unreasonably understand this.

But it has already been explained to you elsewhere by me that it is impossible
that the soul of a child come from the soul of the parent.[200] But in Aristotle
and his followers it is not thought to be problematic that /803a/ an intelligence
should come from an intelligence until one comes to the last, which they call
the mover of the heaven or of the sphere of the moon.[201] But <they say that>
the first intelligence is only from the creator by way of creation, while the
second is from the first, as I have told you elsewhere.[202] It follows, therefore,
that they do not think it problematic that the soul of the second heaven comes
from the first soul or from the intelligence of the first heaven. They were also
not afraid to say that our souls are created by the intelligences, misusing in an
intolerable way the word "create" and "creation," which is an operation proper
to and possible for the blessed creator, attributing it to a creature in a most
impious error.[203]

---

199 Aristotle, *On the Soul* 2.2.412b18–21.

200 See William, *On the Soul* ch. 5, pt. 1; Paris-Orléans ed., II, 110a–112b.

201 Here William attributes Avicenna's emanation of the intelligences to Aristotle
himself, as he does elsewhere. See Avicenna, *Metaphysics* 9.4.; ed. Van Reit, p.
487, and see also William, *The Universe* Ia-IIae, chs. 2–4; Paris-Orléans ed., I,
808a–811b.

202 See William, *The Universe* Ia-Iae, ch. 24; Paris-Orléans ed., I, 618b–619a.

203 See William, *The Universe* Ia-IIae, ch. 31; Paris-Orléans ed., I, 833a–833b.

CHAPTER 30

The Error of Those Who Hold that the Soul of the World Is Composed
Of Numbers and Musical Harmonies Is Destroyed,
And the Explanation of Plato's Comparison

Plato applied and adapted numbers to the form of that soul, and he stated that they enter, as it were, into its composition from the very fabric of the world, for which he held such a soul, as he is seen to have admitted. For he held that the distances that stretch from the earth up to the ninth, in fact, up to eighth heaven, according to him, are proportional to the numbers that he put in its shape, and he held that the whole world and its parts are musical, according to what I could understand about him, naturally suited and connected to one another in harmonious proportions and, for this reason, the soul of the world itself, which necessarily had to harmonize with and fit its body, was naturally united and somehow composed by similar connections, as I touched upon for you above when I spoke about the same and the other of it.[204] He was guided by the force and power of harmonious proportions, which are, as he said, so powerful in our souls that our whole souls seemed to be placed in their power. They do, of course, change them with a marvelous ease in terms of the dispositions that are in the concupiscible and irascible power,[205] and they do this at the desire or pleasure of the musician, if he is trained and clearly expert in the musical art. For they change them with an incredible speed from sorrow to joy, and the converse, from turbulence to tranquility and serenity, from fear to hope or confidence, from pusillanimity to magnificence, and the converse. Hence it is that, since Plato believed that nothing is naturally delighted save by its like, he believed, on account of the very powerful delights that our souls have in harmonies, that our souls are very similar to them and for this reason are composed of musical harmonies. And for this reason he thought the same thing about the soul of the world, adding, as it were, a twofold music to the world. For, since human music does not exceed twice the octave, he stated that the heavenly music rises to four times the whole octave. But because he was a philosopher, Philolaus, was moved by the same reason and held that the human soul was a harmony and consequently that the soul of the world was.[206]

---

204 See above ch. 29; 801b.

205 The concupiscible and irascible powers were sense appetites concerned with immediately attractive sensible goods and with difficult sensible goods respectively.

206 Philolaus of Croton (ca. 470–ca. 385 BC) was a Pythagorean philosopher who held that the whole world and everything in it had or was a harmony.

This position, however, is destroyed in many ways and manners, and first of all because similar things are not merely distasteful to, but cause sadness to our souls. For only someone who is cold is delighted by heat, and only someone hot <is delighted> by cold. And only someone who is hungry or thirsty is delighted by food or drink. Thus motion makes rest delightful, and the converse. And in this way it is possible to find the same thing in many other cases.

Moreover, according to this view, our souls would have delight only in things that can be counted and measured. /803b/ Hence, they would have no delight in simple and incorporeal things, namely, in ones that do not have bodily quantity; hence, <they would have no delight> in the sciences, in the virtues, or even in the creator, in whom it is agreed there is the ultimate of delight and the beatific health of our souls.

Moreover, as our souls seek harmonies by such great desires and make musical instruments for themselves out of a love for musical sweetness, so that soul will seek to a much greater extent those harmonies, and especially ones most fitting its nature and composition, so that, if it were possible, it would make all the heavens resound with harmonious melodies.

But Aristotle has already explained that the heaven cannot resound with or have a musical sound or any other.[207] For sounds have no place there, just as musical instruments do not. But every sound is produced by a violent striking. In the heavens, however, violence or striking have no place and, on this account, neither does sound, especially since air, when compressed by such a striking, emits sound. But it is impossible that there be air in the heavens since its natural place is within the sphere of the moon beneath the sphere of fire. Aristotle also explained that sound is a disposition impressed[208] upon the air by a striking and that for this reason it bears such an impression for so long, that is, for as long as the striking impels it, after which it is no longer heard.[209] Hence it is that neither hair nor fur nor wool makes or impresses a sound unless it is condensed and compacted, because otherwise it is unable to produce a striking of the air, nor does it seem that sound can be produced in water, and the sound of the sea that is heard does not come from the striking of water on water or from the collision of sea water on the shores or cliffs without air in between. For air is receptive of this disposition in every way, and on this account many of the ancients defined sound as air that has been struck or beaten, which account is clearly material. A soul, therefore, would have been unsuitably collocated in the higher part of the bodily world, that

---

207 See Aristotle, *On the Heavens* 2.9.290b12-291a25.

208 I have conjectured "*impressa*" instead of "*impressam*."

209 See Aristotle, *On the Soul* 2.8.419b4–420b4.

is, in something so dissimilar to its nature that, although it is composed of harmonious numbers, there would be no harmony in that region of it.

But if someone says that there is a spiritual or intellectual harmony there in the numbers of motions and their proportions, I say that this is a statement of an obvious impossibility. For the motion of the eighth sphere in relation to the motion of the sphere or star of Saturn is in a proportion of thirty years to one day. I mean diurnal motion. For on each natural day the eighth sphere describes or passes through its whole self, as it were. But, according to Plato, the star of Saturn passes through the same distance in no less than thirty years. But the star of Jupiter passes through the whole circle of the signs in twelve years.

But it is evident that these proportions are not harmonious. He also held that the heavenly music does not exceed four times the whole octave, but four times the whole octave is only the proportion contained in sixteen or in accord with it. For the proportion in sixteen continuously contains four doubles, of which the first is from sixteen to eight, the second from eight to four, the third from four to two, the fourth from two to one.[210] But the previously mentioned proportions are much greater.

But if someone says that between the spheres of the planets or their motions there are harmonious proportions, this statement too is likewise obviously erroneous. For the proportion of the motion of the sphere or star of Saturn to the motion of the sphere or star of Jupiter is the proportion of thirty to twelve. But this is double once and a half according to their mean course. But, if made equal, the course produces a far different proportion between them and one not at all harmonious according to the truth. For if the equaled course /804a/ and the mean course were of precisely the same quantity, there would really be a proportion between the motions of these two planets, namely, Saturn and Jupiter, composed of an octave and a fifth. In the other planets too, after you have examined their motions with a true equalization, you will find that proportions of their motions are not at all harmonious, and if you make a more careful consideration through their retrogressions and pauses, you will find that the proportions of their motions are different from harmonious dispositions and, if there were other <proportions> between those motions, they would in many ways turn them away.

But it is up to you to see whether what he held concerning distances and proportions agrees with the proofs of Ptolemy and others, although the proportions of the distances are seen to have to be more, as I touched upon for you in the preceding. For all the mobile heavens are seen to be proportional in

---

210 See Plato, *Timaeus* 35B as the possible source, where Plato has the series 1, 2, 4, and 8.

magnitude and thickness or density. The contrary, that is, a contrary relation, seems an unfitting deformity for the higher world. There will not, therefore, be those proportions of distances that Plato held. I think these and similar things should be left to your consideration.

Moreover, that other, which he held to be a part of the soul, is either other according to its essence, that is, having in itself this part and that part, or it is other only in terms of its powers and operations. But if it is other according to its essence, the same question will arise about those parts, that is, whether they are divisible into parts and gathered together from a multitude or not. And that other is not composed of a continuation or continuity of parts, for such a composition is only that of a body. For such a composition belongs only and essentially to a body. Hence, those parts will be gathered together from simple or indivisible parts and those, of course, finite. Otherwise, the being of that soul would be infinite and unintelligible and interminable for the intellect and non-traversable. But this and every other philosophy rejects such positions. For no one who is truly wise philosophizes about unintelligible things. Therefore, that other will be gathered together from finite simple parts, and they will necessarily be substances, since they are parts of that substance, which is this other.

These substances, therefore, will be either living or not living, and again either intelligent or not intelligent. But if they are intelligent and living, they will, then, be noble substances and will be souls, intelligences, or angelic spirits. Hence, part of that soul will be composed of souls, intelligences, or angelic spirits. But you know full well how problematic and as yet unheard of this is. But if those parts were not living, the whole, therefore, will for much better reason be not living. It is impossible, however, that something living be composed of not living and dead things.

But if he says that the other is not other by a diversity of parts gathered together in its composition, but by a diversity of powers and operations that come from it, then the remaining part of the same soul will for much better reason not be the other, since of necessity there comes from it a greater diversity and multitude of operations, as from one higher and more noble than that other is. For the higher and the more noble every power is, the more multiple it is in powers and operations, and especially if it is united to a body, as is clearly seen in the rational soul, which is far more multiple in its powers and operations than the brute soul, and the brute soul more than the vegetative soul. But how could someone maintain that one <soul> was gathered together or composed in any other way from some substances or powers unless because of a defect and feebleness of the intellect he could not see? I say this, however, on account of the feeble-minded and misguided /804b/ folk who dare to hold that either the rational soul or any other noble substance is gathered together from simple substances or powers, from whose operations or powers it is impossible that one \<soul\> be composed. For this is as if someone said that one power was gathered together or in some other manner composed from the power of sight and the power of hearing.

Moreover, if according to the truth, numbers entered into the composition of the soul of the world, it would be composed from them, according to the truth of its essence. Hence, of necessity the number would be in the truth of its essence, and on this account it would not be a true substance; in fact, its essence, both in its truth and genus, would be quantity, and on this account it would be in a subject and would not itself be a genuine subject.

Moreover, the unities from which that number would exist would be either substances or accidents. If they were substances, the question I raised earlier returns, because they are either living and intelligent or not, and so on. But if they are accidents, it is impossible that anything but an accident be made from them.

Moreover, as there are harmonious proportions in those numbers, so there are also the contrary proportions. For, just as there are in them nine and eight, and six and four, three and two and one,[211] which have harmonious proportion to one another, so there are in them nine or seven, and five and three, and nine and five, and seven and four, whose proportions are completely contrary to harmonies. Hence, just as the first numbers produced a resonance in that soul in relation to one another, so these latter produce a contrary dissonance in it and a greater dissonance, inasmuch as they have more discordant proportions than those which are connected to one another by harmonious proportions. Therefore, this composition will be no less inept by reason of such dissonances than it is apt by reason of the consonances.

It is evident to you, therefore, through those things that have gone before that Plato did not hold such a composition for the heavenly soul according to reality and the truth, and this is clearly seen from his other statements.[212] For, since he said that it is more excellent than all who understand, he obviously understood that it is simple, since simple substances are necessarily more excellent than composite ones. It is likewise seen from the mixtures and divisions, from which he said that it was composed. For spiritual substances can be neither mixed nor cut, but bodily substances also cannot be mixed with non-bodily ones, nor the converse, as you have learned elsewhere. And in whatever way they are joined together to produce that one, it is impossible, nonetheless, that

---

211 I suspect that the proportions of numbers should be the same as above on fol. 803b.

212 See *Timaeus* 34C for the excellence of soul.

what is composed from them be divisible, just as man as man is not able to be divided or cut. For, in whatever way it would be divided, it is necessary that the soul move to one of the parts. For it is indivisible by such a division. It is, therefore, clearly seen according to reality and the truth that neither Plato nor another intelligent person thought in that way about the soul.

But to pursue one by one Plato's comparisons that he listed wants a longer explanation than my present plan allows. Nor do I think anything else should be understood in his having held a bodily form for that soul but that he imagined that the powers of that soul were extended and spread out in the body of the heaven in accord with those heavenly shapes, just as if someone says that the human soul has the shape of two equal straight lines intersecting at right angles, because the human body obviously has such a shape. But this is as if someone held that it was composed of the intellective power as the first and higher part and of the operative power as the lowest—I mean operative in the body and through the body—but /805a/ of the concupiscible and irascible powers as the intermediate parts, one on the right, the other on the left. And certain people held that the seat for the concupiscible power was the liver or in the liver, and they said that the liver was the seat of love. Hence, they said that those are great-hearted or small-hearted who had magnanimity and pusillanimity, which are undoubtedly dispositions of our irascible power.

But if anyone held for this reason, namely, because the powers of the human soul are extended, as if from above to below and from left to right, and the converse, in accord with the shape of the human body, that it spiritually has such a shape, he will be seen to hold this in the manner of Plato, and if he wishes to proceed further in such a position, he will be able to adapt the whole shape of the human body to it in this way. But its forces and[213] powers are spread out and extended through all the members to all the extremities of the body, as is evident concerning the sun, because its luminosity is poured out in the world around it in every direction and into every part, following the form of the solar body, and it is generally true that bodily powers imitate the form of their origin, that is, of the body from which they arise, by the extension and diffusion of their operations. Perhaps it seemed so to Plato that spiritual powers imitated the form of their origin, that is, of the substances from which they emerge.

It has also seemed to many philosophers that bodies are adapted to spiritual powers and substances, which can be joined to bodies, in accord with the exigence or aptness of their operations and that they are configured, that is, are made like them by their configuration, and on this they certainly thought correctly, that is, concerning the adaptation of shapes. For the soul of a snake

---

213 I have conjectured "*et*" instead of "*si*."

or of another <reptile> is found to be unable to exist in an upright body that is naturally suited for walking, as the human soul cannot exist in the body of a snake. The powers and operations of souls, therefore, require bodily shapes suited to them. Hence, souls are seen to have potentially or virtually such shapes or some likeness of them.

It could also be that Plato considered the vital or vivifying power in the human soul as the center or middle[214] of the soul and then the intellective power as proceeding from that middle upwards, but the power operative through the body as if proceeding from that middle downward, and again the concupiscible and irascible powers proceeding from that middle, one to the right side and the other to the left. And perhaps on this account he thought that the shape of the human body ought to have such lines, for this is explicitly seen in the heavenly orbs. For there are four powers in number, and they seems to be the principal ones in the human soul.

But if someone says that the power to walk is like one of such lines, that is, one that stretches downward from the vital power, while the power productive of artifacts or of any other necessities stretches to each side like arms, and such a power is undoubtedly in arms and hands, for which reason the law and teaching of Christians placed no slight proof of human salvation and reformation in such a shape.[215] For reformation ought to correspond to and fit the form or formation.

Because, therefore, Plato understood circular motion to be the first and most noble of motions and thought it is two-formed, /805b/ both one, or the same, and other, or straight and oblique, according to the statements of Aristotle,[216] he maintained for the soul of the higher world a form congruent with these motions and their shapes, as if, in accord with the examples given, the soul were in its first and most excellent power potentially one and the same and potentially circular, that is, naturally capable of such circular motion, he held on the basis of this that the first motion was that straight one, that is, one and the same and equal, in which there was no diversity. But for the second part he held circular motion, but other and oblique, as naturally capable of oblique motion and subject to many diversities. On these things that he and his followers thought about motions, you have heard a refutation, and if it is true, this position of Plato cannot stand, either according to the truth or as a comparison.

---

214 I have conjectured "*medium*" instead of "*modicum.*"

215 See, for example, Augustine, *Letters* 55.14.24–25: PL 33: 216, where he uses the form of the cross to exemplify Christian salvation.

216 See Aristotle, *On the Soul* 1.2.404b7-404b26 p. 644

You have also heard my intention on this, that is, on the heavenly motions, as the brevity of the chapter permitted. You have heard the proofs and ideas of Ptolemy. From all of them it is easy for you to destroy this position of Plato, as well as from these things that you have heard from me here, although I helped his comparison with what examples I could, and I think these suffice here for you to have certitude about this position of Plato that is considered so famous and so profound both by Greeks and by Latins up to today.

CHAPTER 31
Whether That Higher World Is One Living Being or Many
And Whether the Heavens Themselves and Their Souls Are Rational

But whether that higher world is one living being or many and whether the heavens themselves are animated and whether their souls are rational is considered to have been settled among Aristotle and his followers and also among many of the Italian philosophers.[217] But the teaching of the Hebrews and Christians have not as yet cared about such things. For the people of the Hebrews used to be content with the books of its law and the prophets. But long ago they turned to incredible myths and gave themselves wholly to them, with the exception of the few who mingled with the people of the Saracens and philosophized.[218] But the people of the Christians, subjecting themselves wholly to the virtues, holiness, and veneration of the creator, embraced philosophy to a small degree, except insofar as the perversity of those in error and the contradiction of the foolish forced them both to the defense of the law and of the faith and to the destruction of those by whom either the salvation they hope for or the honor of the creator was attacked. And people of this law, concerned about their own souls, refused to pay attention to the souls of the heavens, because they thought that the knowledge of them helped neither their profession nor their salvation and that an ignorance of them did not hinder them, whether that world was one living being or whether the heaven was a living being or the heavens living beings. That people stood in horror of it as a monster completely unknown to them, and they stood in awe

---

217 Here as elsewhere, William most probably refers mainly to Avicenna by the expression, "Aristotle and his followers," and he perhaps refers to Cicero who reported Plato's views on the world soul.

218 William perhaps alludes to the Jewish people who followed the Talmud and its teaching and distinguishes them from those who were influenced by Islamic philosophical thought. See R. Valois's chapter on William's condemnation of the Talmud.

of it as a novelty, about which they thought that nothing pertained to them. And they even took flight from it, although one of the more noble and wiser among the teachers of that people was not ashamed to admit ignorance of it in a certain book of his,[219] and in another he said that he doubted this.[220] To believe Aristotle, therefore, or anyone else in this matter is no danger to the law, faith, or teaching /806a/ of the Christians. But it involves no small danger, namely, to hold concerning those souls that they are governors of lower things and especially of human affairs and of human beings and likewise that they are causes, either through themselves or through their bodies, of human events and of the perfect laws or of other things that astronomers ascribed to them. And I do not in any way think that they are signs of such things or that the heavenly bodies should be consulted in any way on behalf of human affairs. And you have already heard my intention of this in many chapters.[221]

You should have no doubt that, whether the heavens are animated or are even living beings, the rule of their bodies and motions has been naturally entrusted to them, but nothing concerning governance in other things has been naturally entrusted to them. For they do none of the things that pertain to governors or rulers. For they neither pass nor promulgate laws, and they do not command or forbid anything, nor do they show care or, suggest, persuade, or dissuade anything. Hence, the human race is entrusted to its own choice and governance with the helps that it has from the side of the creator on account of natural things, such as judges, kings, princes, consuls, magistrates, councilors, teachers, priests, and the offices of priests. And among these helps are the law, teaching, and prophesy, and I understand under prophecy visions and revelations, and under the helps also of the creator, which I am unable to list—in fact unable even to understand—I understand miracles, scourges, and terrors, and their contraries.

---

219 Augustine, for example, knew of the Platonic doctrine of the world-soul, but he expressed skepticism about its existence in a number of places. William either does not know or simply ignores the fact that Augustine himself seems to have held a world soul in some of his early writings. See my "The World-Soul and Time in St. Augustine," *Augustinian Studies* 14 (1983): 75–92.

220 See Augustine, *Revisions* (*Retractationes*) 1, 11, 4; PL 32: 601–602, where in commenting on his *On Music* (*De musica*) Augustine acknowledges that Plato did hold a soul of the world, but that he himself does not know whether the world is a living being or not.

221 See above chs. 20 and 28.

CHAPTER 32
That Some Erroneously Hold That There Is a Ruling Power in the Universe
Besides the Creator and His Helpers

B ut those who held that there is a ruling power in the universe besides
the creator and his assistants, as I have named and taught them, have
held this absolutely superfluously since these suffice for the governance
of the universe. But among the assistants of the creator there are also the holy
angels who by their many offices /806b/ care for human affairs and direct
and help human beings, as you will hear in the treatise following this.[222] And
concerning such a ruling power, one would have to ask those who held it
whether it is a substance or an accident and where it is and what its operation
is besides those that I listed. And if you choose to investigate it, you will find
that is utterly superfluous, otiose, and doing nothing or that it is a figment
of people dreaming in an incredible error. And when you have listed and
have carefully considered the roles of governance, you will not find that such
a figment causes or helps any of them to come about because you will find
that it produces no command or prohibition or any of the other things that
I already mentioned.

CHAPTER 33
On the Wicked Error of Those Who Say that the Holy Spirit
Is the Soul of the World

B ut those who held that the Holy Spirit, that is, the third person in the
blessed and glorious Trinity, is the soul of the world[223] showed that they
did not know the Holy Spirit at all and were evidently ignorant of the
nature and character of the soul, since every soul is a perfection and a part of
what it animates and is bound to the body it animates. But the Holy Spirit is
so far from each of these to the extent that the ultimate degree of freedom and

---

222 In the second principal part of *The Universe of Creatures*, William deals with the
spiritual universe, that is, with the Aristotelian separate substances, the good
angels, and the bad angels. The second part of the second principle part runs to
170 folio pages and has 163 chapters.

223 Roland De Vaux identifies these thinkers as Thierry of Chartres and William of
Conches. See his *Notes et textes sur l'Avicennisme latin aux confines des XIIe–XIIIe
siècles* (Paris: J. Vrin, 1934), p. 25. Peter Abelard also clearly held this view; see
his *Christian Theology* (*Theologia Christiana*) I, 5; PL 178: 1144.

glory, by which he is the true and only God, permits him to be bound to or included in no body. And in the first part of this treatise it was explained to you by certain proofs that the one Trinity is the only and true God and that each of the three persons is the pure, true, and only God.[224] But if those who held this were led them into that error because the Holy Spirit is the giver and fountain of life wherever there is life, and because the whole life of the world comes from him, it is necessary that they hold the same thing concerning each of those three persons, since each of them gives life to everything living, and for this reason each is said to be the life of the ages, that is, the fountain of the life that is given to everything that lives in every age.

---

224 See William, *The Trinity or the First Principle*, chs. 14–23; Switalski pp. 82–124.

BIBLIOGRAPHY

Primary Sources

William, of Auvergne. *Opera Omnia.* 2 vol. Ed. F. Hotot, with *Supplementum.* Ed. Blaise Le Feron. Orléans-Paris, 1674; repr. Frankfurt am Main: Minerva, 1963.

———. *De trinitate.* An Edition of the Latin Text with an Introduction by Bruno Switalski. Toronto: Pontifical Institute of Mediaeval Studies, 1976.

———. *The Trinity, or the First Principle.* Trans. Roland J. Teske, S.J. and Francis C. Wade, S.J.; introduction and notes by Roland J. Teske, S.J. Medieval Philosophical Texts in Translation 28. Milwaukee: Marquette University Press, 1989.

———. *De Universo.* Nuremberg: Georg Stuchs, 1496.

———. *The Universe of Creatures.* Selections Translated from the Latin with an Introduction and Notes by Roland J. Teske, S.J. Mediaeval Philosophical Texts in Translation 35. Milwaukee: Marquette University Press, 1998.

———. *Guillaume d'Avergne: De L'Âme (VII, 1-9).* Introduction, traduction et notes par J.-B. Brenet. Paris: J. Vrin, 1998.

———. "Tractatus Magistri Guilielmi Alvernensis de bono et malo." Ed. J. Reginald O'Donnell. *Mediaeval Studies* 8 (1946): 245–299.

———. "Tractatus Secundus Guilielmi Alvernensis de bono et malo." Ed. J. Reginald O'Donnell. *Mediaeval Studies* 16 (1954): 219–271.

———. *De immortalitate animae.* Ed. Georg Bülow. In *Des Domininicus Gundissalinus Schrift von der Unsterblichkeit der Seele nebst einem Anhange, enthaltend die Abhandlung des Wilhelm von Paris (Auvergne) "De immortalitate animae."* In *Beiträge zur Geschichte der Philosophie des Mittelalters*, II, 3. Münster: Aschendorff, 1897.

———. *The Immortality of the Soul.* Trans. Roland J. Teske, S.J., with an Introduction and Notes. Mediaeval Philosophical Texts in Translation 30. Milwaukee: Marquette University Press, 1991.

———. *The Soul.* Trans. Roland J. Teske, S.J., with an Introduction and Notes. Mediaeval Philosophical Texts in Translations 37. Milwaukee: Marquette University Press, 2000.

———. *Il "Tractatus de Gratia" di Gugliemo d'Auvergne.* Ed. Guglielmo Corti. Rome: Lateran University, 1966.

Secondary Sources

Books

Averroes. *Averroes' Destructio Destructionum Philosophiae Algazelis in the Latin Version of Calo Calonymous.* Ed. B. H. Zedler. Milwaukee: Marquette University Press, 1961.

Avicebron. *Avencebrolis Fons Vitae.* Ex arabico in latinum translatus ab Johanne Hispano et Dominico Gundissalino. Ed. Clemens Baeumker. In *Beiträge zur Geschichte der Philosophie des Mittelalters* I. Münster: 1892-1895.

Autour de Guillaume d'Auvergne (1249). Ed. Franco Morensoni and Jean-Yves Tilliette. Turnhout: Brepols, 2005.

Avicenna. *Avicenna Latinus: Liber de Anima seu Sextus de Naturalibus.* Edition critique de la traduction latine médiévale par Simone van Riet. Introduction sur la doctrine psychologique d'Avicenne par Gerard Verbeke. 2 vols. Louvain: E. Peeters; Leiden: E. J. Brill, 1973 and Louvain: Editions Orientalists; Leiden: E. J. Brill, 1968.

————. *Avicenna Latinus: Liber de Philosophia Prima sive Scientia Divina.* Edition critique de la traduction latine médiévale par Simone van Riet. Introduction doctrinale par Gerard Verbeke. 3 vols. Louvain-La-Neuve: E. Peeters; Leiden: E. J. Brill, 1977, 1983.

————. *Avicennae Metaphysices Compendium.* Ed. Nematallah Carame. Rome: Pontificum Institutum Orientalium Studiorum, 1926.

Bianchi, Luca. *L'errore di Aristotele. La polemica contro l'eternità del mondo nel XIII secolo.* Firenze: La Nuova Italia Editrice, 1984.

Boethius. *The Theological Treatises.* Trans. and ed. H. F. Stewart and E. K. Rand. Cambridge: Harvard University Press; London: Wm. Heinemann, 1946.

Borok, Helmut. *Der Tugendbegriff des Wilhelm von Auvergne (1180-1249): Eine moralhistorische Untersuchung zur Ideengeschichtliche Rezeption der aristotelischen Ethik.* Düsseldorf: Patmos-Verlag, 1979.

Bridges, John Howell. *The Philosophy of William of Auvergne with respect to Thirteenth Century Christian Aristotelianism.* Ph.D. dissertation, Emory University, 1969.

Caffrey, Mary Carol. *Realism and Knowledge according to William of Auvergne.* Ph.D. dissertation, Fordham University, 1944.

Caster, Kevin J. *The Real Distinction in Creatures between Being and Essence according to William of Auvergne.* Ph.D. dissertation, Marquette University, 1995.

Dales, Richard C. *Medieval Discussions of he Eternity of the World.* Leiden: E. J. Brill, 1990.

Davidson, Herbert A. *Proofs for Eternity, Creation and the Existence of God in Medieval Islamic and Jewish Philosophy.* New York: Oxford University Press, 1987.

Denys l'Areopagite. *La hiérarchie céleste.* Sources chrétiennes 58. Intro. René Roques; ed. Günter Heil, trans. and notes by Mauricè de Gandillac. Paris: Du Cerf, 1958.

Dondaine, A. *Le Liber de Duobus Principiis.* Rome: Instituto Storico Dominicano, 1939. 2nd ed. C. Thouzellier. Paris: Editions du Cerf, 1973.

Giles of Rome. *Errores Philosophorum.* Ed. J. Koch, trans. by J. Reidl. Milwaukee: Marquette University Press, 1944.

Gilson, Étienne. *History of Christian Philosophy in the Middle Ages.* New York: Random House, 1955.

Hissette, Roland. *Enquête sur les 219 articles condamnées à Paris le 7 mars 1277.* Louvain: Publications universitaires, 1977.

Jeck, Udo Reinhold. *Aristoteles contra Augustinum: Zur Frage nach dem Verhältnis von Zeit und Seele bei den antiken Aristoteleskommentatoren, im arabischen Aristotelismus und im 13. Jahrhundert.* Amsterdam: B. R. Gründer, 1994.

Jourdain, Amable. *Recherches critiques sur l'âge et l'origine des traductions latines d'Aristote.* Paris: Delaunay, 1819.

Kretzmann, Norman and Anthony Kenny and Jan Pinborg, eds. *The Cambridge History of Later Medieval Philosophy from the Rediscovery of Aristotle to the Disintegration of Scholasticism 1100-1600.* Cambridge: Cambridge University Press, 1982.

Marrone, Steven P. *William of Auvergne and Robert Grosseteste: New Ideas of Truth in the Early Thirteenth Century.* Princeton: Princeton University Press, 1983.

Masnovo, Amato. *Da Guglielmo d'Auvergne a S. Tommaso d'Aquino.* 3 vols, 2nd ed. Milan: Vita et Pensiero, 1946.

Nelli, R. *La philosophie du catharisme: Le dualisme radical au XIIIe siecle.* Paris: Payot, 1978.

Padgett, Alan. *God, Eternity, and the Nature of Time.* New York: St. Martin's Press, 1992.

Quentin, Albrecht. *Naturkenntnisse und Naturanschungen bei Wilhelm von Auvergne.* Hildesheim: Gerstenberg, 1976.

Renan, Ernst. *Averroès et l'Averroïsme.* Paris: A. Durand, 1866.

Rohls, Jan. *Wilhelm von Auvergne und der mittelalterliche Aristotelismus.* München: Chr. Kaiser, 1980.

Schindele, Stephan. *Beiträge zur Metaphysik des Wilhelm von Auvergne.* Munich, 1900.

Sorabji, Richard. *Time, Creation and the Continuum: Theories in Antiquity and the Early Middle Ages*. Ithaca, N.Y.: Cornell University Press, 1983.

Valois, Noël. *Guillaume d'Auvergne, Évêque de Paris (1228-1249): Sa vie et ses ouvrages*. Paris: Picard, 1880.

Walter of Bruges. *Quaestiones Disputatae*. IV. Ed. E. Longpré. In: *Les Philosophes Beiges*, X. Louvain, 1928.

William of Conches. *Glossae super Platonem: Texte critique avec introduction, notes et tables*. Ed. Edouard Jeauneau. Paris: J. Vrin, 1965.

Articles and Chapters in Books

Allard, Baudoin C. "Additions au *Répertoire des maîtres en théologie de Paris au XIIe siècle*." *Bulletin de la société internationale pour l'étude de la philosophie médiévale* 5 (1963): 147–149.

———. "Note sur le 'De immortalitate animae' de Guillaume d'Auvergne." *Bulletin de philosophie médiévale* 18 (1976): 68–72.

———. "Nouvelles additions et corrections au *Répertoire* de Glorieux: A propos de Guillaume d'Auvergne." *Bulletin de philosophie médiévale* 10–12 (1968–1970): 98–118.

Anciaux, P. "Le sacrement de pénitance chez Guillaume d'Auvergne." *Ephemerides theologicae lovaniensis* 24 (1948): 98–118.

Baldner, Stephen. "St. Bonaventure on the Beginning of the Temporal World." *The New Scholasticism* 63 (1989): 206–28.

Barzán, Bernardo C. "Pluralisme de formes ou dualisme de substances?" *Revue philosophique de Louvain* 67 (1969): 30–73.

Berlioz, Jacques. "La voix de l'évêque Guillaume d'Auvergne dans les *Exempla* (XIIIe–XIVe siècles)," pp. 9–34. In *Autour de Guillaume d'Auvergne*.

Bernstein, Alan E. "Esoteric Theology: William of Auvergne on the Fires of Hell and Purgatory." *Speculum* 57 (1982): 509–531.

———. "Theology between Heresy and Folklore: William of Auvergne on Punishment after Death." *Studies in Medieval and Renaissance History* 5 (1982): 4–44.

———. "William of Auvergne and the Cathars," pp. 271–292. In *Autour de Guillaume d'Auvergne*.

Beuchot, Mauricio. "La distinción entre esencia y existencia en los escolasticos anteriores a Tomas de Aquino." *Revista de Filosofía* 19 (1986): 71–88.

Bianchi, Luca. "Gli articoli censurati nel 1241/1244 e la loro influenza da Bonaventura a Gerson," pp. 155–171. In *Autour de Guillaume d'Auvergne*.

Boglioni, Pierre. "Saints, miracles et hagiographie chez Guillaume d'Auvergne," pp. 323–339. In *Autour de Guillaume d'Auvergne*.

Boccadoro, Brenno. "La musique, les passions, l'âme et le corps," pp. 75–93. In *Autour de Guillaume d'Auvergne*.

Caster, Kevin J. "The Distinction between Being and Essence according to Boethius, Avicenna, and William of Auvergne." *The Modern Schoolman* 73 (1996): 309–332.

———. "The Real Distinction between Being and Essence According to William of Auvergne." *Traditio* 51 (1996): 201-223.

———. "William of Auvergne's Adaptation of Ibn Gabirol's Doctrine of the Divine Will." *The Modern Schoolman* 74 (1996): 31–42.

Casagrandi, Carla. "Gugliemo d'Auvergne e il buon uso delle passioni nella penitenza," pp. 189–201. In *Autour de Guillaume d'Auvergne*.

Cesalli, Laurent. "Guilaume d'Auvergne et l'enunciable: La soluton profane d'un problème théologique," pp. 117–136. In *Autour de Guillaume d'Auvergne*.

Christe, Yves. "Grossement," pp. 341–367. In *Autour de Guillaume d'Auvergne*.

Collumb, Pascal. "Guillaume d'Auvergne au banquet sacré? La messe et le corps du Christ dans le *De missa*," pp. 217–236. In *Autour de Guillaume d'Auvergne*.

Contenson, P.-M., de. "La théologie de la vision de Dieu au début du XIIième siècle: Le 'de retributione sanctorum' de Guillaume d'Auvergne et la condamnation de 1241." *Revue de sciences philosophiques et théologiques* 46 (1962): 409–444.

Corti, Guglielmo. "Le sette parte del *Magisterium diuinale et sapientiale* di Guglielmo di Auvergne." In *Studi e richerche di scienze religiose in onore dei santi apostoli Petro et Paulo nel XIX centenario del loro martirio*, pp. 289–307. Rome: Lateran University, 1968.

Dahan, Gilbert. "L'exégese de la Bible chez Guillaume d'Auvergne," pp. 237–270. In *Autour de Guillaume d'Auvergne*.

Dales, Richard C. "Robert Grosseteste's Place in Medieval Discussions of the Eternity of the World." *Speculum* 61 (1986): 544–563.

———. "Robert Grosseteste's Treatise *De finitate motus et temporis*." *Traditio* 19 (1963): 245-266.

Davidson, Herbert A. "John Philoponus as a Source of Medieval Islamic and Jewish Proofs of Creation." *Journal of the American Oriental Society* 89.2 (1969): 357–391.

Davis, Leo D. "Creation according to William of Auvergne." In *Studies in Mediaevalia and Americana*. Ed. by G. Steckler and L. Davis, pp. 51–75. Spokane: Gonzaga University Press, 1973.

De Porter, A. "Un manuel de prédication médiévale: Le ms. 97 de Bruges." *Revue néoscolastique de philosophie* 25 (1923): 192–209.

Faes de Mottoni, Barbara. "Gugliemo d'Alvernia et l'anima rapita," pp. 55–74. In *Autour de Guillaume d'Avergne*.

Forest, Aimé. "Guillaume d'Auvergne, critique d'Aristote." In *Études médiévales offertes à Augustin Flictie*, pp. 67–79. Paris: Presses Universitaires de France, 1952.

Gauthier, René A. "Notes sur les débuts (1225-1240) du prémier 'Averroisme.'" *Revue des sciences philosophiques et théologiques* 66 (1982): 321–234.

Gilson, Etienne. "La notion d'existence chez Guillaume d'Auvergne." *Archives d'histoire doctrinale et littéraire du moyen age* 21 (1946): 55–91.

———. "Les 'Philosophantes.'" *Archives d'histoire doctrinale et littéraire du moyen age* 19 (1952): 135–140.

———. "Pourquoi saint Thomas a critiqué saint Augustin." *Archives d'histoire doctrinale et littéraire du moyen age* 1 (1926): 5–127.

———. "Les sources gréco-arabes de l'augustinisme avicennisant." *Archives d'histoire doctrinale et littéraire du moyen age* 4 (1929): 5–149.

Glorieux, Palemon. "Le tractatus novus de poenitentia de Guillaume d'Auvergne." In *Miscellanea Moralia. Bibliotheca Ephemeriarum Theologicarum Lovaniensium*. Series 1, vol. 3, pp. 551–565. Louvain: Nauwelaerts, 1949.

Hamilton, B. "The Albigensian Crusade." In *Monastic Reform, Catharism and the Crusades, (900-1300)*. London: Variorum Reprints, 1979.

Heinzmann, Richard. "Wilhelm von Auvergne." In *Lexikon für Theologie und Kirche*. 2 ed. Vol. 10, 1127. Freiburg im Breisgau: Herder, 1965.

———. "Zur Anthropologie des Wilhelm von Auvergne." *Münchener Theologische Zeitschrift* 16 (1965): 27–36.

Judy, Albert. "Avicenna's 'Metaphysics' in the *Summa contra Gentiles*." *Angelicum* 52 (1975): 340–384 and 541–586.

Jüssen, Gabriel. "Aristotles-Rezeption and Aristoteles-Kritik in Wilhelm von Auvergne's *Tractatus De anima*." In *Knowledge and the Sciences in Medieval Philosophy: Proceedings of the Eighth Congress of Medieval Philosophy*. Ed. Monika Asztalos, John E. Murdoch, Ilkka Niiniluoto. Vol. 3, pp. 87–96. Helsinki: Yliopistopaino, 1990.

———. "Die Tugend und der gute Wille: Wilhelm von Auvergnes Auseinanderstezung mit der aristotelischen Ethik." *Philosophisches Jahrbuch* 102 (1995): 20–32.

———. "Wilhelm von Auvergne." In *Contemporary Philosophy. A New Survey*. Volume 6. *Philosophy and Science in the Middle Ages*, Part I, pp. 177–185. Dordrecht: Kluwer Academic Publishers, 1990.

———. "Wilhelm von Auvergne und die Entwicklung der Philosophie in Übergang zur Hochscholastik" and "Von Wilhelm von Auvergne zu Thomas von Aquin—und zurück." In *Thomas von Aquin im philosophischen Gesprach*. Ed. Wolfgang Kluxen, pp. 185–203 and pp. 262–265. Freiburg and Munich, 1975.

————. "Wilhelm von Auvergne und die Transformation der scholastischen Philosophie im 13. Jahrhundert." In *Philosophie im Mittelalter. Entwicklungslinien und Paradigmen.* Ed. Jan P. Beckmann et. al., pp. 141–164. Hamberg: Felix Meiner, 1987.

Kneale, William C. "Modality De Dicto and De Re." In *Logic, Methodology and Philosophy of Science: Proceedings of the 1960 International Congress.* Ed. E. Nagel, P. Suppes and A. Tarski, pp. 622–633. Stanford: Stanford University Press, 1962.

Knowles, David, "William of Auvergne." In *The Encyclopedia of Philosophy.* 8 Vols. New York: Macmillan, 1967. Vol. 8, p. 302–303.

Kramp, Josef. "Des Wilhelm von Auvergne 'Magisterium Divinale.'" *Gregorianum* 1 (1920): 538–613, 2 (1921): 42–103 and 174–195.

Landry, Bernard. "L'originalité de Guillaume d'Auvergne." *Revue d'histoire de la philosophie* 3 (1929): 441–463.

Landgraf, A. "Der Tracktat de 'De errore Pelagii' des Wilhelm von Auvergne." *Speculum* 5 (1930): 168-180.

Laumakis, John A. "The Voluntarism of William of Auvergne and Some Evidence to the Contrary." *The Modern Schoolman* 76 (1999): 303-312.

Lewis, Neil. "William of Auvergne (c. 1180–1249)." In *Encyclopedia of Philosophy.* Ed. Donald Borchert. 2nd ed. Vol. 9, pp. 765–767. Detroit: Macmillan Reference, USA, 2006.

————. "William of Auvergne's Account of the Enuntiabile: Its Relation to Nominalism." *Vivarium* 33 (1995): 113-136.

Longpré, Ephrem. "Guillaume d'Auvergne et Alexandre de Halès." *Archivum Franciscanum Historicum* 16 (1923): 249-250.

————. "Guillaume d'Auvergne et l'Ecole Franciscaine de Paris." *La France Franciscaine* 5 (1922): 426-429.

————. "Thomas d'York et Matthieu d'Aquasparta. Textes inédits sur le problème de la création." *Archives d'histoire doctrinale et littéraire du moyen âge* 1 (1926): 269–308.

Macken, Raymond. "Heinrich von Gent im Gespräch mit seinen Zeitgenossen über die menschliche Freiheit." *Franziskanishe Studien* 59 (1977): 125–182.

Masnovo, Amato. "Guglielmo d'Auvergne e l'universita di Parigi dal 1229 al 1231." In *Mélanges Mandonnet* , II, 191–232. Paris: Librairie J. Vrin, 1930.

McGinnis, Jon. "Ibn Sina on the Now." *American Catholic Philosophical Quarterly* 73 (1999): 73–106.

Michaud-Quantin, P. and M. Lemoine. "Pour le dossier des 'philosophantes.'" *Archives d'histoire doctrinale et littéraire du moyen age* 35 (1968): 17–22.

Miller, Michael. "William of Auvergne and Avicenna's Principle 'Natures Operates in the Manner of a Servant." In *Medieval Philosophy and the*

Classical Tradition :In Islam, Judaism and Christianity. Ed. John Inglis, pp. 263–276. Richmond, Surrey: Curzon, 2002.

———. "William of Auvergne on Primary and Secondary Causality." *The Modern Schoolman* 75 (1998): 265-277.

Moody, Ernest A. "William of Auvergne and his Treatise De Anima." In *Studies in Medieval Philosophy, Science, and Logic,* pp. 1–109. Berkeley and Los Angeles: The University of California Press, 1975).

Morenzoni, Franco. "Predicatio est rei predicate humanis mentibus presentatio: Les sermons pour la dédicas de l'église de Guillaume d'Auvergne," pp. 293–322. In *Autour de Guillaume d'Auvergne.*

O'Donnell, J. Reginald, "The Notion of Being in William of Auvergne." *Proceedings and Addresses of the American Philosophical Association* 21 (1946): 156-165.

———. "The Rhetorica Divina of William of Auvergne. A Study in Applied Rhetoric." In *Images of Man in Ancient and Medieval Thought.* Ed. F. Bossier et al., pp. 323–333. Leuven: Leuven University Press, 1976.

———. "William of Auvergne (of Paris)." In *The New Catholic Encyclopedia,* Vol. 14, p. 921. New York: McGraw-Hill, 1967.

Ottman, Jennifer R. "List of Manuscripts and Editions," pp. 375–399. In *Autour de Guillaume d'Auvergne.*

Riet, Simone van. "L'immortalité de l'âme dans le 'De anima' d'Avicenne. Une synthèse de l'Aristotélisme et du Néoplatonisme." *Pensamiento* 25 (1969): 271–90.

Rosier-Catach, Irène. "Signes sacramentals et signes magiques: Guillaume d'Auvergne et la théorie du pacte," pp. 93–116. In *Autour de Guillaume d'Auvergne.*

Rosheger, John P. "Is God a 'What'? Avicenna, William of Auvergne, and Aquinas on the Divine Essence." In *Medieval Philosophy and the Classical Tradition: In Islam, Judaism, and Christianity.* Ed. John Ingles, pp. 277–297. Richmond, Surrey: Curzon, 2002.

Salmon, Dominique. "Algazel et les Latins." *Archive d'histoire doctrinale et littéraire du moyen âge* 10 (1935–36): 101–127.

———. "Note sur la première influence d'Averroes." *Revue néoscolastique de philosophie* 40 (1937): 203–12.

Sannino, Antonella. "La dottrina della causalità nell'universo di Gugliemo d'Alvernia: Percorsi di lettura." *Studi filosofici* 27 (2004): 31–68.

———. "Ermete mago et alchimista nelle biblioteche di Guglielmo d'Alvernia e Ruggero Bacone." *Studi medievali* 41 (2000): 151–209.

Santi, Francesco. "Gugliemo d'Auvergne et l'ordine dei Domenicani tra filosofia naturale et tradizione magica," pp. 137–153. In *Autour de Guillaume d'Auvergne.*

Smalley, Beryl, "William of Auvergne, John of La Rochelle and Saint Thomas on the Old Law." In *St. Thomas Aquinas 1274-1974 Commemora-*

tive Studies. 2 vols. Ed. A. Maurer, 2, pp. 11–71. Toronto: Pontifical Institute of Medieval Studies, 1974.

Stadter, E. "Die Seele als 'Minor Mundus' and als 'Regnum.' Ein Beitrag zur Psychologie der mittleren Franziskanerschule." In: *Universalismus and Partikularismus im Mittelaller*. Miscellanea Mediaevalia 5. Ed. Paul Wilpert, pp. 56–72. Berlin: De Gruyter, 1968.

Storck, Alfredo. "Eternidade, possibilidade e emanacao: Guilherme de Auvergne e Tomas de Aquino leitores de Avicenna." *Analytica* 71 (2003): 113-159.

Teske, Roland J. "The Identity of the 'Italici' in William of Auvergne's Discussion of the Eternity of the World." *Proceedings of the PMR Conference* 15 (1990): 189–201.

———. "The Will as King over the Powers of the Soul: Uses and Sources of an Image in Thirteenth Century Philosophy." *Vivarium* 32 (1994): 62-71.

———. "William of Auvergne." In *A Companion to Philosophy in the Middle Ages*. Ed. Jorge J. E. Gracia and Timothy B. Noone, pp. 680–687. Malden, MA: Blackwell Publishing, 2002.

———. "William of Auvergne." In *Dictionary of Literary Biography*: Vol. 115: *Medieval Philosophers*. Ed. Jeremiah Hackett, pp. 344–353. Detroit: Gale Research, 1992.

———. "William of Auvergne and the Manichees." *Traditio* 48 (1993): 63-75.

———. "William of Auvergne on *De re* and *De dicto* Necessity." *The Modern Schoolman* 69 (1992): 111–121.

———. "William of Auvergne on Freedom of the Will." In *Moral and Political Philosophies in the Middle Ages*. Proceedings of The Ninth International Conference on Medieval Philosophy. Ed. B. Carlos Bazán, et al., 2, pp. 932–938. New York: Legas, 1996.

———. "William of Auvergne on Philosophy as 'Divinalis' and 'Sapientialis.'" In *Was ist Philosophie im Mittelalter?* Ed. Jan A. Aertsen and Andreas Speer, pp. 475–481. Berlin: De Gruyter, 1998.

———. "William of Auvergne on the Eternity of the World." *The Modern Schoolman* 67 (1990): 187–205.

———. "William of Auvergne on the Individuation of Human Souls." *Traditio* 49 (1994): 77–93.

———. "William of Auvergne on the 'Newness of the World.'" *Mediaevalia: Textos e Estudios* 7-8 (1995): 287–302.

———. "William of Auvergne on the Relation between Reason and Faith." *The Modern Schoolman* 75 (1998): 279–291.

———. "William of Auvergne on the Various States of our Nature." *Traditio* 58 (2003): 201–218.

———. "William of Auvergne on Time and Eternity." *Traditio* 55 (2000): 125–141.

———. "William of Auvergne's Debt to Avicenna." In *Avicenna and His Heritage*. Acts of the International Colloquium. Leuven–Louvaine-La-Neuve September 8–September 11, 1999. Ed. Jules Janssens and Daniel De Smet, pp. 153–170. Leuven: Leuven University Press, 2002.

———. "William of Auvergne's Rejection of the Agent Intelligence." In *Greek and Medieval Studies in Honor of Leo Sweeney, S.J.* Ed. William J. Carroll and John J. Furlong, pp. 211–235. New York: Peter Lang, 1995.

———. "William of Auvergne's Rejection of the Platonic Archetypal World." *Traditio* 55 (1998): 117–130.

———. "William of Auvergne's Spiritualist Conception of Man," pp. 35–53. In *Autour de Guillaume d'Auvergne*.

———. "William of Auvergne's Use of the Avicennian Principle: 'Ex Uno, In Quantum Unum, Non Nisi Unum.'" *The Modern Schoolman* 71 (1993): 1–15.

Tillette, Jean-Yves. "Oraison et art oratoire: Les sources et le propos de la *Rhetorica divina*," pp. 203–215. In *Autour de Guillaume d'Auvergne*.

Vannest, Alfred, "Nature et grâce dans la théologie de Guillaume d'Auxerre et de Guillaume d'Auvergne." *Ephemerides theologicae lovanienis* 53 (1977): 83–106.

Vaux, Roland de, "La première entrée d'Averroës chez les Latins." *Revue de sciences philosophiques et théologiques* 22 (1933): 193–245.

Vecchio, Silvana. "*Passio, Affectus, Virtus:* Il sistema delle passioni nei Trattati morali di Gugliemo d'Alvernia," pp. 173–187. In *Autour de Guillaume d'Auvergne*.

Verger, Jacques. "Conclusion," pp. 369–374. In *Autour de Guillaume d'Auvergne*.

Vernet, F., "Guillaume d'Auvergne, Évèque de Paris." In *Dictionnaire de théologie catholique*, 7, 1967–1976. Paris: Letzouy, 1923–1950.

Viard, P., "Guillaume d'Auvergne." In *Dictionnaire de spiritualité* 6, 1182–1192. Paris: Beauchesne, 1937– .

Weisheipl, James A., "Albertus Magnus and Universal Hylomorphism." *Southwestern Journal of Philosophy* 10 (1979): 239–260.

Wood, Rega. "Richard Rufus of Cornwall on Creation: The Reception of Aristotelian Physics in the West." *Medieval Philosophy and Theology* 2 (1992): 1–30.

· NAME INDEX

A

Abelard, Peter, 183
Abumasar, 26, 154, 167–168
Apuleius of Madaura, 18, 93
Archytas of Tarentum, 15, 58–59
Aristotle, 12, 26–27, 41–42, 45–49,
  53, 57, 59, 91, 95, 98, 105, 108,
  114, 123, 128–129, 131, 146–147,
  154–157, 162, 164, 169, 172, 174,
  179–181, 187
Augustine of Hippo, 21, 27, 34, 60–61, 86,
  95, 98, 100, 127, 168, 179, 181
Avicenna, 12, 21, 24, 26, 29, 148, 155,
  167, 186, 189–190, 192–194

B

Boethius, Anicius Manlius, 13, 26, 117,
  169–170, 186, 189

C

Cicero, Marcus Tullius, 13, 21, 23, 34,
  58,106. 119. 122. 138, 154, 168,
  170, 180

D

De Vaux, Roland, 167, 183, 194

E

Epicurus of Samos, 82

G

Galen of Pergamum, 16, 73
Gerard of Cremona, 154, 167

H

Herman of Carinthia, 154
Hermes Trismegistos, 21, 90, 127

I

Italian philosophers, 13, 27, 34, 117, 122,
  132, 138, 168–169, 180

J

Jerome of Bethlehem, 36, 156

K

Klubertanz, George P., 36

L

Lactantius, Lucius, 86

M

Matthew of Aquasparta, 191
Miller, Michael, 22, 46, 192
Mutakallimum, 91

P

Philolaus of Croton, 173–174
Plato, 25–27, 93, 106, 151, 154–156,
  158–162, 164, 166–173, 175–181
Ptolemy, Claudius, 26, 161, 176, 180

S

Seneca, Lucius, 13, 132
Socrates, 35, 50, 142, 144–146, 161,
  164, 169

SUBJECT INDEX

A

accident, 13, 42, 68, 92-93, 144, 146-147, 177, 182
adversity, 22, 67, 137, 153
angels 12, 18, 22, 27, 32, 38-39, 49, 78, 105, 129-131, 151, 167, 182

B

barbarian nations, 17, 74, 78
beneficence, 17, 72, 76, 80, 135

C

care, 14, 16-19, 29-40, 54, 60, 62-65, 68, 72, 74-77, 79, 81-87, 89, 92-93, 96-99, 121, 154, 181-182
causality, 39, 120, 125, 131, 192
cause, 13, 15-17, 21-23, 39, 45-46, 55, 60-61, 64, 71, 75, 79, 82-84, 88, 105, 109, 113, 117-118, 121-123, 125-127, 132-137, 139, 145, 147-148, 157, 159, 163, 174
chance, 13, 16, 18, 32-33, 47, 68-69, 88, 92-93, 127
compositions, 20, 113, 148-149
conservation, 32-33, 49, 66, 75, 88-89, 160
contradictories, 19, 105, 109, 115, 119, 141, 144
creator, 13-25, 27, 29-46, 48-50, 52, 54-87, 89-95, 97-99, 103-119, 127-131, 135-142, 145-148, 151-153, 155, 161-162, 167, 172-174, 180-182

D

death, 15-16, 33, 39, 62, 64, 67, 69-72, 80, 139, 141, 188

divine generosity, 80
divisions, 20, 27, 113, 148-149, 170, 177
duplicity, 19-20, 100-101, 106-108, 110, 115, 140

E

efficient cause, 17, 22, 45, 117, 125-126, 132-133
err, 19, 68, 103-104, 106, 122, 163
error, 16-20, 22-23, 26-27, 29, 31, 43, 47, 56, 82, 92-93, 99, 103, 106, 113-115, 117, 119-122, 126, 135, 139, 142, 148, 156, 166-167, 169, 173, 180, 182-183
eternal, 12, 20, 63, 79, 113-115, 144
eternity, 11-12, 19-21, 23-24, 104, 106-107, 109, 113-116, 118, 138, 140, 142, 146, 148, 150, 187, 189, 193-194
evil, 15, 17-18, 21, 30-31, 57, 60-64, 67, 69-73, 80-83, 91, 93, 98, 117, 120, 127, 129-130, 135, 139, 165
evils, 13, 15-17, 21, 23, 30-31, 43, 59-60, 62-63, 65, 67, 69-73, 76, 79-83, 97, 117-118, 122, 127, 129, 139, 165

F

falsity, 24, 61, 63, 103, 112, 140, 143, 145-148
fate, 21-23, 25, 30, 120, 137-140, 151-152
Fates, 30, 137, 151-152
fear, 14, 16, 47, 50, 56-58, 71, 79, 85, 88, 124, 128, 173
foreknowledge, 13, 30, 99
freedom, 21-22, 62, 72, 87, 123-124, 128-131, 134, 136, 167, 183, 193

Liber De Pomo: *The Apple, or Aristotle's Death.* Mary F. Rousseau, Tr. ISBN 0-87462-218-2. (Translation No. 18, 1968). 96 pp. $5

St. Thomas Aquinas: *On the Unity of the Intellect against the Averroists.* Beatrice H. Zedler, Tr. ISBN 0-87462-219-0. (Translation No. 19, 1969). 96 pp. $10

Nicholas of Autrecourt. *The Universal Treatise.* Leonard L. Kennedy, C.S.B., Tr. ISBN 0-87462-220-4. (Translation No. 20, 1971). 174 pp. $15

Pseudo-Dionysius Areopagite: *The Divine Names and Mystical Theology.* John D. Jones, Tr. ISBN 0-87462-221-2. (Translation No. 21, 1980). 320 pp. $25

Matthew of Vendome: *Ars Versificatoria.* Roger P. Parr, Tr. ISBN 0-87462-222-0. (Translation No. 22, 1981). 150 pp. $15

Francis Suárez. *On Individuation.* Jorge J.E. Gracia, Tr. ISBN 0-87462-223-9. (Translation No. 23, 1982). 304 pp. $35

Francis Suárez: *On the Essence of Finite Being as Such, on the Existence of That Essence and Their Distinction.* Norman J. Wells, Tr. ISBN 0-87462-224-7. (Translation No. 24, 1983). 248 pp. $20

The Book of Causes (Liber De Causis). Dennis J. Brand, Tr. ISBN 0-87462-225-5. (Translation No. 25, 1984). 56 pp. $5

Giles of Rome: *Errores Philosophorum.* John O. Riedl, Tr. Intro. by Josef Koch. ISBN 0-87462-429-0. (Translation No. 26, 1944). 136 pp. $10

St. Thomas Aquinas: *Questions on the Soul.* James H. Robb, Tr. ISBN 0-87462-226-3. (Translation No. 27, 1984). 285 pp. $25

Under the Editorship of Richard C. Taylor

William of Auvergne. *The Trinity.* Roland J. Teske, S.J. and Francis C. Wade, S.J. ISBN 0-87462-231-X (Translation No. 28, 1989) 286 pp. $20

Under the Editorship of Roland J. Teske, S.J.

Hugh of St. Victor. *Practical Geometry.* Frederick A. Homann, S.J., Tr. ISBN 0-87462-232-8 (Translation No. 29, 1991) 92 pp. $10

William of Auvergne. *The Immortality of the Soul.* Roland J. Teske, S.J., Tr. ISBN 0-87462-233-6 (Translation No. 30, 1992) 72 pp. $10

Dietrich of Freiberg. *Treatise of the Intellect and the Intelligible.* M. L. Führer, Tr. ISBN 0-87462-234-4 (Translation No. 31, 1992) 135 pp. $15

Henry of Ghent. *Quodlibetal Questions on Free Will.* Roland J. Teske, S.J., Tr. ISBN 0-87462-234-4 (Translation No. 32, 1993) 135 pp. $15

Francisco Suárez, S.J. *On Beings of Reason. Metaphysical Disputation LIV.* John P. Doyle, Tr. ISBN 0-87462-236-0 (Translation No. 33, 1995) 170 pp. $20

Francisco De Vitoria, O.P. *On Homicide,* and *Commentary on Thomas Aquinas: Summa theologiae IIaIIae, 64.* Edited and Translated by John Doyle. ISBN 0-87462-237-9. (Translation No. 34, 1997) 280 pp. $30

William of Auvergne. *The Universe of Creatures.* Edited, Translated, and with an Introduction by Roland J. Teske, S.J. ISBN 0-87462-238-7 (Translation No. 35, 1998) 235 pp. $25

Francis Suarez, S.J. *On the Formal Cause of Substance. Metaphysical Disputation XV.* Translated by John Kronen & Jeremiah Reedy. Introduction & Explanatory Notes by John Kronen. ISBN 0-87462-239-5 (Translation No. 36, 2000) 218 pp. $25

William of Auvergne. *The Soul.* Translated from the Latin with an Introduction and Notes by Roland J. Teske, S.J. ISBN 0-87462-240-9 (Translation No. 37, 2000) 516 pp. $50

The Conimbricenses: Some Questions on Signs. Translated with Introduction and Notes by John P. Doyle.ISBN 0-87462-241-7 (Translation No. 38, 2001) 217 pp. $25

Dominicus Gundissalinus. *The Procession of the World (De processione mundi).* Translated from the Latin with an Introduction & Notes by John A. Laumakis. ISBN 0-87462-242-5 (Translation No. 39, 2002) 87 pp. $10

Francisco Suárez. *A Commentary on Aristotle's Metaphysics or "A Most Ample Index to the Metaphysics of Aristotle" (Index locupletissimus in Metaphysicam Aristotelis).* Translated with an Introduction & Notes by John P. Doyle. ISBN 0-87462-243-3 (Translation No. 40, 2003) 430 pp. $45

Henry of Ghent. *Quodlibetal Question on Moral Problems.* Translated from the Latin with an Introduction and Notes by Roland J. Teske, S.J. ISBN 0-87462-244-1 (Translation No. 41, 2005) 82 pp. $10

Francisco Suárez, S.J. *On Real Relation (Disputatio Metaphysica XLVII).* A Translation from the Latin, with an Introduction and Notes by John P. Doyle. ISBN 0-87462-245-X (Translation No. 42, 2006) 432 pp. $45

William of Auvergne. *The Providence of God regarding the Universe. Part Three of the First Principal Part of The Universe of Creatures.* Translated from the Latin with an Introduction and Notes by Roland J. Teske, S.J. ISBN 978-0-87462-XXX-X (Translation No. 43, 2007) 204 pp. $23

MEDIÆVAL PHILOSOPHICAL TEXTS IN TRANSLATION
Roland J. Teske, S.J., Editor

This series originated at Marquette University in 1942, and with revived interest in Mediæval studies is read internationally with steadily increasing popularity. Available in attractive, durable, colored soft covers. Volumes priced from $5 to $50 each. Complete Set [0-87462-200-X] receives a 40% discount. John Riedl's *A Catalogue of Renaissance Philosophers*, hardbound with red cloth, is an ideal reference companion title (sent free with purchase of complete set). New standing orders receive a 20% discount and a free copy of the Riedl volume. Regular reprinting keeps all volumes available. Recent volumes are also available as ebooks.

See our web page: http://www.marquette.edu/mupress/
Order from:
   Marquette University Press
   30 Amberwood Parkway
   Ashland OH 44805
      Tel. 800-247-6553 Fax: 419-281-6883

Editorial Address for **Mediæval Philosophical Texts in Translation**:
   Roland J. Teske, S.J., Editor MPTT
   Department of Philosophy
   Marquette University
   Box 1881
   Milwaukee WI 53201-1881

Marquette University Press office:
   Marquette University Press
   Dr. Andrew Tallon, Director
   Box 3141
   Milwaukee WI 53201-1881
      Tel: (414) 288-1564 FAX: (414) 288-7813
         email: andrew.tallon@marquette.edu.

Web Page: **http://www.marquette.edu/mupress/**